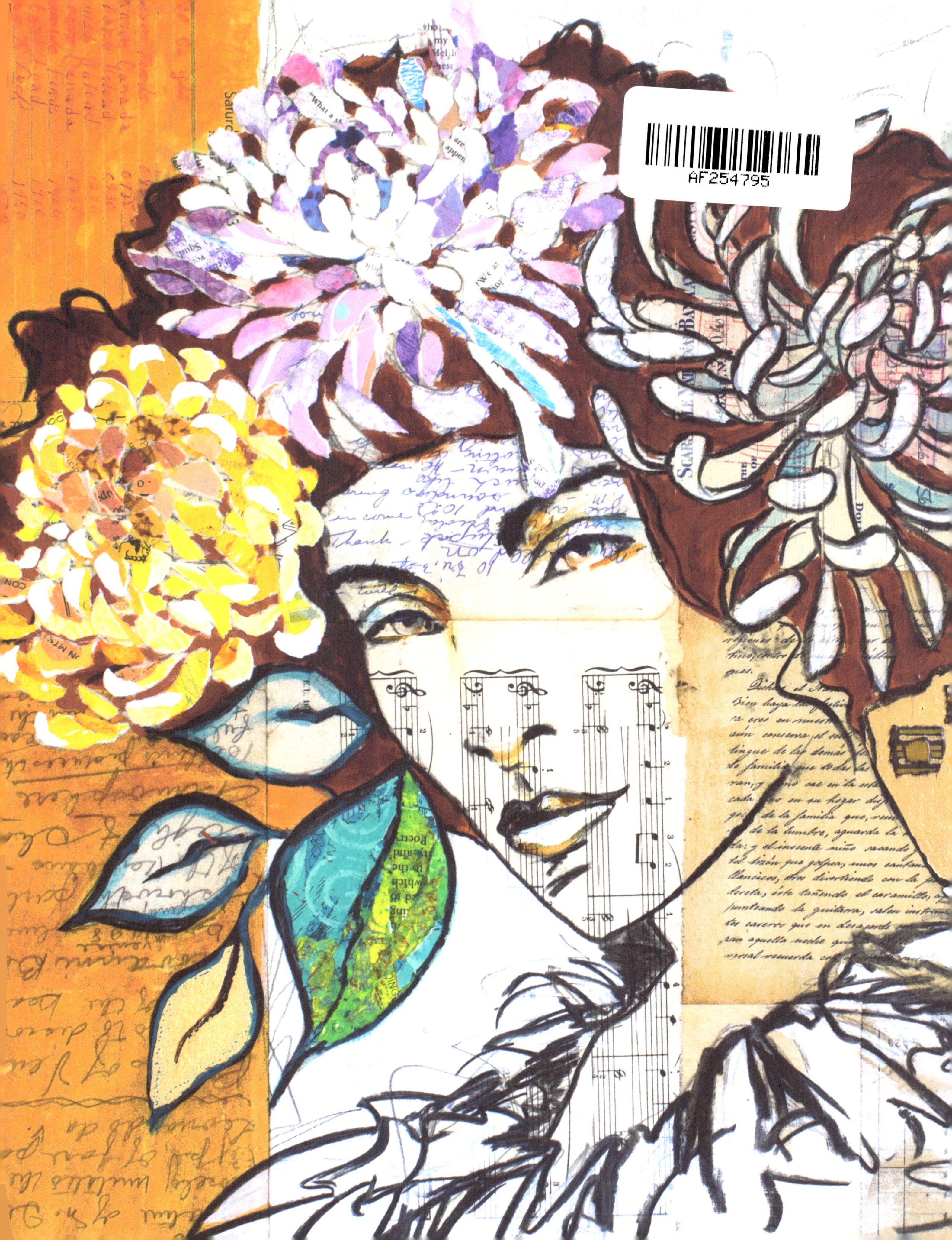

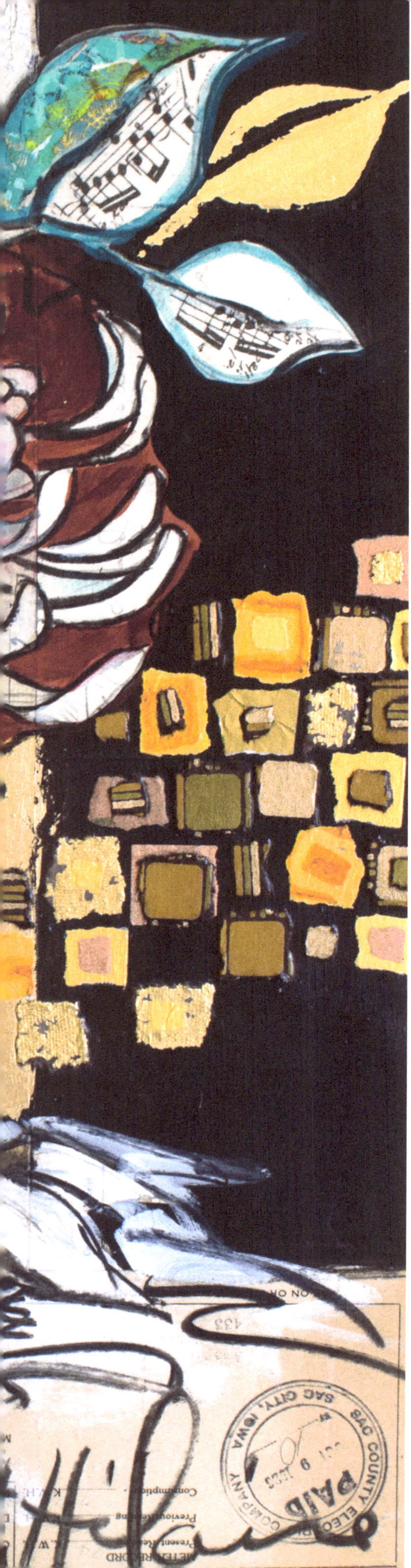

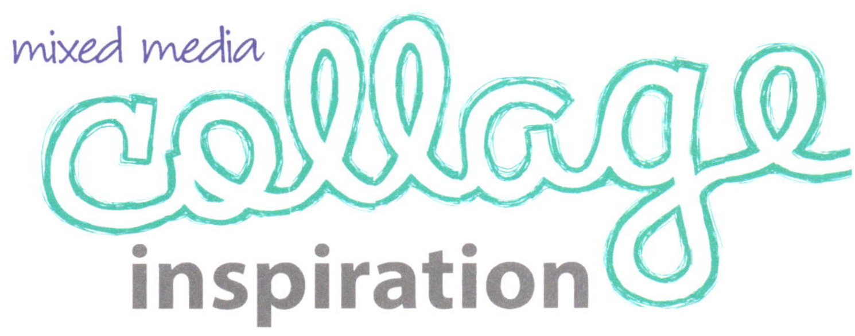

ELIZABETH ST. HILAIRE

Mixed Media Collage Concepts to Jump-Start Your Creativity

Stretch your imagination and experiment with new techniques for inspired results.

©2017 Elizabeth St. Hilaire,
Photography and Artwork ©2017 St Hilaire

For Emilie and Connor

Thank you for loving me for who I am, for supporting me in what I do, and for understanding both.

–Elizabeth St. Hilaire

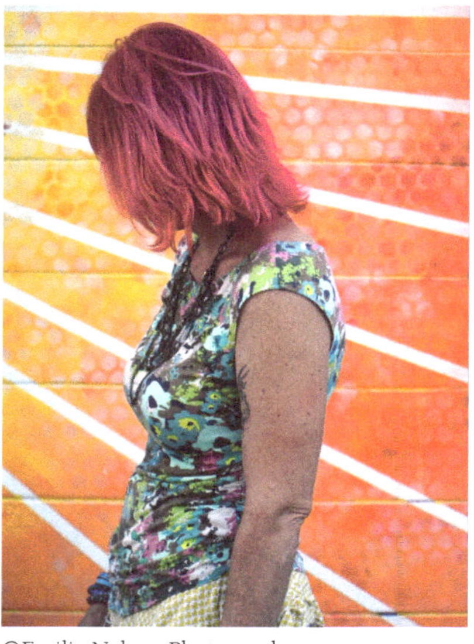

©Emilie Nelson Photography

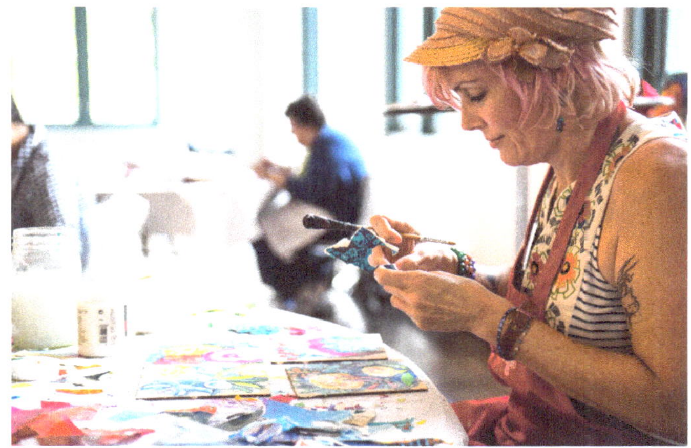

©Ryan Lawrence Photography

introduction

FOR THE LAST 10 YEARS my collage technique has evolved from an exercise in loosening up my acrylic painting style, to being my signature medium. Over the years I have kept my work fresh through experimentation with mixed media. I have tried everything from colored gesso primer, to InkTense and Prismacolor colored pencils, to vine charcoal and soft pastel, to metallic leaf; if it's in the studio, it's fair game!

It is my hope that you will experiment with some or all of the techniques presented, before you pick your favorites—sometimes the least likely combination yields the best success.

In this book I'm also featuring strategies for loosening up. I have made it my artistic goal to be *more* loose and painterly in my collage application, something that's in the forefront of my mind every time I put a wood panel up on my easel.

I hope this book leaves you inspired and ready to paint!

Thank You
For Being a Part of
My Art Journey,

Elizabeth

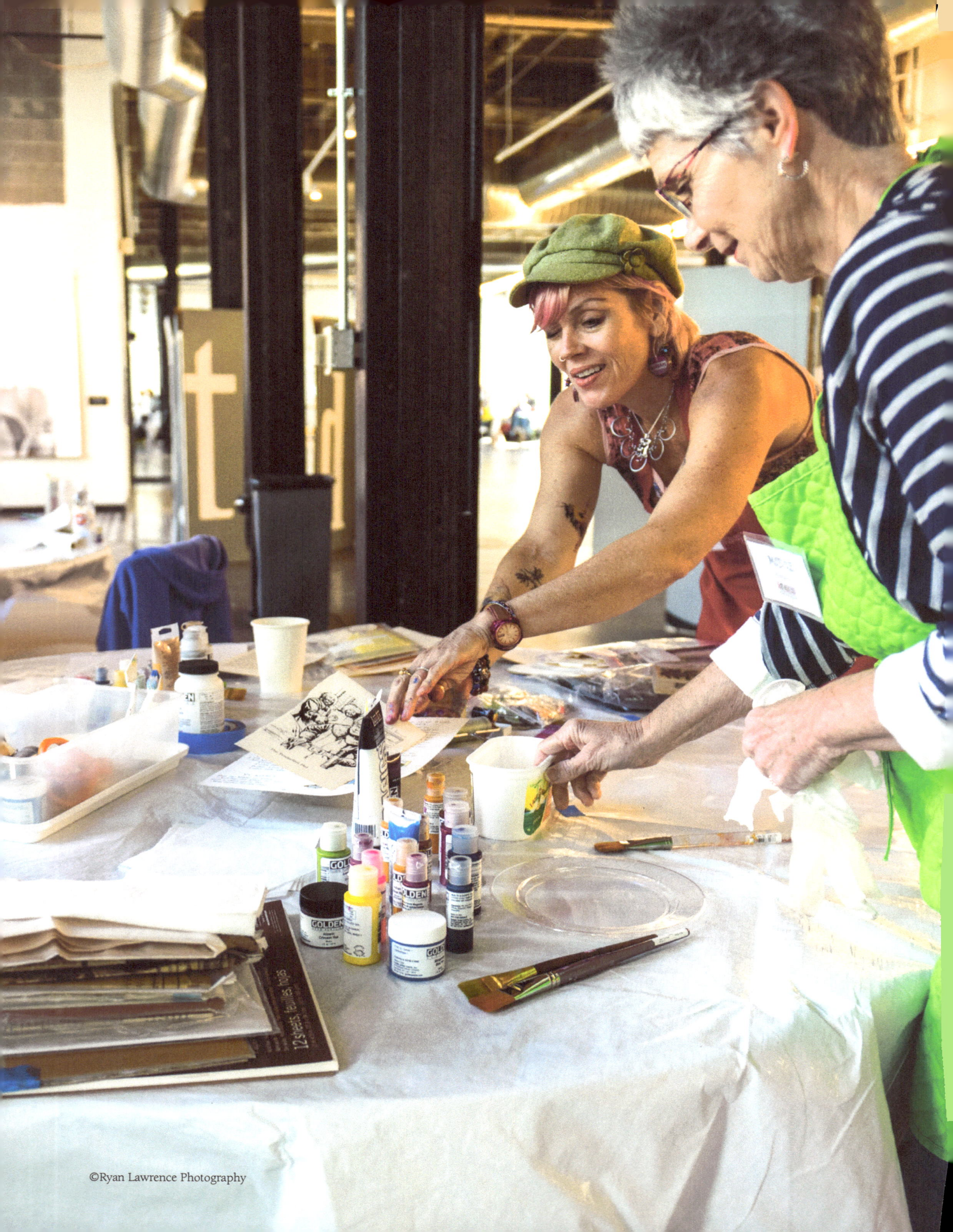
©Ryan Lawrence Photography

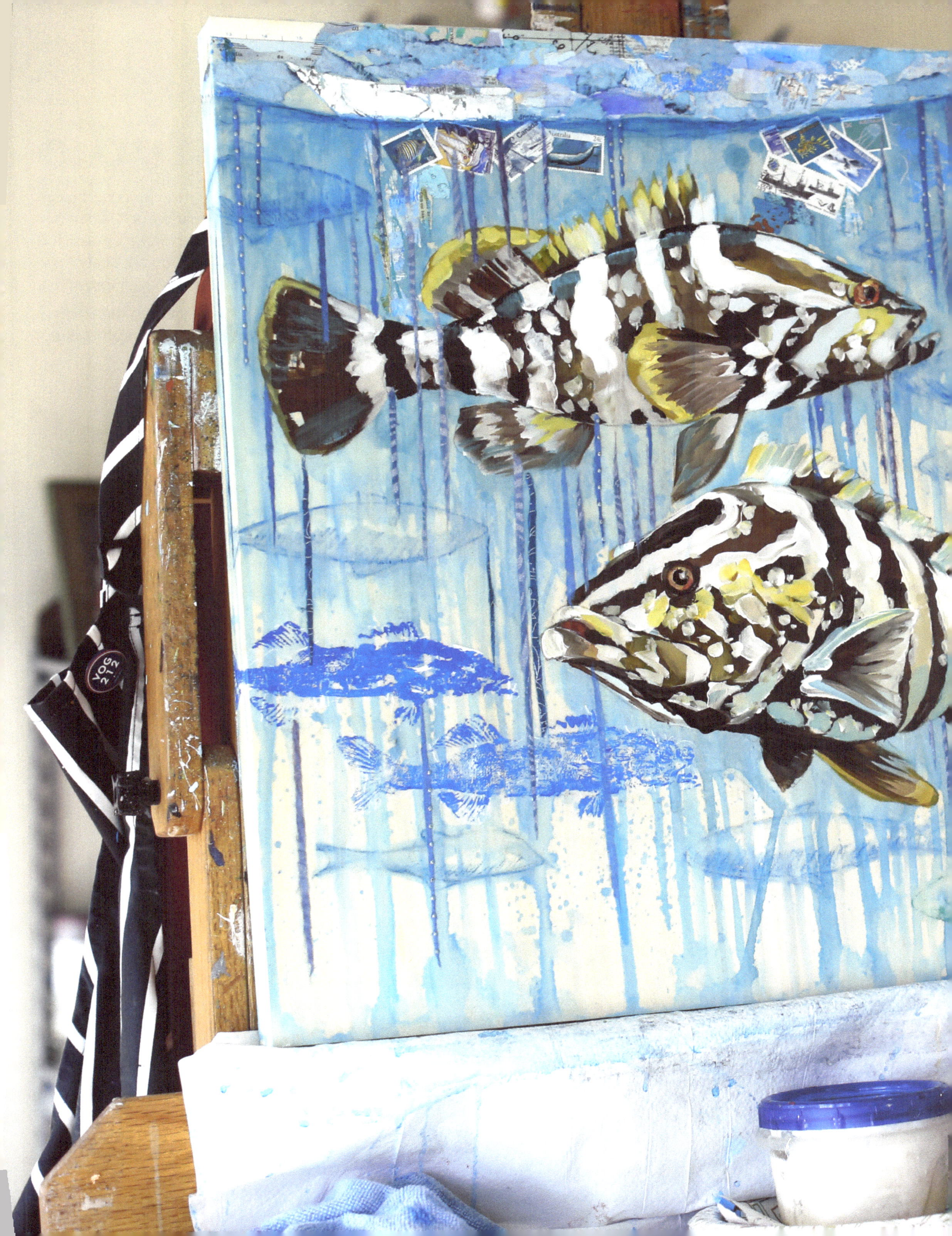

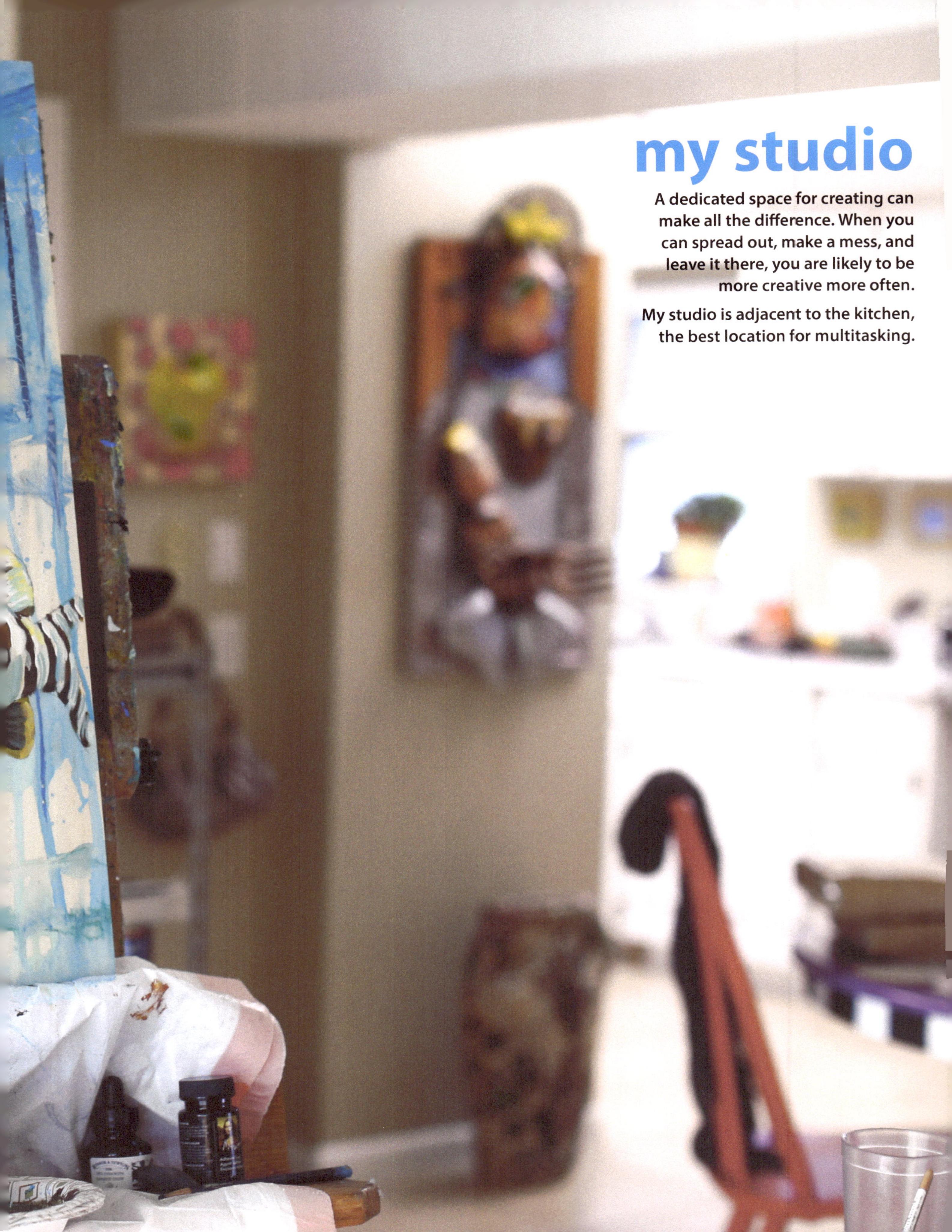

my studio

A dedicated space for creating can make all the difference. When you can spread out, make a mess, and leave it there, you are likely to be more creative more often.

My studio is adjacent to the kitchen, the best location for multitasking.

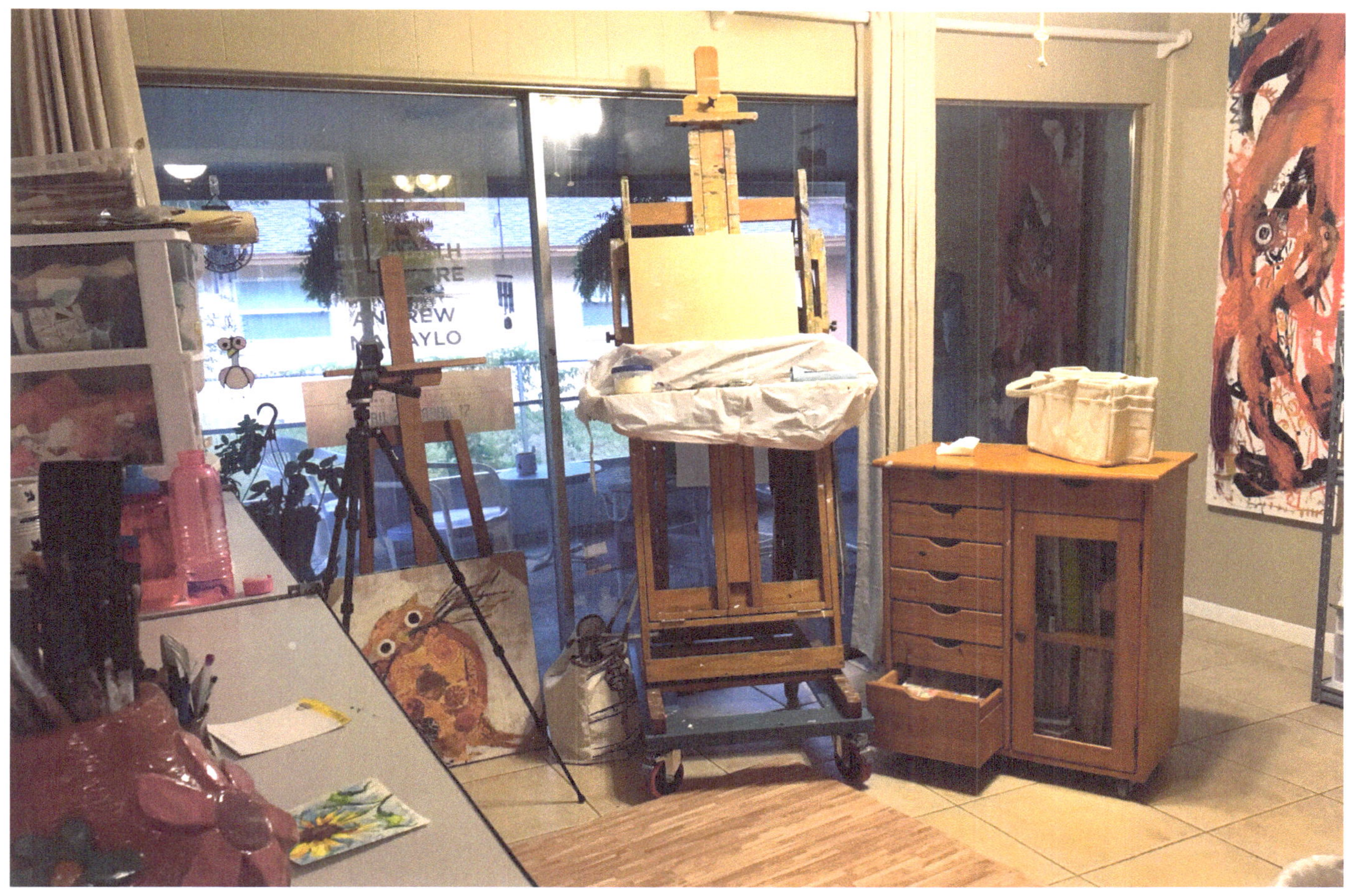

My current studio is adjacent to my kitchen and patio, filled with plenty of natural light.

A Dedicated Space

A PLACE TO CALL YOUR OWN, to leave messy and not have to clean up in order to set the table for dinner, can be an inspiration all its' own. I have artist friends who use an extra bedroom, and some who just go all-out and have set up shop in the living room (some have flip-flopped—sleeping in the living room and working in the bedroom). Even if you have to start out like I did, with an air conditioned corner of the garage, (the predecessor to that space was a louver-doored closet) it can make all the difference. When inspiration strikes, whether it's 4:00 a.m. or the middle of the night, having the ability to act on it is key. Consider setting up your easel and taboret in the corner of an occupied room of the house, to start. Carve out a bit of dedicated space and leave yourself set up to create at a moment's notice, you'll be amazed at how it affects your productivity!

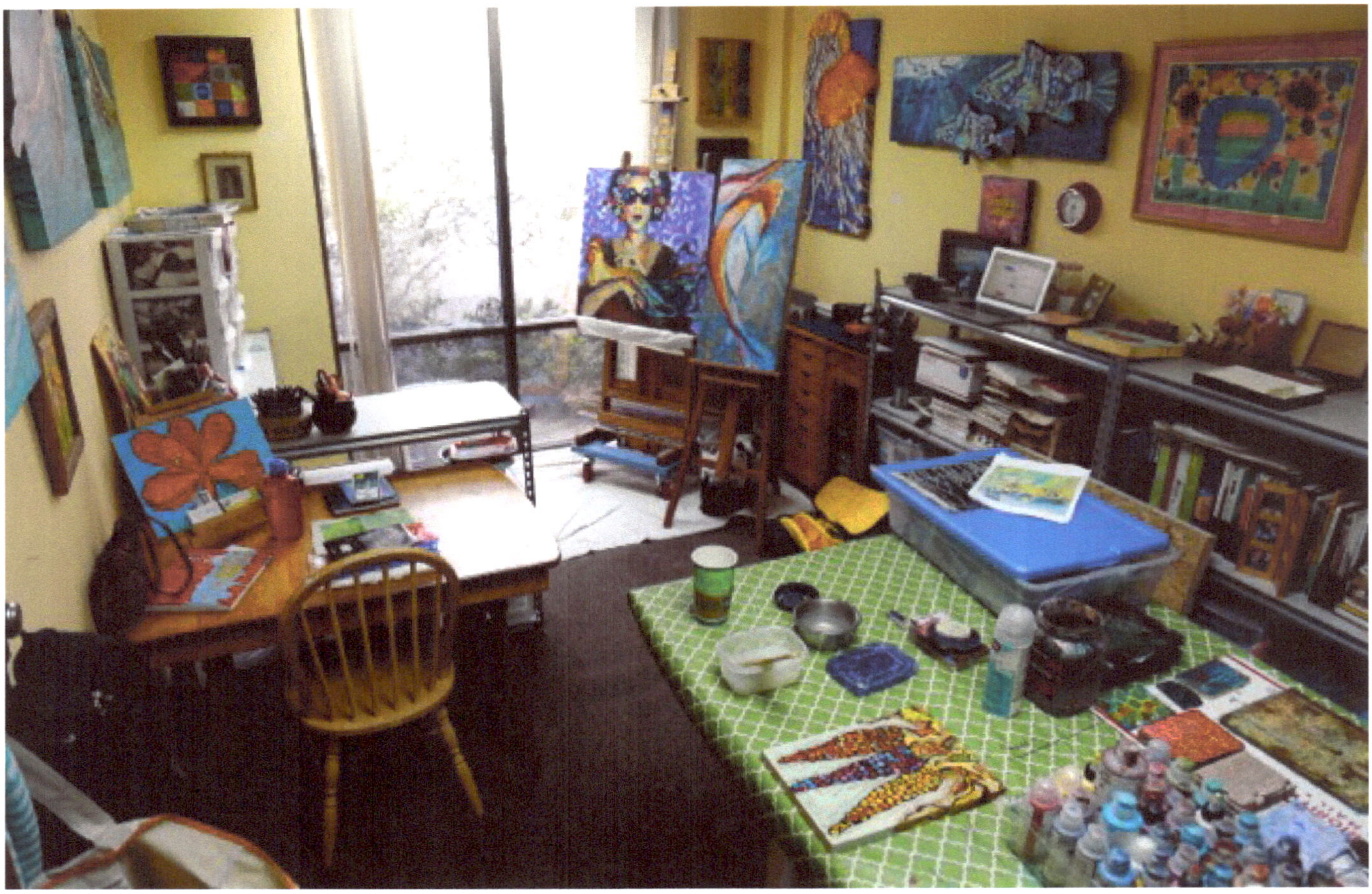

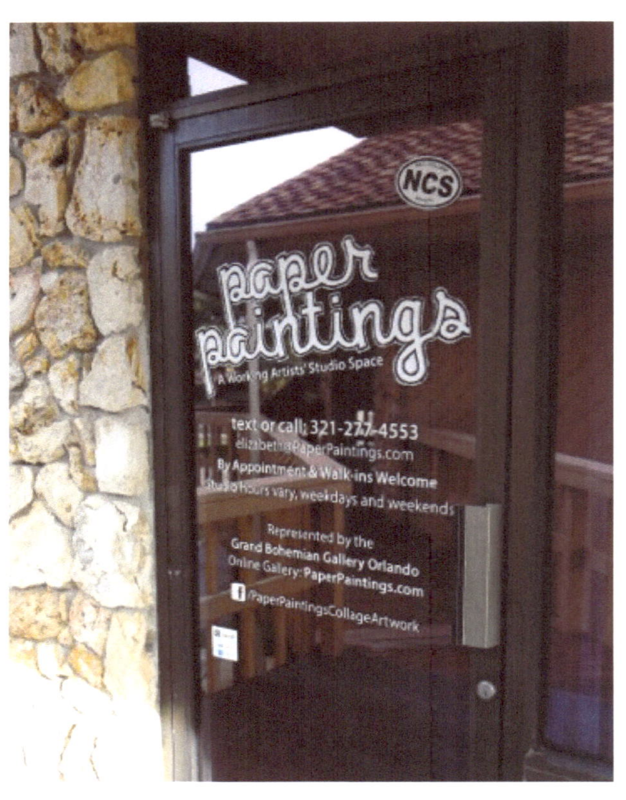

Off-site space above a retail environment provided a reason to get dressed and out of the house.

I HAVE BEEN FORTUNATE ENOUGH to have occupied an air conditioned corner of the garage, a detached free standing studio in my back yard, an off-site studio space (featured above), and a dedicated room adjacent to my kitchen (featured on the left and previous spread).

Off all three scenarios I would say that the ladder is the most productive. The garage was quite small and offered no natural light, the backyard space offered the ability to work from home, but left me feeling a little disconnected from the family. The off-site space was a wonderful way to visit with other shop owners during the day, and a great reason to get dressed and leave the house (painting in your pajamas can be a slippery slope) but it came at the price of monthly rent payments and having to close up shop when it was time to go home and make dinner or let the dogs out.

My in-home space is a converted sun room, adjacent to my kitchen and laundry room; talk about perfect for multitasking! I am able to let the dogs out, run a load of laundry, and put dinner (or a batch of cookies in the oven) without missing a beat. My son often does his homework at the kitchen table while I'm at the easel.

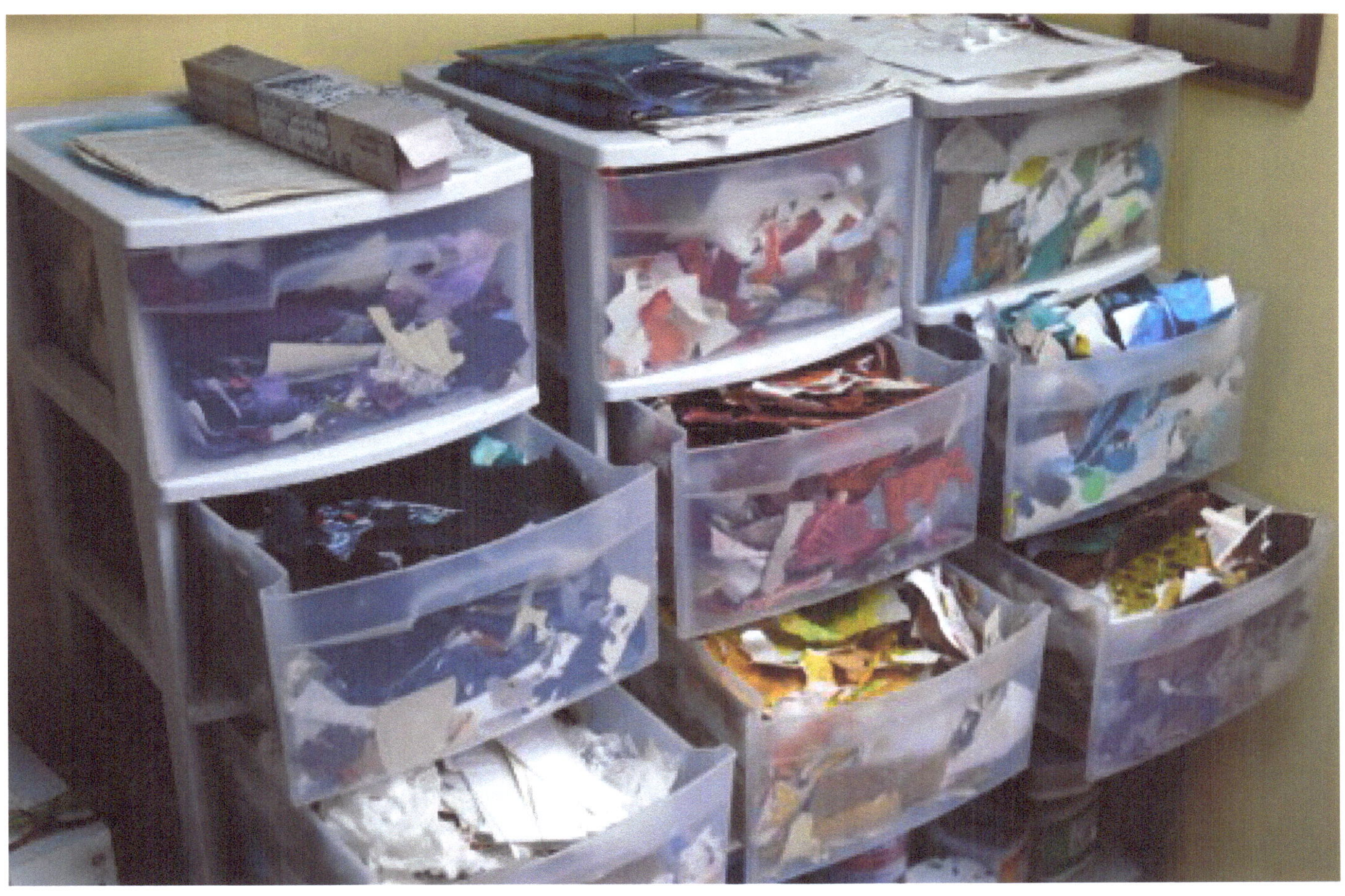

My collage papers are separated by color in nine clear-front plastic drawers that I purchased at my local Target store.

Tools of the Trade

ORGANIZATION IS KEY for mixed media, if you can't find it you can't use it. My taboret has several shallow drawers where I store the things I use the most. Behind my easel I have an old set of oak card catalog drawers that I scored from an antique store. All of the drawers are labeled as to what is in each one of them, eliminating guess work when I'm looking for vine charcoal, pencils, fine point markers, game tiles, or wooden thread spools.

Recently I purchased a second easel, so that I could work on more than one project at a time. I found that the larger pieces, which took more hours to complete, were more accessible left on my big work horse easel—while the smaller, more timely paintings were easier to produce with a second dedicated easel. Both easels and my taboret are on wheels, allowing me to roll them around for the best light, and for cleaning the floor beneath them. (I installed good quality, swivel locking wheels purchased at the Home Depot.)

                    MIXED MEDIA COLLAGE INSPIRATION

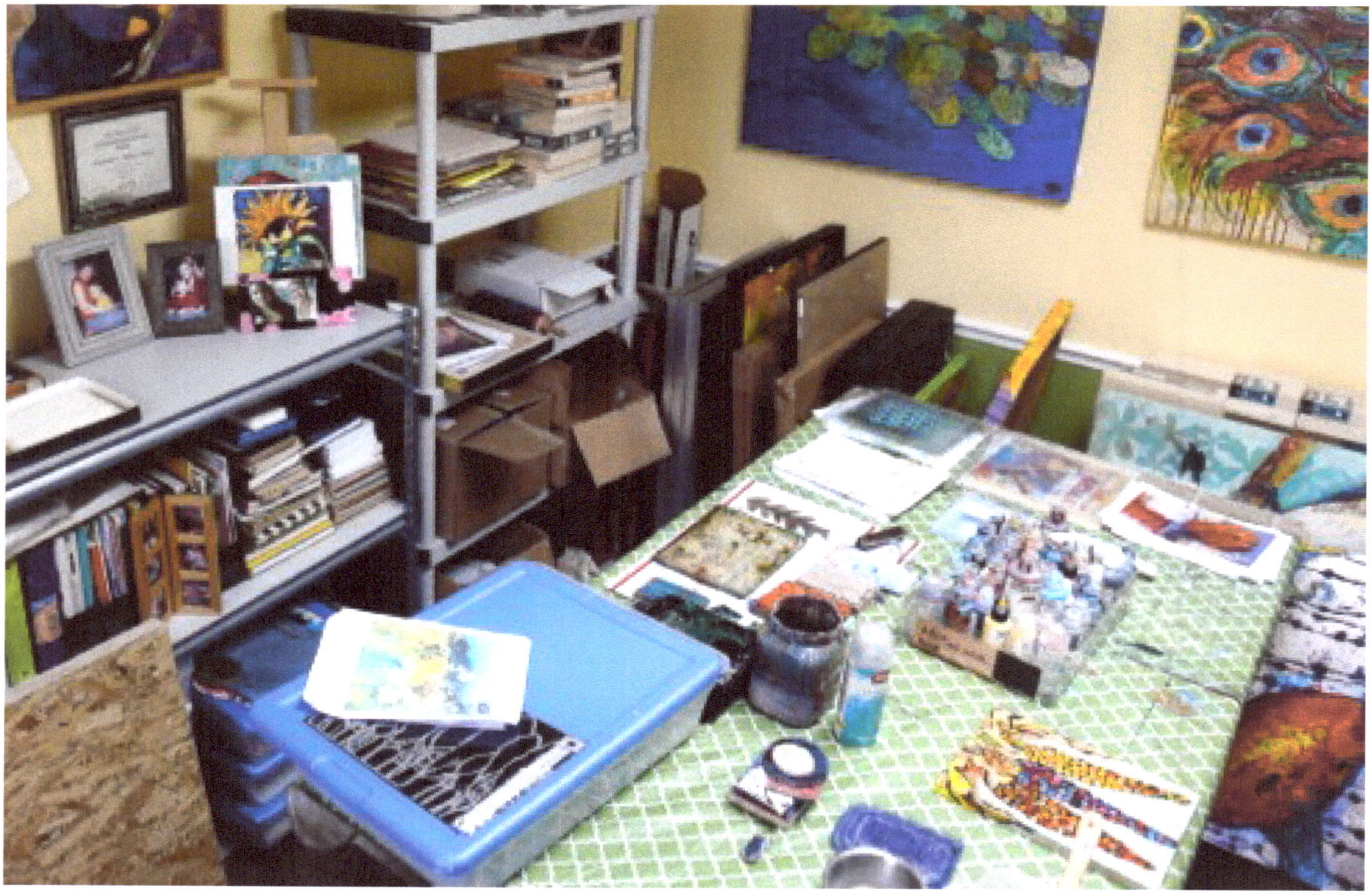

A dedicated table where I can prime panels and varnish finished work offers storage underneath with adjacent open she'ving for supplies.

STORAGE IS ALWAYS A CHALLENGE, when it comes to keeping inventory artwork and organizing art supplies. I have found that Tupperware-type plastic bins with locking lids on industrial shelving works best for me. The bins are clear plastic, making it easy to determine what's inside, and they stack nicely on top of each. Open shelving allows good visibility and easy access.

I hang as much inventory artwork as I can both in my studio and in my home (hanging salon style makes for a very colorful and fun living environment). Regardless of good sales and creative hanging, I still have work that needs to be stored. My work table was made by a local handy-man who put it on wheels and added shelving for storage underneath. The table top has a large overhang, allowing me to stand close to the edges while still storing a good number paintings below.

Speaking of inventory, after you have created more than a handful of work, you may want to seek out an application for your phone or computer (or both) that will help you to keep track of your artwork, where it is, dimensions, medium, and cost; organization is the key to success.

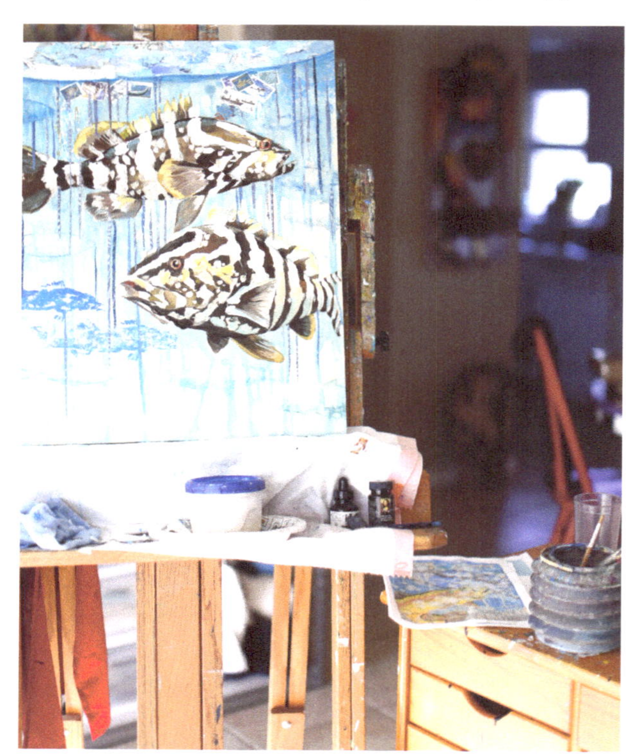

My taboret and easel are on wheels, allowing me to easily move them for proximity to one another and the best light.

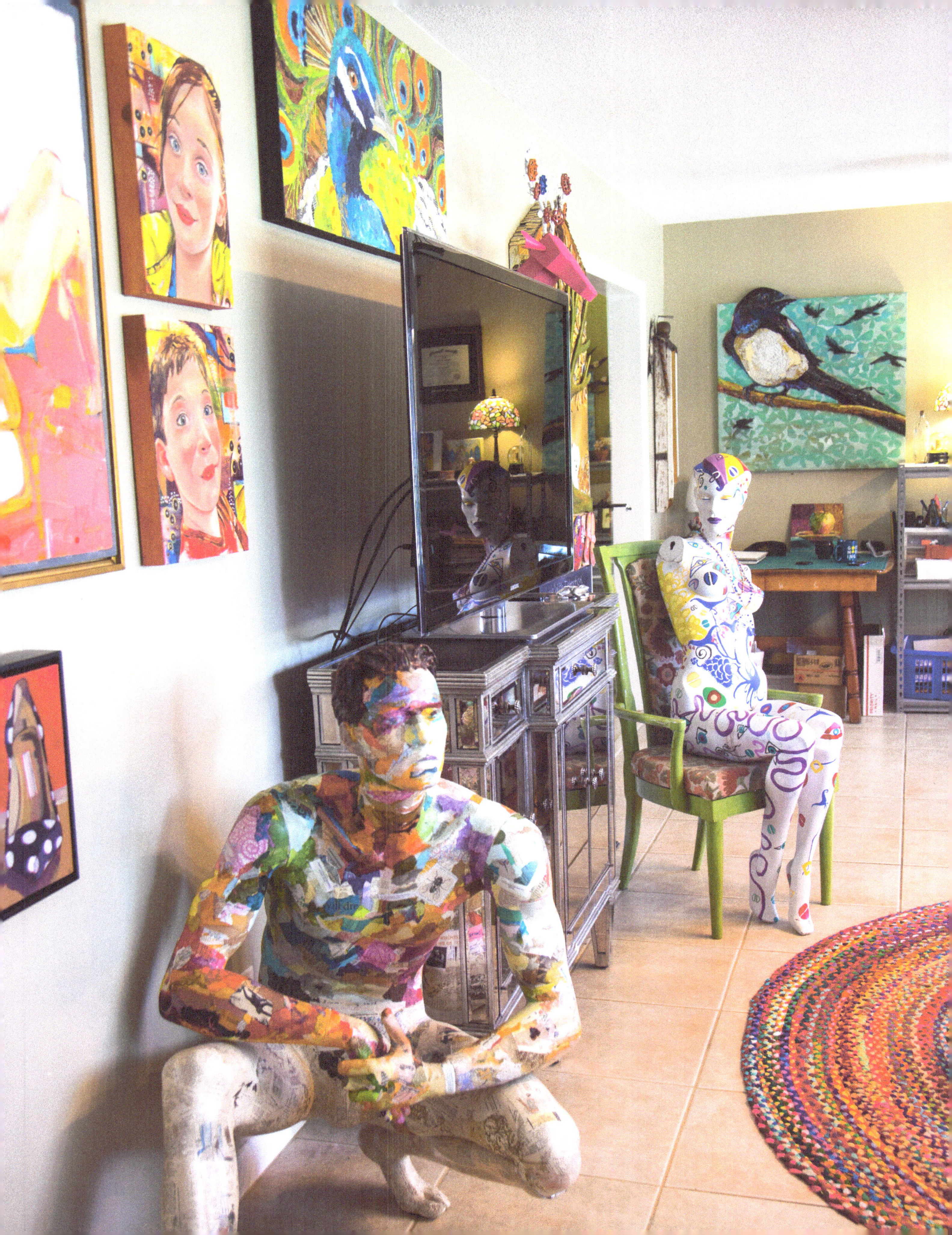

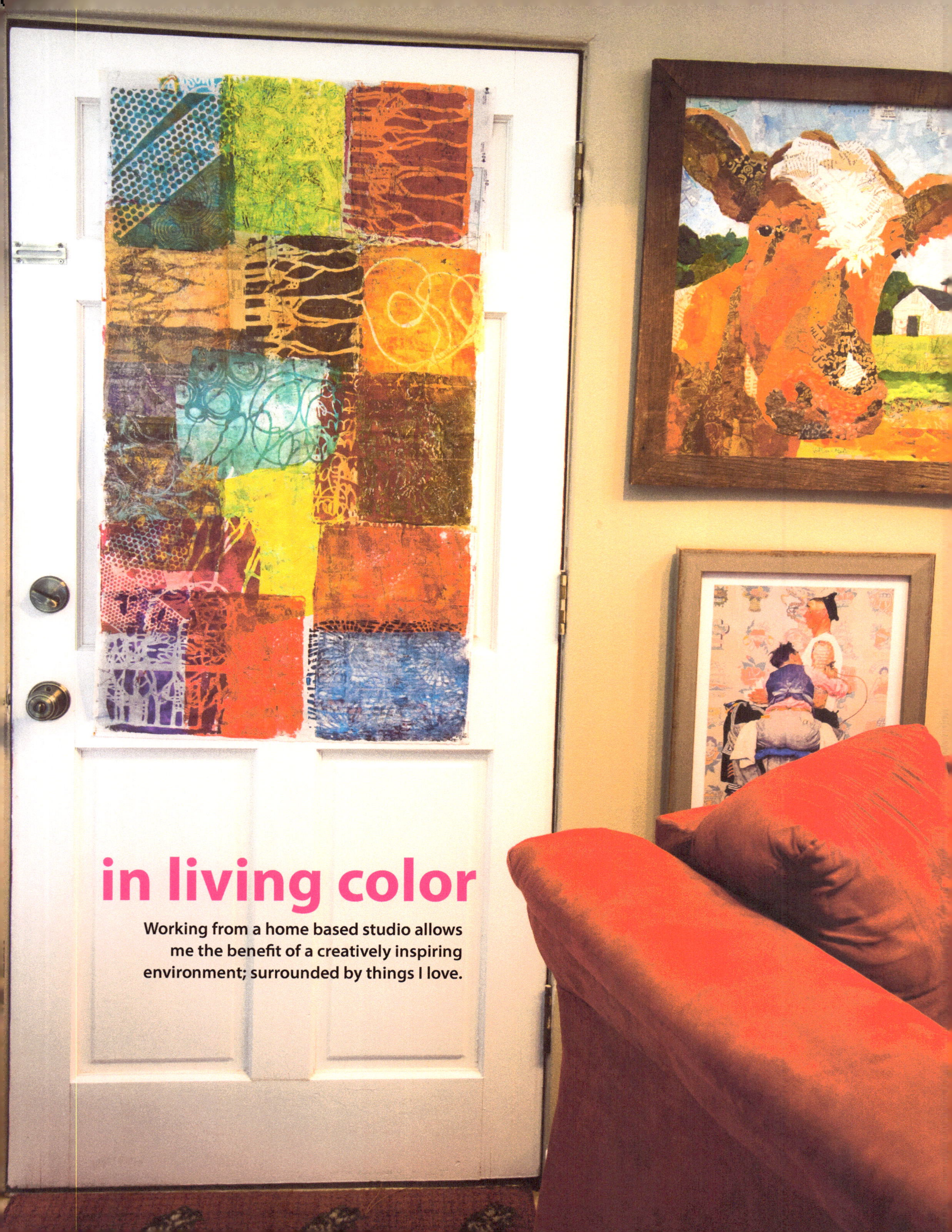

in living color

Working from a home based studio allows me the benefit of a creatively inspiring environment; surrounded by things I love.

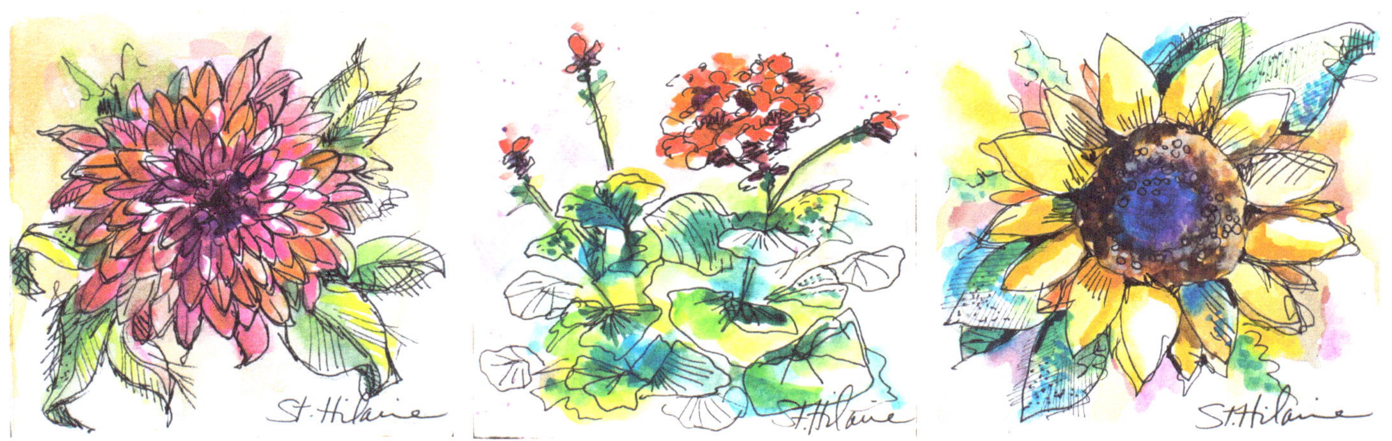

practice

I AM OFTEN ASKED to present to a group about art as a successful career. I have spoken to continuing education groups of 400, Womens Club groups of 50, University Club groups of 30, high school advanced placement art classes of 25, and summer art camp groups of 12. I've volunteered with 5th graders for years, seven classrooms at a time. The common advice I give aspiring artists of all ages, including and *especially* my Paper Paintings workshop students, is to *practice, practice practice*.

What does that mean exactly? To practice means to be creative every day; to draw, sketch, or paint for at least 20 minutes a day. How do you accomplish this? Get a sketchbook. If you keep a sketchbook and a small, dedicated pouch of pencils, erasers, and fine point markers, you can practice anywhere. I have been known to use my Sakura Koi® Water Color Field Sketch Travel Kit and pencil pouch on the airplane seat back tray table, in the doctor's waiting room, and on the sidelines of dance competitions and regattas. I am creative every single day, and my painting benefits from it.

Keeping your sketchbook and dedicated pencil pouch ready to go makes it easy to be creative at home and away. When you are looking for things to draw, look no further than what's around you; salt and pepper shakers, a tea kettle, flowers in the yard.

When people ask me how to improve their painting skills, I tell them to draw more–to practice every day. Drawing is the foundation to painting just as ballet is the foundation of dance. My daughter practiced three hours of ballet per week for years, though her primary focus was modern and contemporary; even hip-hop benefits from ballet.

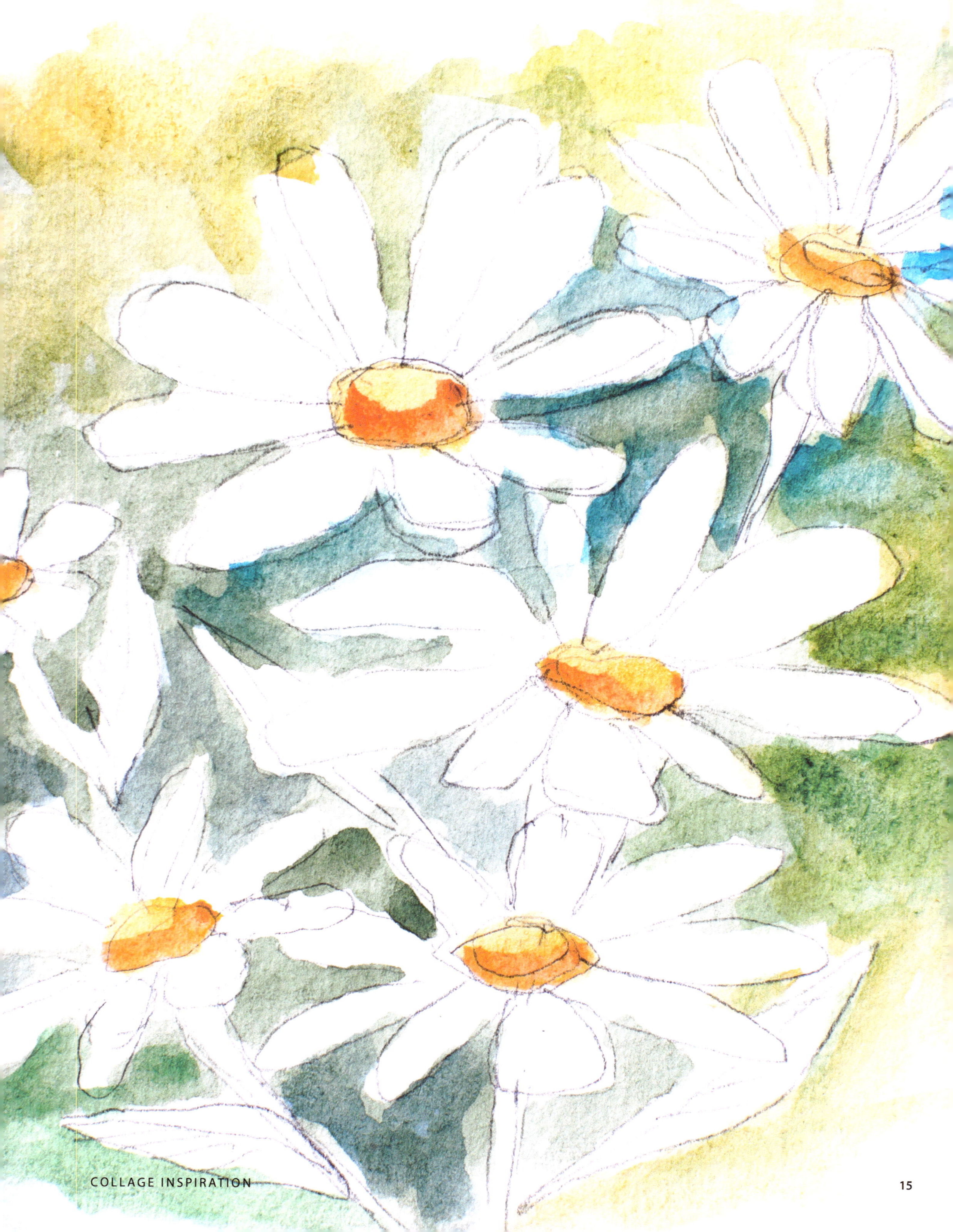

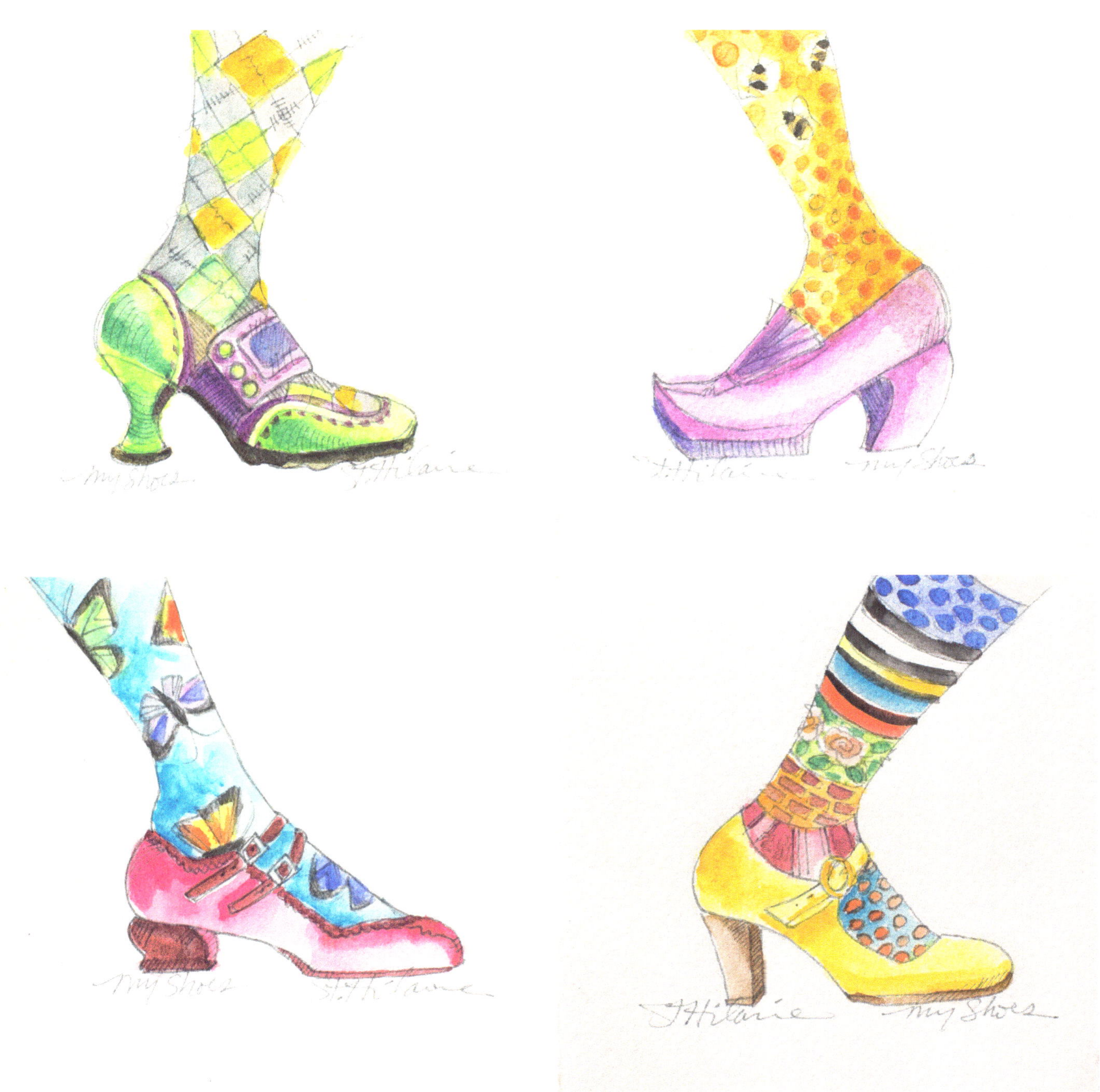

My Shoes (and socks)

THIS SERIES WAS CREATED on seat back tray tables over various flights, including a long leg (no pun) to Italy from Atlanta. I started with iPhone photo references of my own shoe and sock combinations, saved to my camera roll. Using a mechanical pencil and a kneaded rubber eraser, all of these watercolors started with a sketch. Once I established a good drawing, I filled it in with color, using my Sakura Koi® Water Color Field Sketch Travel Kit, it's very small and portable, featuring a brush with water in the handle and a removable color mixing tray.

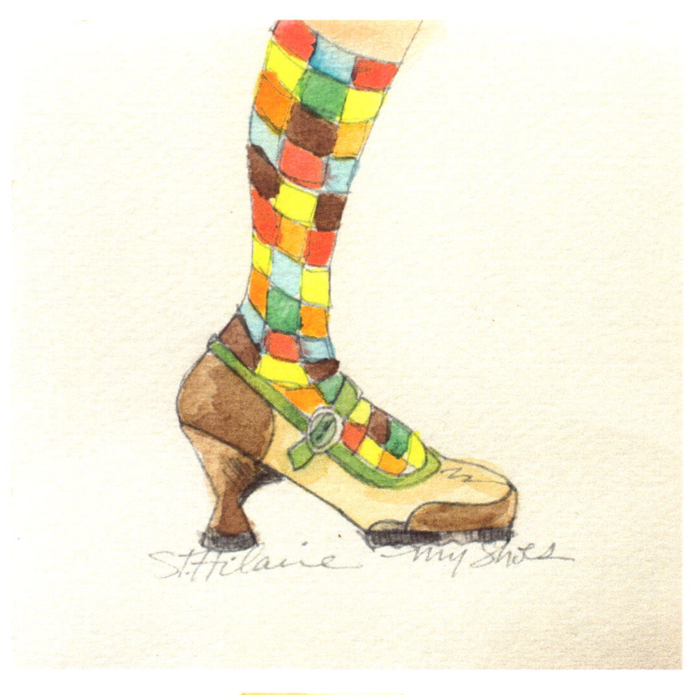

St. Hilaire
my Shoes

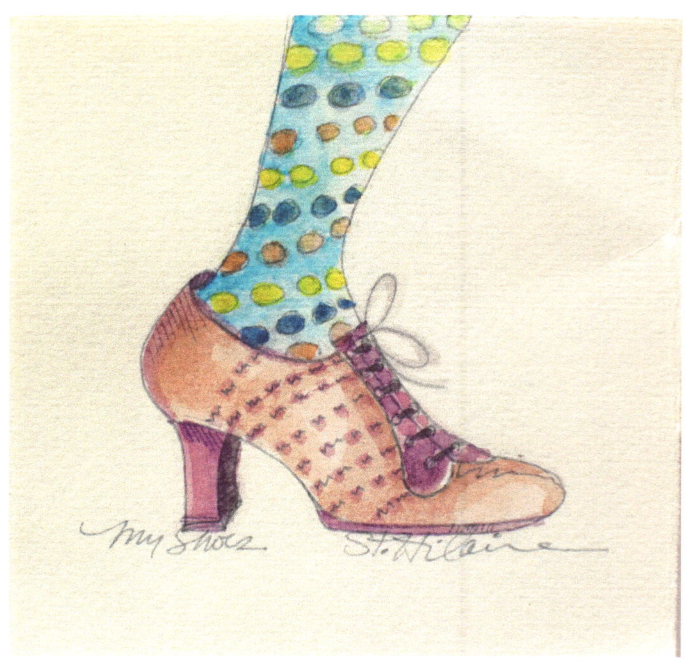

my Shoes
St. Hilaire

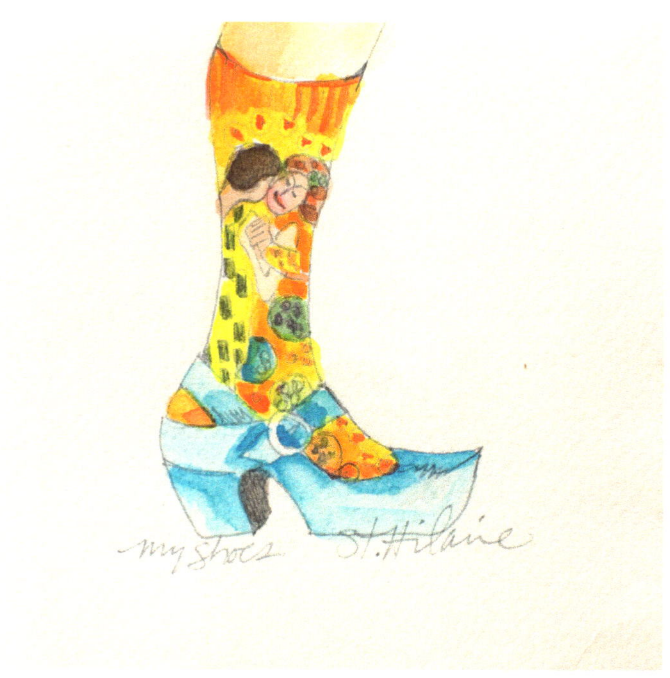

my Shoes
St. Hilaire

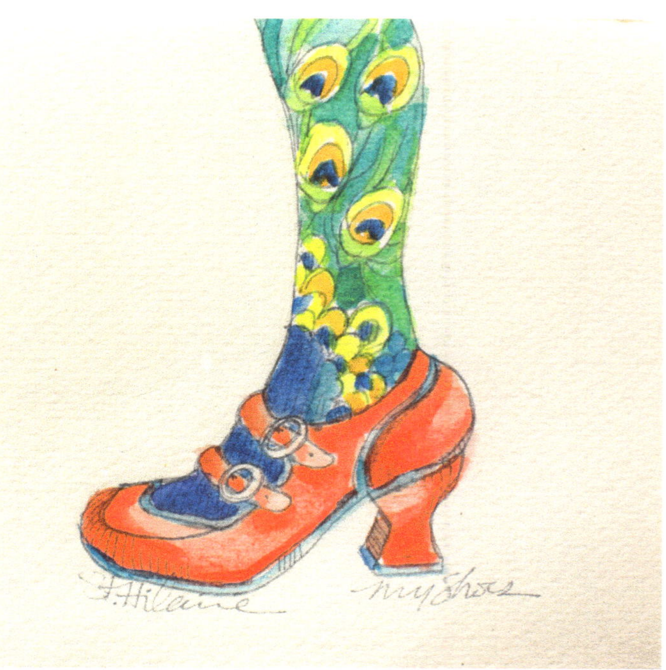

St. Hilaire
my Shoes

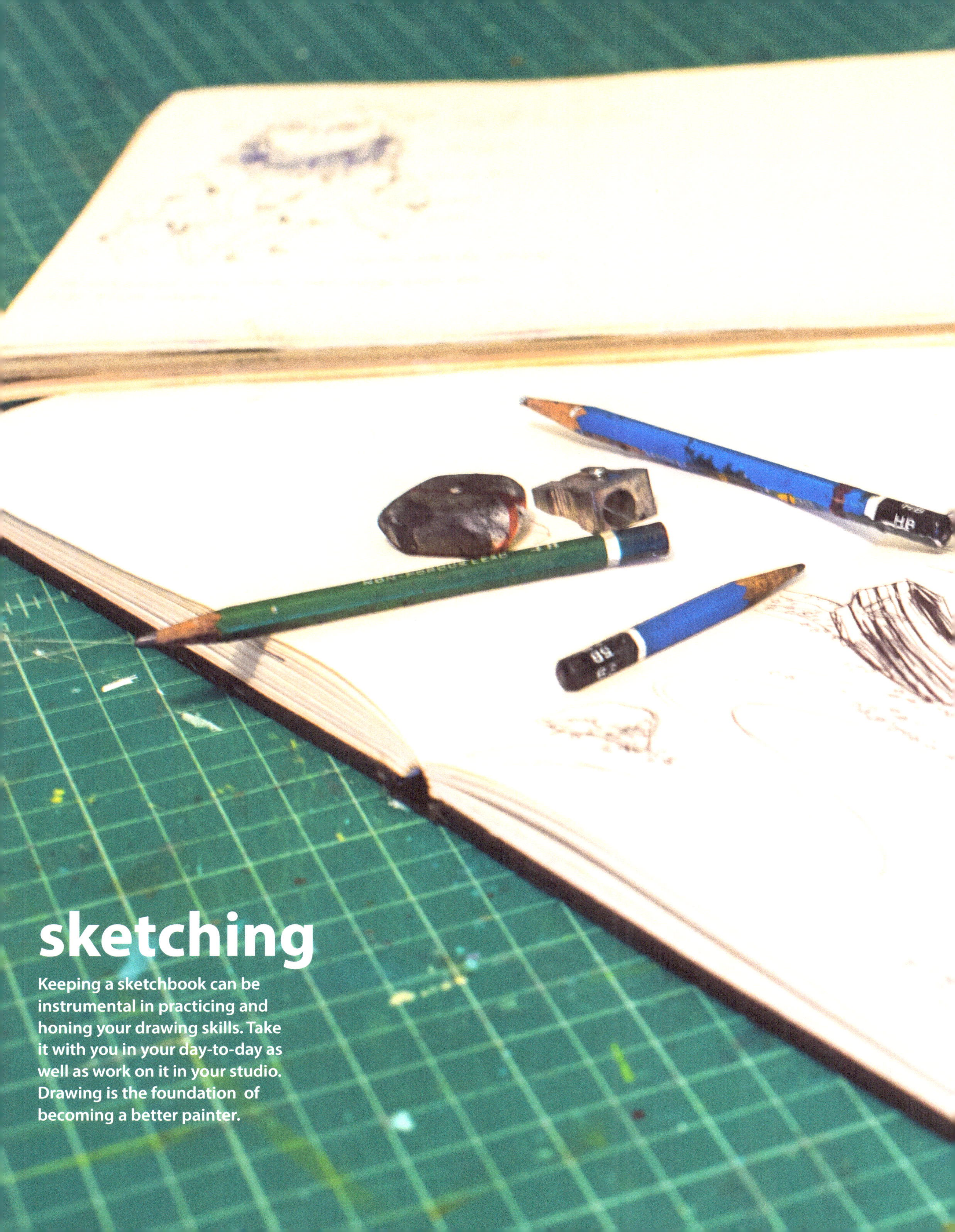

sketching

Keeping a sketchbook can be instrumental in practicing and honing your drawing skills. Take it with you in your day-to-day as well as work on it in your studio. Drawing is the foundation of becoming a better painter.

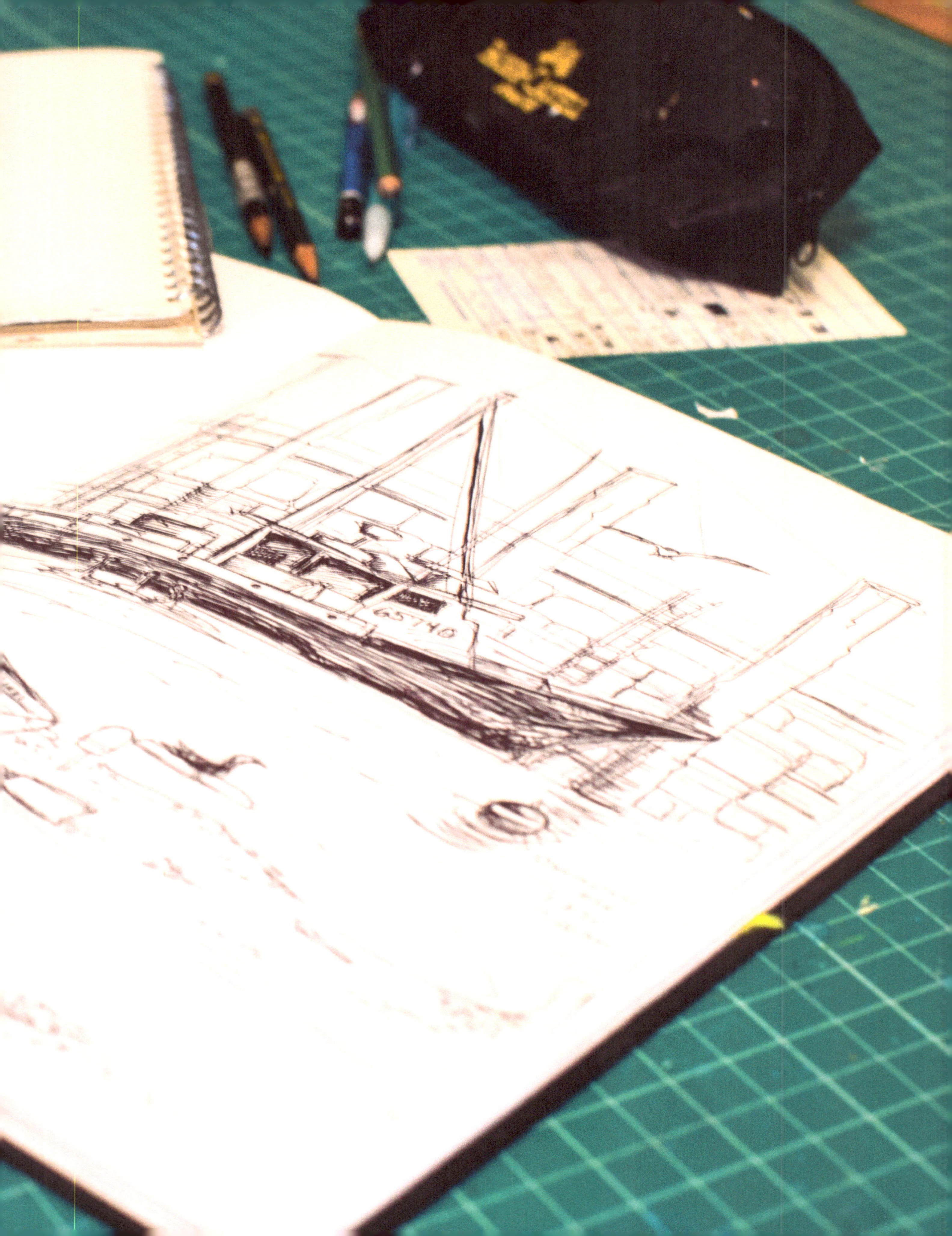

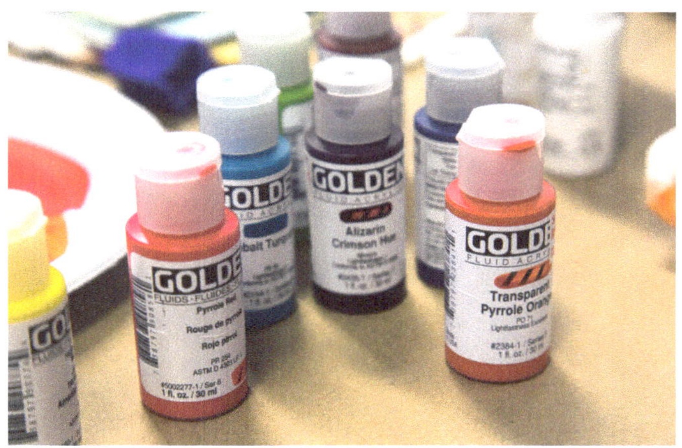

experiment

WHEN I FIRST STARTED hand-painting my own collage papers I used full bodied paint from tubes. I even occasionally used student grade paint in order to keep within a budget. One day a fellow collage artist asked me if I had ever tried acrylic inks or fluid acrylics. I told her that I had stood in front of the fluid acrylic display at the art supply store for a long time, looking and contemplating. The price point had kept me from experimenting.

"Just buy a couple of 1 oz. containers of the Golden fluid acrylics and try them." She suggested. *"You are going to love a translucent medium for layering color and creating depth in your collage papers. Trust me."*

It was a leap of faith, and Jo was right. I never looked back.

I have a plethora of art supplies that I have been carrying around with me for about 30 years. Having earned my Bachelor of Fine Arts (BFA) at Syracuse University, I accumulated more materials with each new year on campus. I still have supplies with SU Bookstore price tags on them; I recently unwrapped a brand-new/old kneaded rubber eraser from those wonderful years. I kid you not.

I experiment constantly with new and different media from my college days as well as things that I come across in the art supply store. I suggest that every now and then you visit a brick and mortar art store (versus always on-line shopping) for inspiration. Wander down the isles, check every shelf, pick up some new supplies that interest you. Experimenting leads to new and different results, and it keeps things interesting.

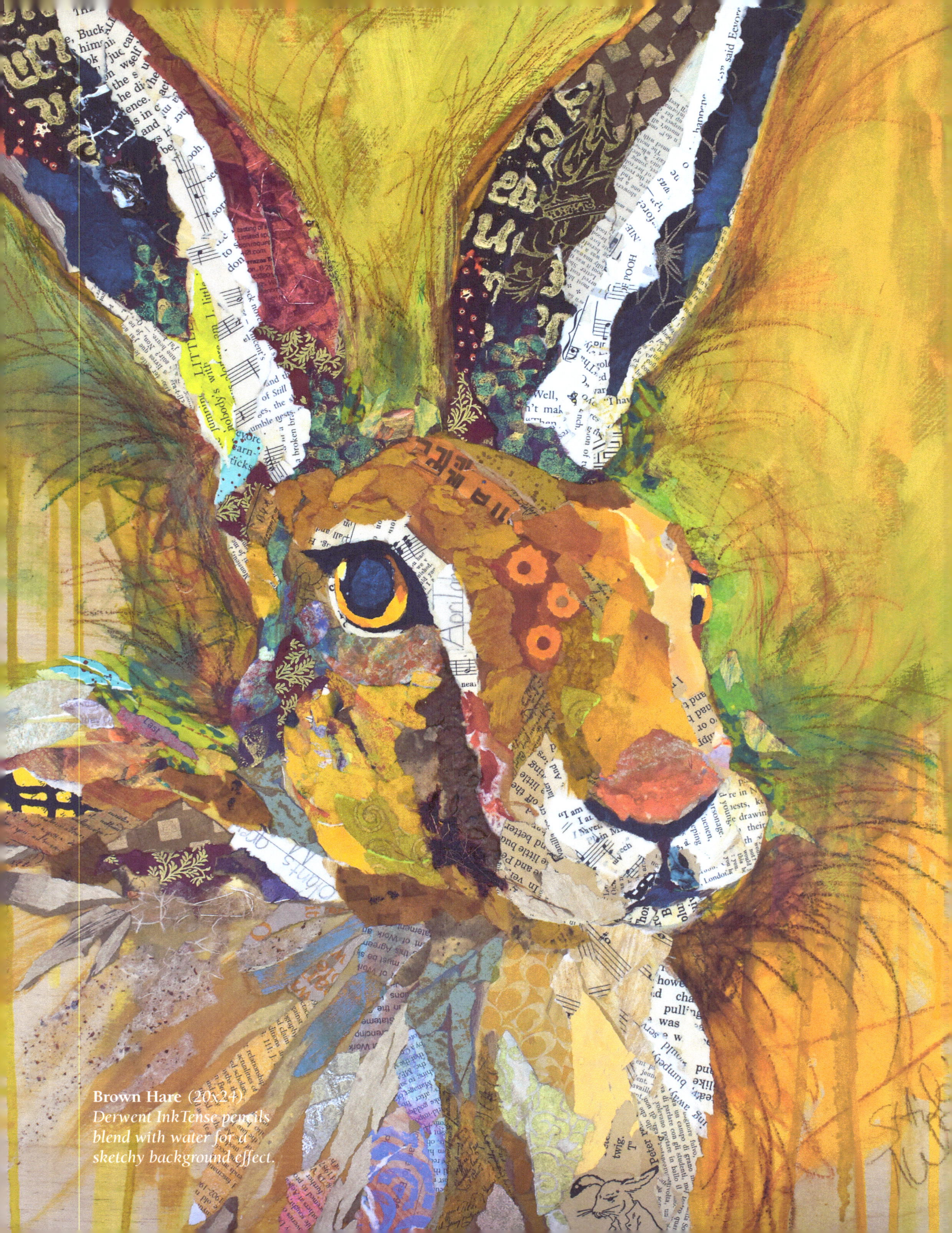

Brown Hare (20x24).
*Derwent InkTense pencils
blend with water for a
sketchy background effect.*

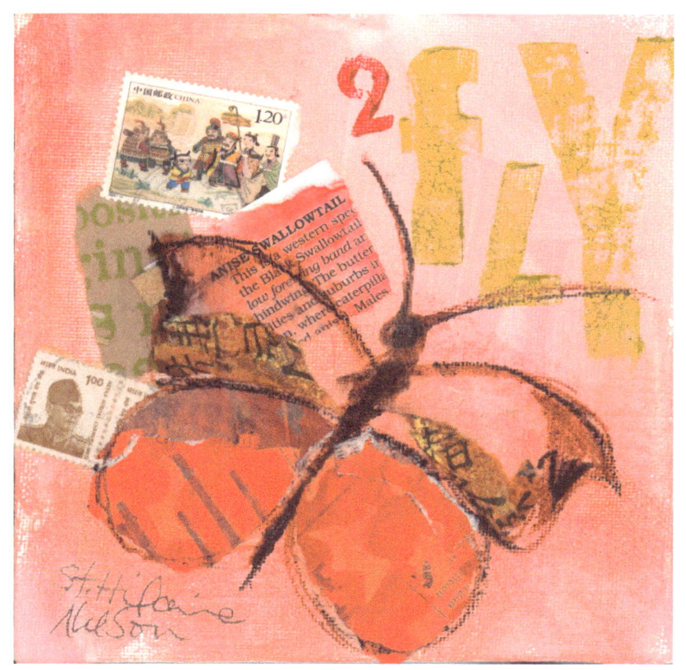

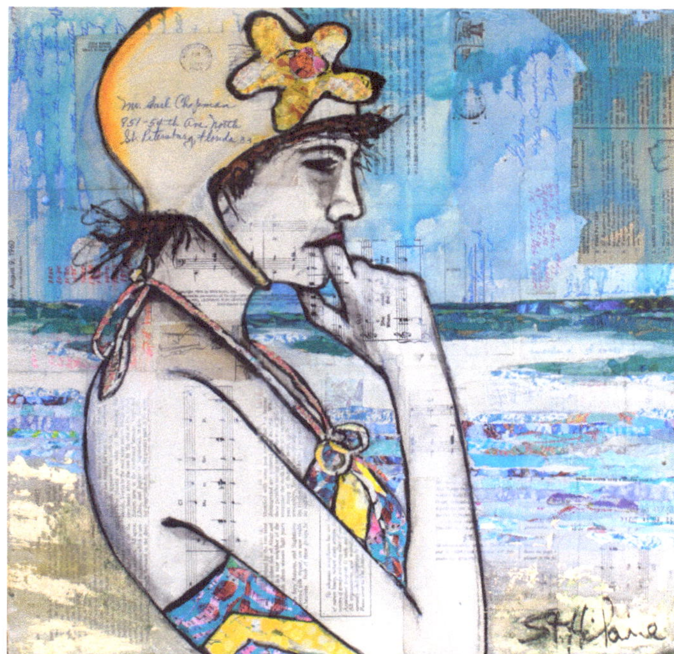

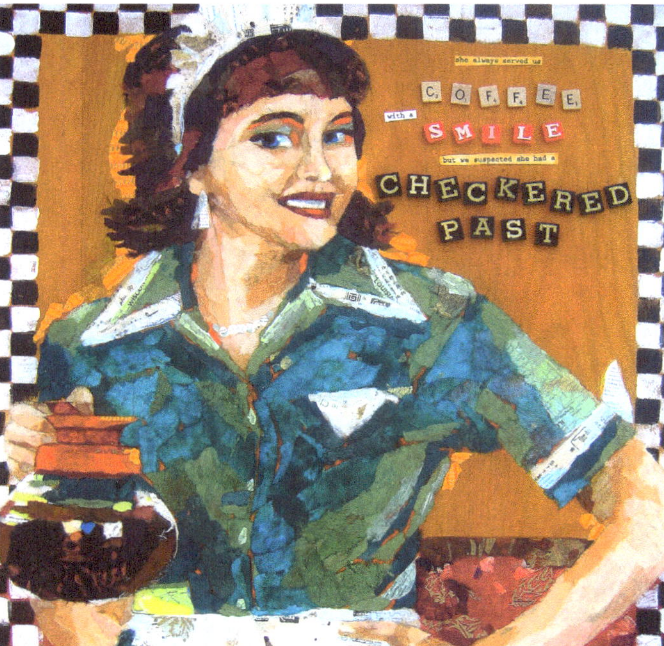

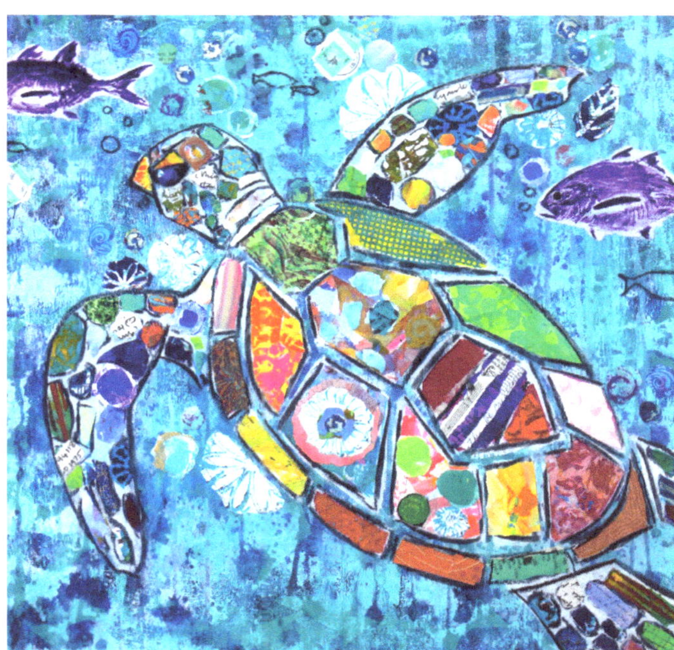

Mixed Media Inspiration

EXPERIMENTING WITH NEW MEDIA is always a gateway to becoming more creative. **Top left:** stamping with Speedball block printing ink and wooden printing press letters directly onto the substrate background. **Top right:** dominant black line through charcoal drawing. Bottom left: incorporating game letter tiles. **Bottom right:** silver metallic leaf applied with specific adhesive (Mona Lisa brand by Speedball) to the background.

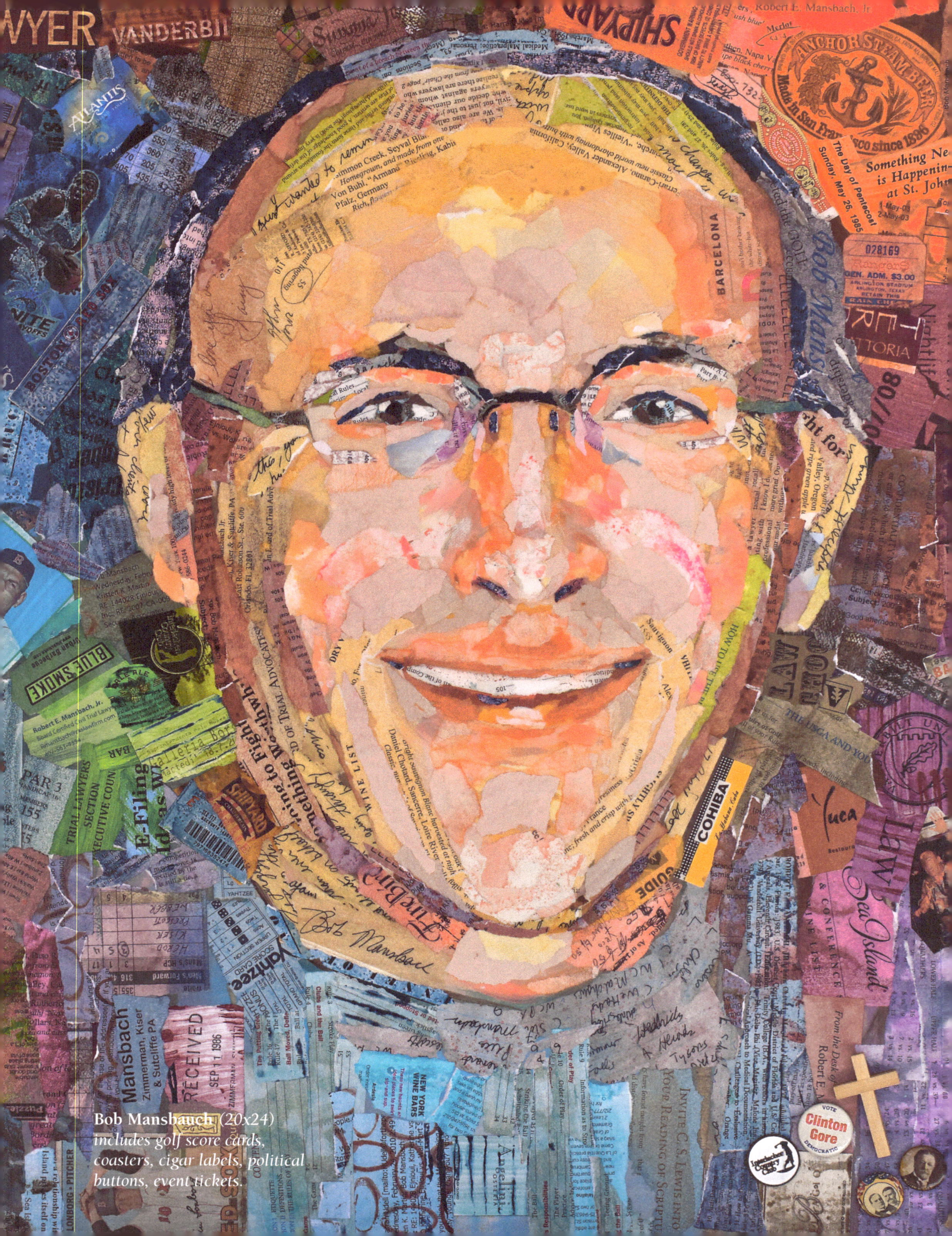

Bob Mansbach (20x24)
includes golf score cards,
coasters, cigar labels, political
buttons, event tickets.

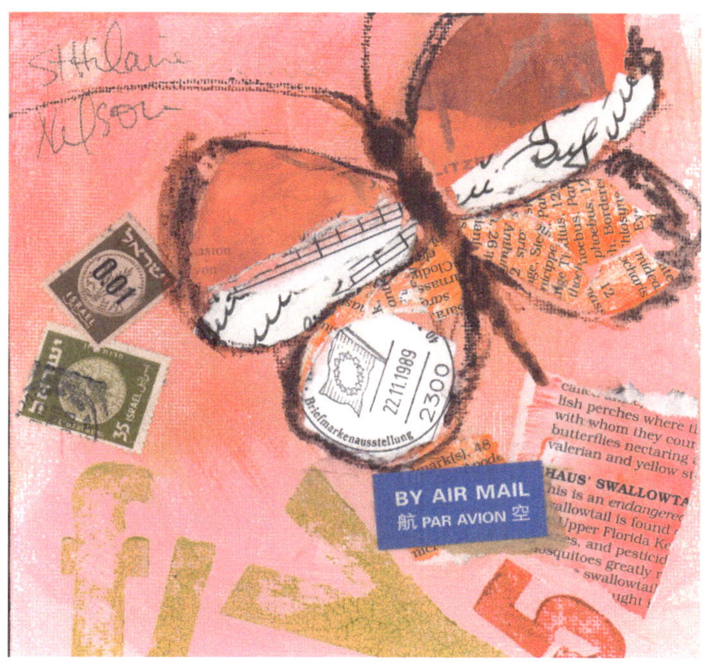

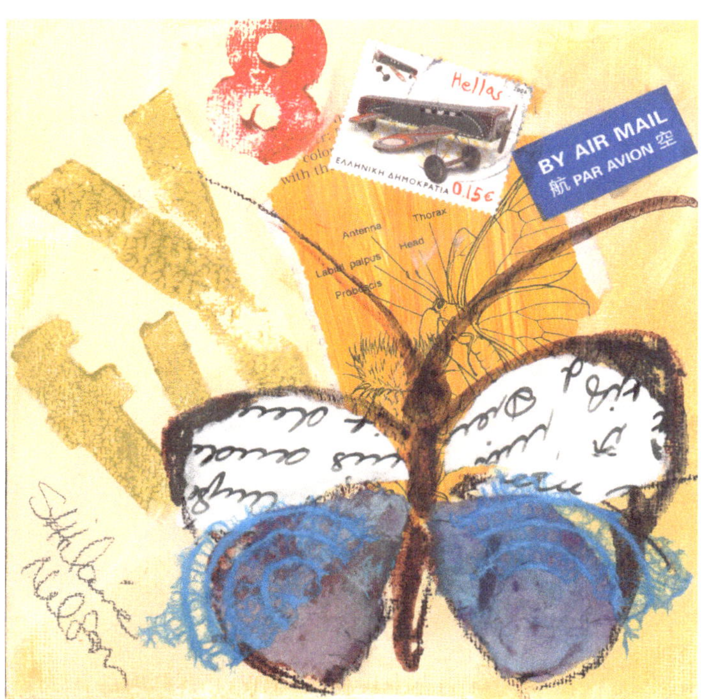

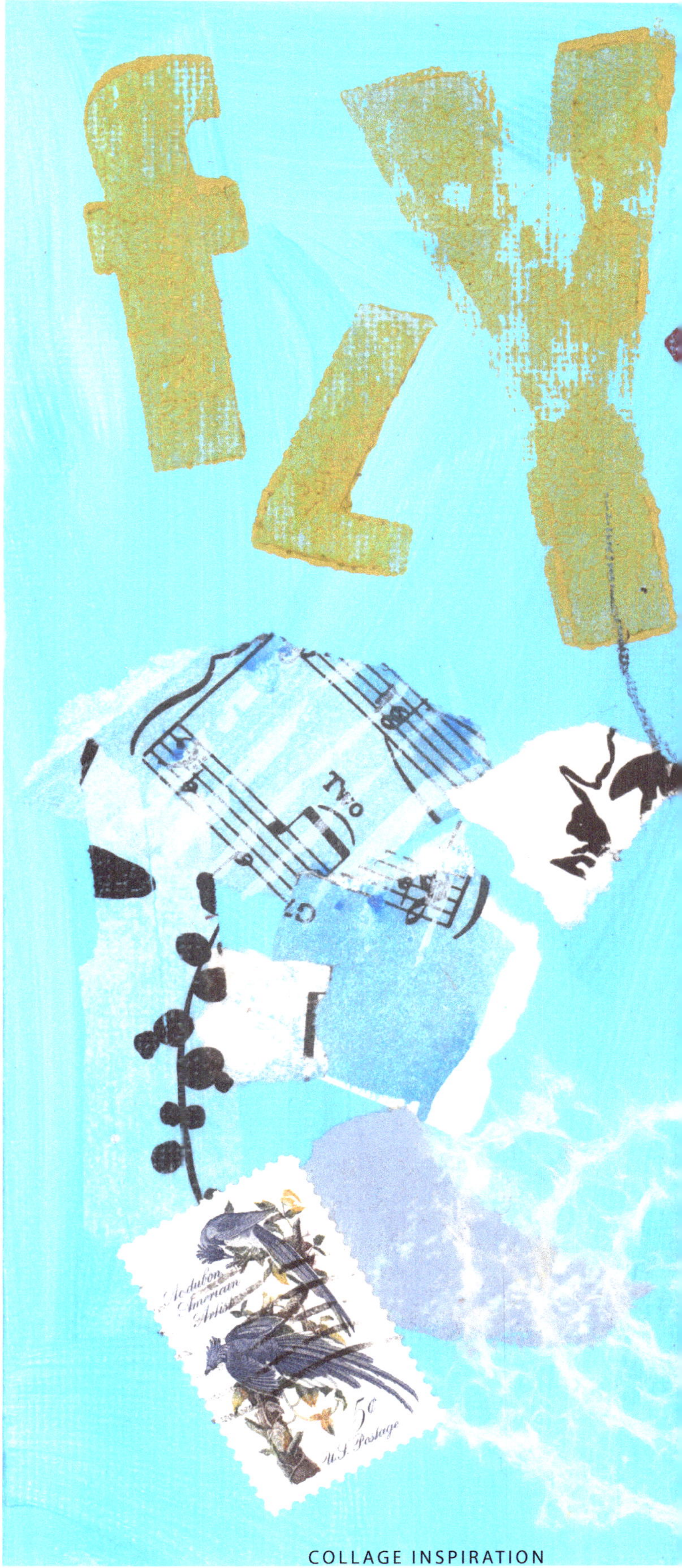

Stamping

The Numbered Butterfly Series *(8X8 and 9x12) was created on solid painted backgrounds with postage stamps and bits of hand-painted paper in combination with soft vine charcoal, and graphite. The letters and numbers were achieved by stamping with Speedball block printing ink and wood printing press letters on top of the established background–a purchased rubber stamp would also suffice.*

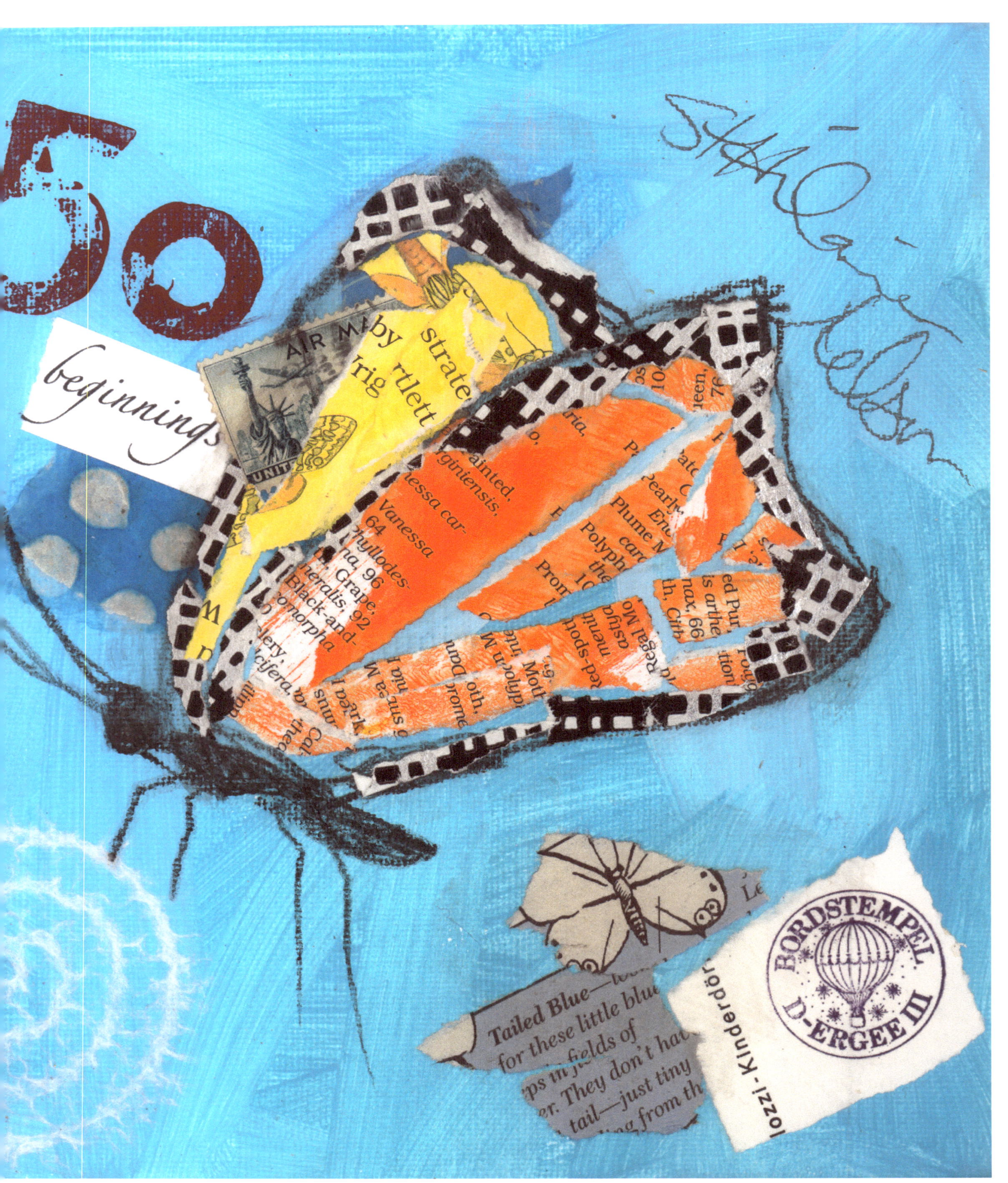
50
beginnings
AIR MAIL
strate
by rtlett
rig
Vanessa car-
Vanessa
Phyllodes
Grape.
Black-and-
Tailed Blue—
for these little blue
ps in fields of
er. They don't ha
tail—just tiny
ing from th
BORDSTEMPEL
D-ERGEE III

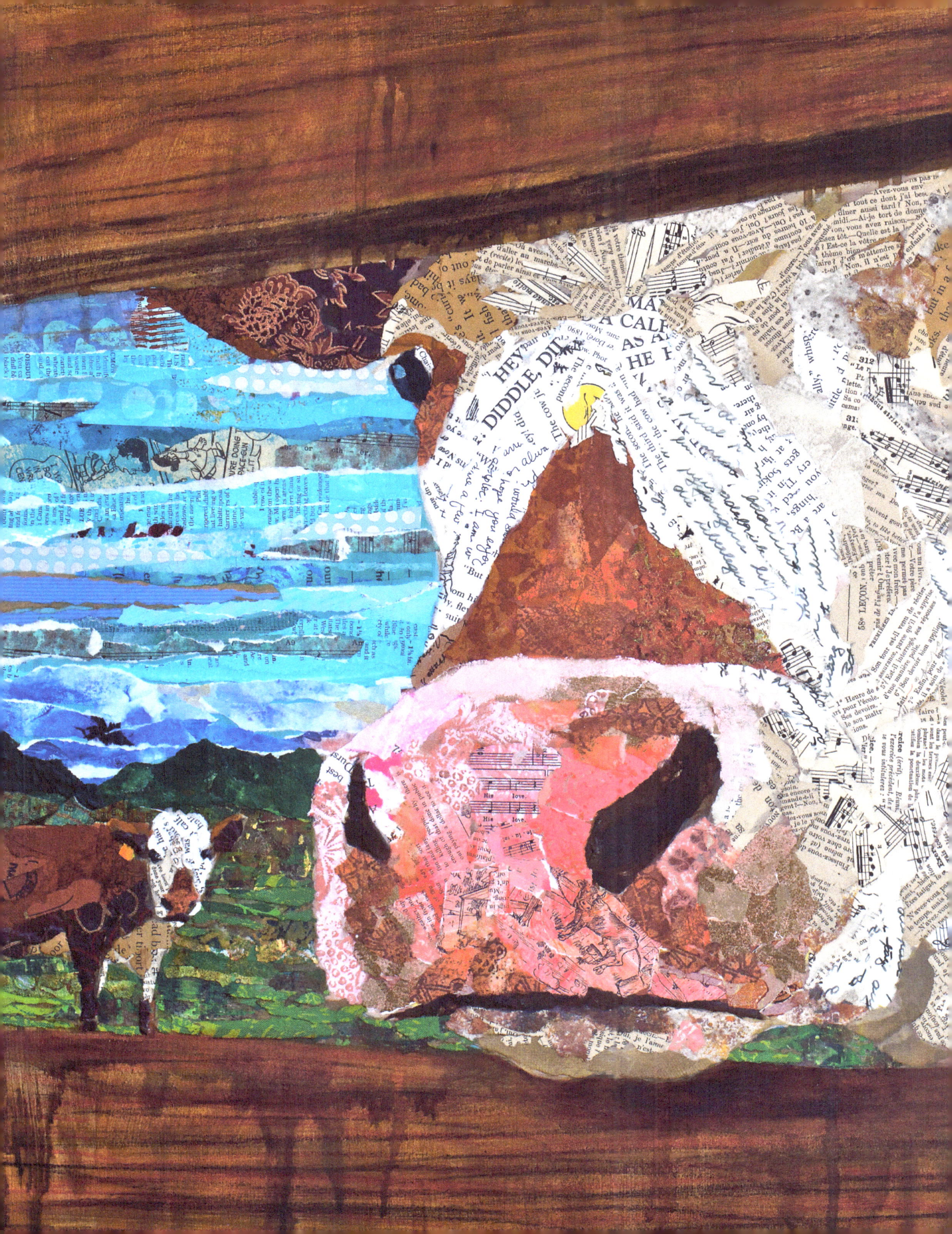

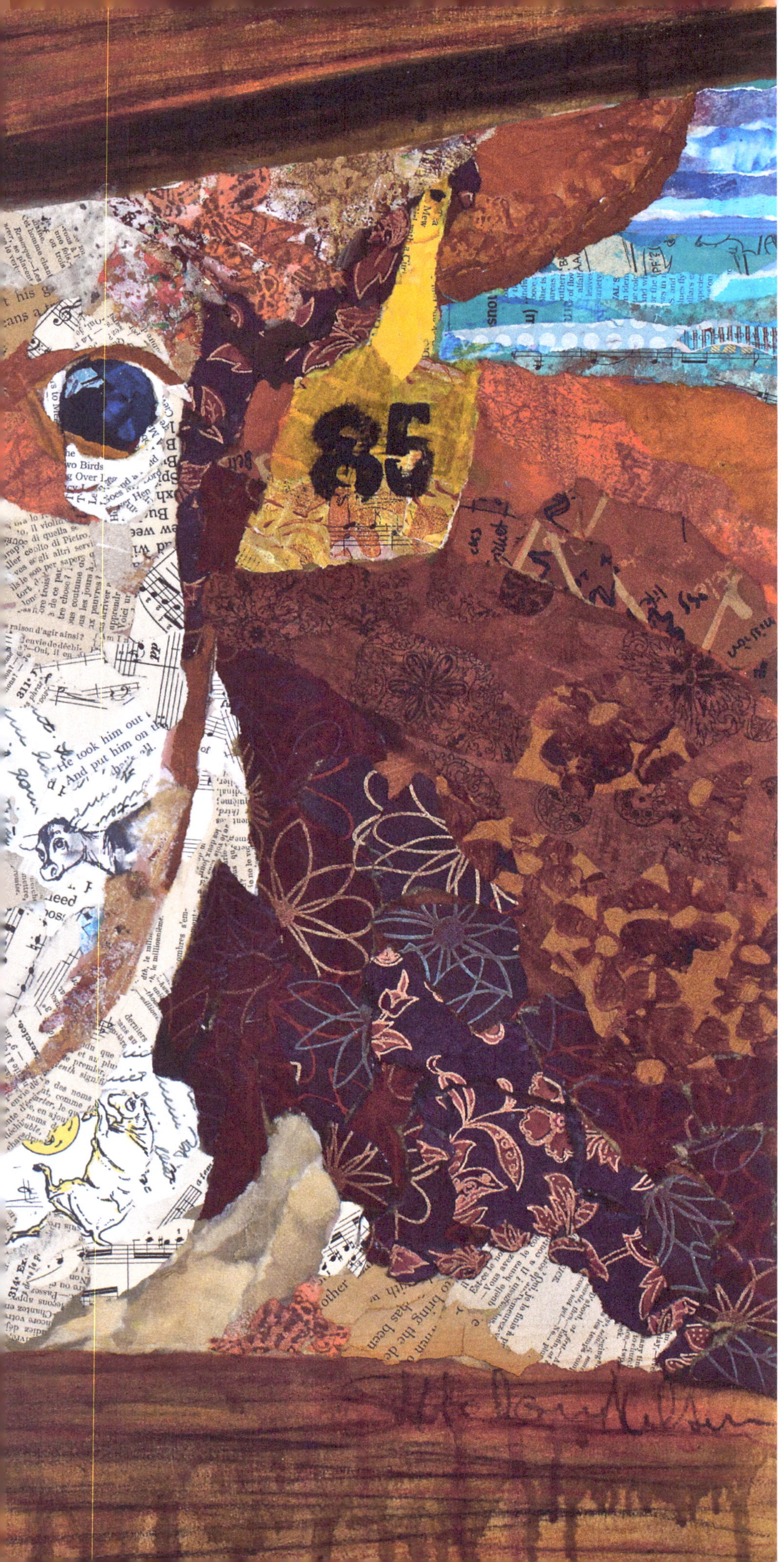

Stamping

Cow #85 *(36x24) makes use of the substrate wood and its grain. I worked on cabinet grade wood and "stained" the fence slat sections of the image with watered down Van Dyke brown fluid acrylic. The translucency of the paint gave it a wonderful color that also exposed the natural striations and grain of the wood.*

#85 is stamped with Speedball block printing ink with wood letter type blocks from an old printing press, on top of the collage paper.

1985 was the year I first traveled to Europe, with the Westfield High School Spanish class; a remarkable experience.

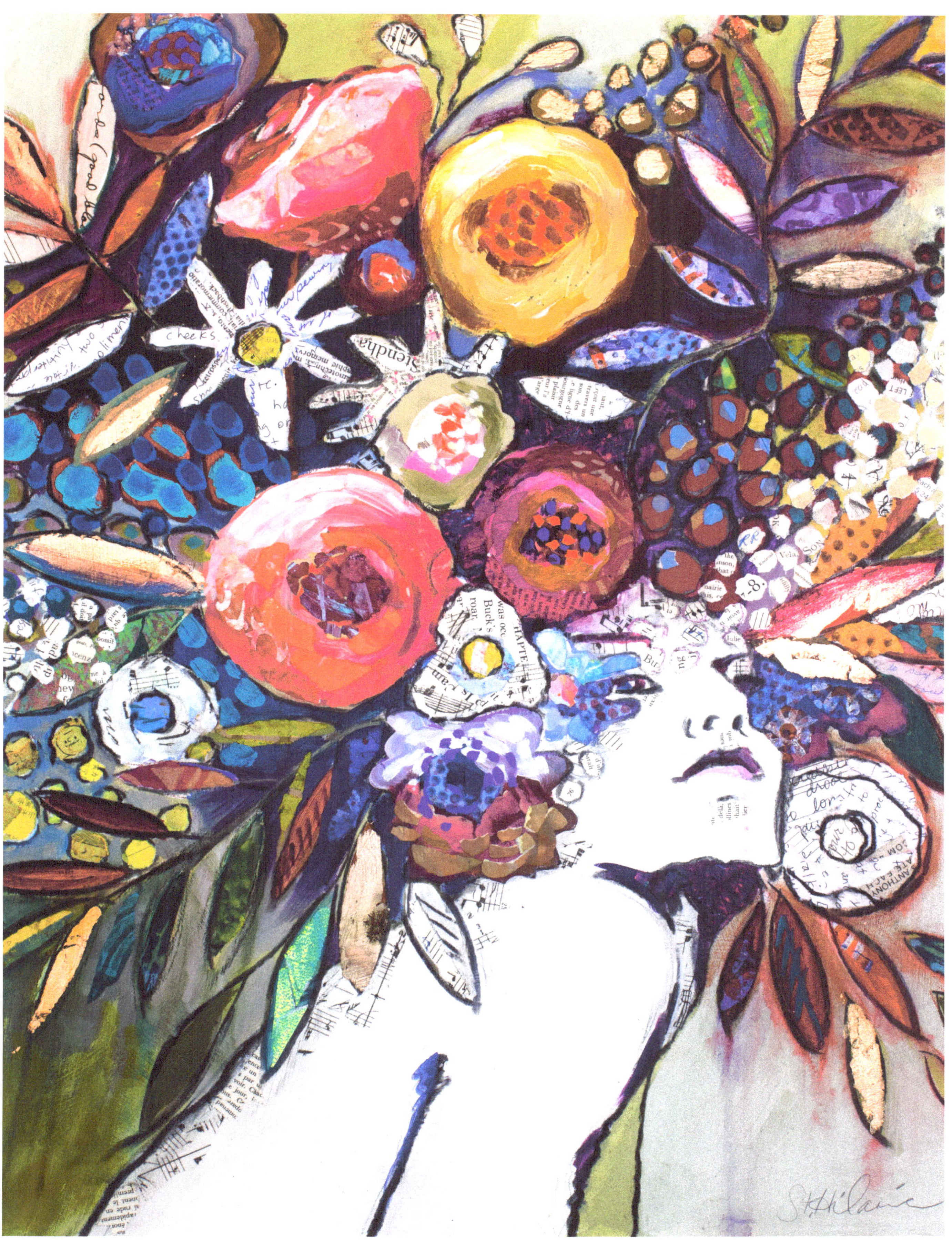

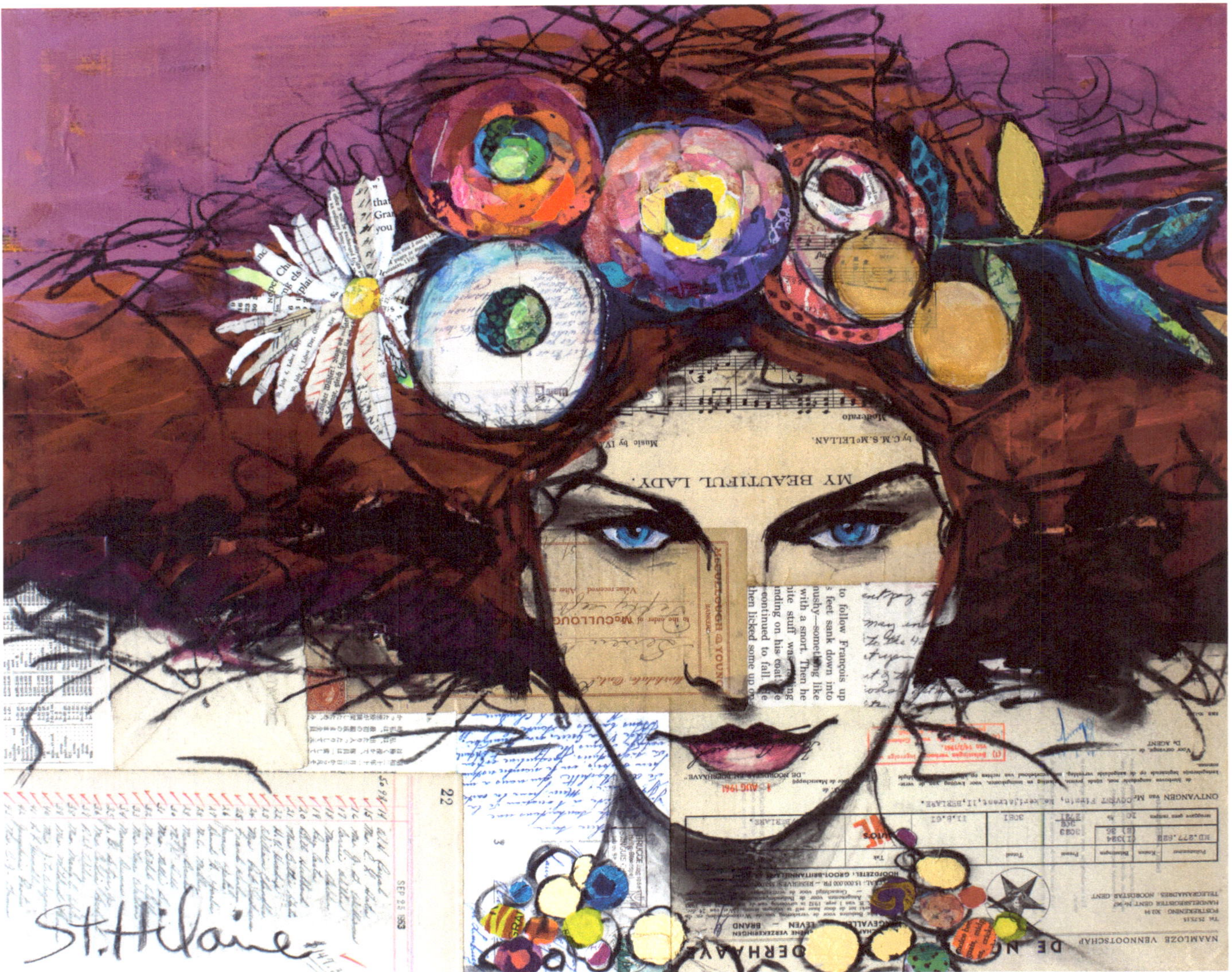

Black Outlines

MY FASHION SERIES incorporates soft vine charcoal and painted-on black gesso in order to yield heavy black outlines on the under-painting layer as well as added on top of the collage. Charcoal lines can also be rubbed and smudged before setting them with acrylic spray varnish.

Left: **Flora and Fauna** *(20x24) makes use of the white gesso primer layer on the substrate to form the skin tone. Soft vine charcoal was used for the outlines.*

Above: **My Beautiful Lady** *(24x20) features a background of various ephemera glued down to the substrate in order to create the skin tone. Smudged soft vine charcoal, acrylic painting, and collage is on top.*

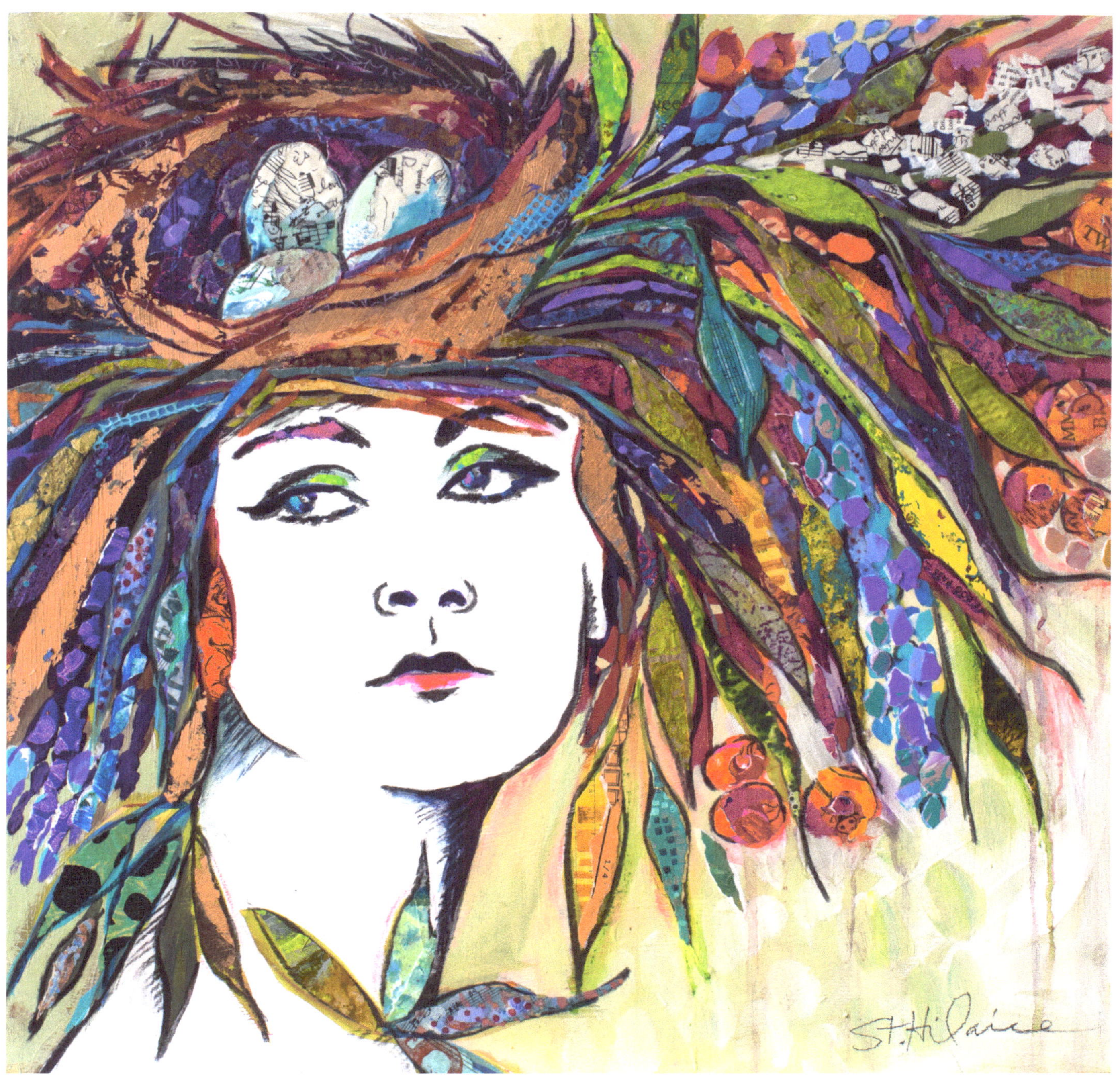

Black Outlines

Above: **Nesting** *(20x20) makes use of the white gesso primer on the substrate to form the skin tone. Soft vine charcoal and black gesso make up the outlines with accents of copper metal leaf.*

Right: **Might I Have a Bit of The Earth?** *(18x36) features a background of various ephemera glued down to the substrate. Soft vine charcoal and black gesso make up the outlines with acrylic paint, and collage on top.*

Overleaf: **Tulip Elephant** *(14x16) and* **Geoff Giraffe** *(14x16) feature backgrounds of various ephemera glued down to the substrate. Smudged soft vine charcoal outline, acrylic paint, combine with collage on top.*

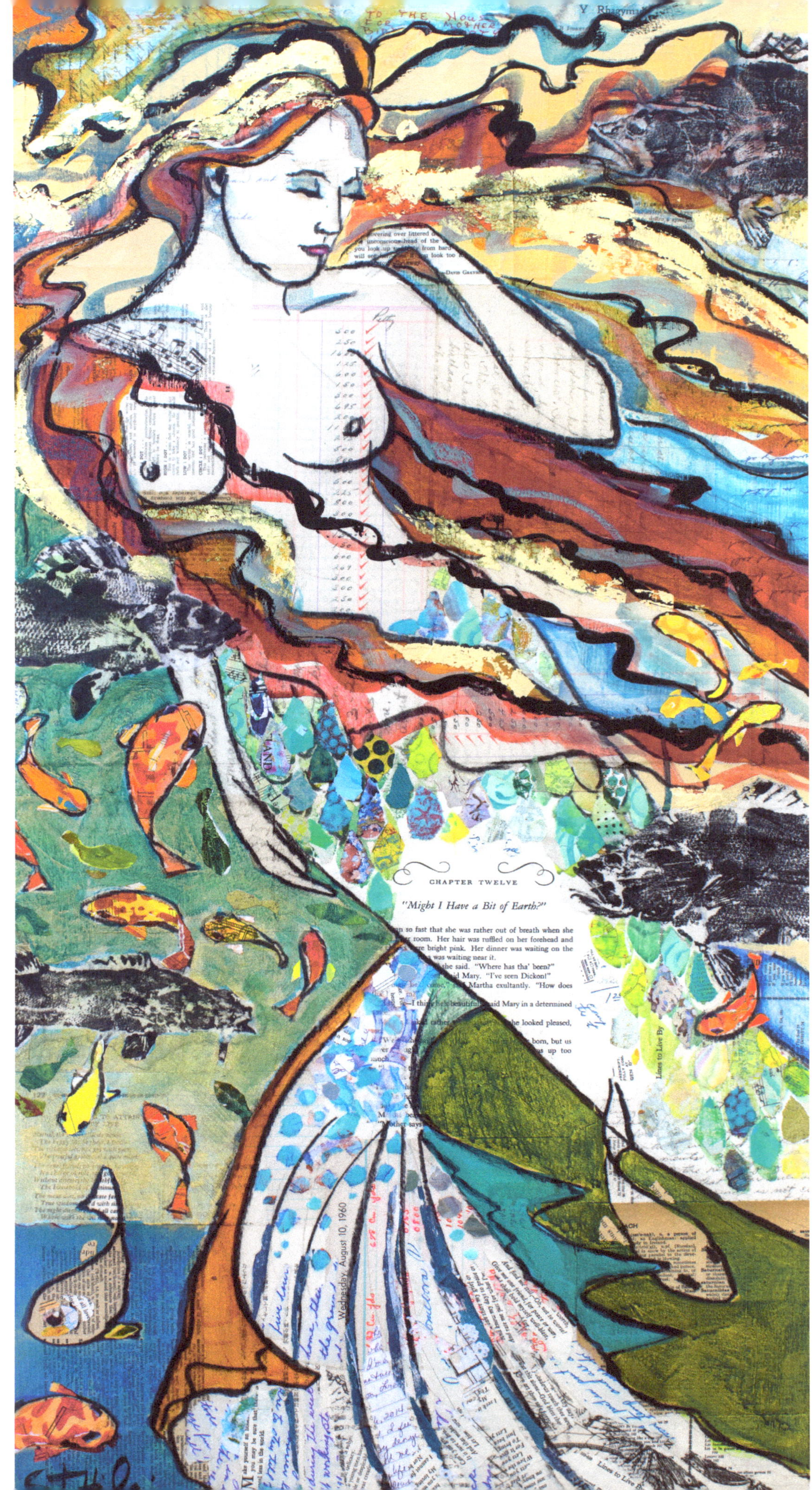

CHAPTER TWELVE

"Might I Have a Bit of Earth?"

n so fast that she was rather out of breath when she
room. Her hair was ruffled on her forehead and
bright pink. Her dinner was waiting on the
was waiting near it.
she said. "Where has tha' been?"
id Mary. "I've seen Dickon!"
Martha exultantly. "How does

I think he's beautiful, said Mary in a determined

she looked pleased,

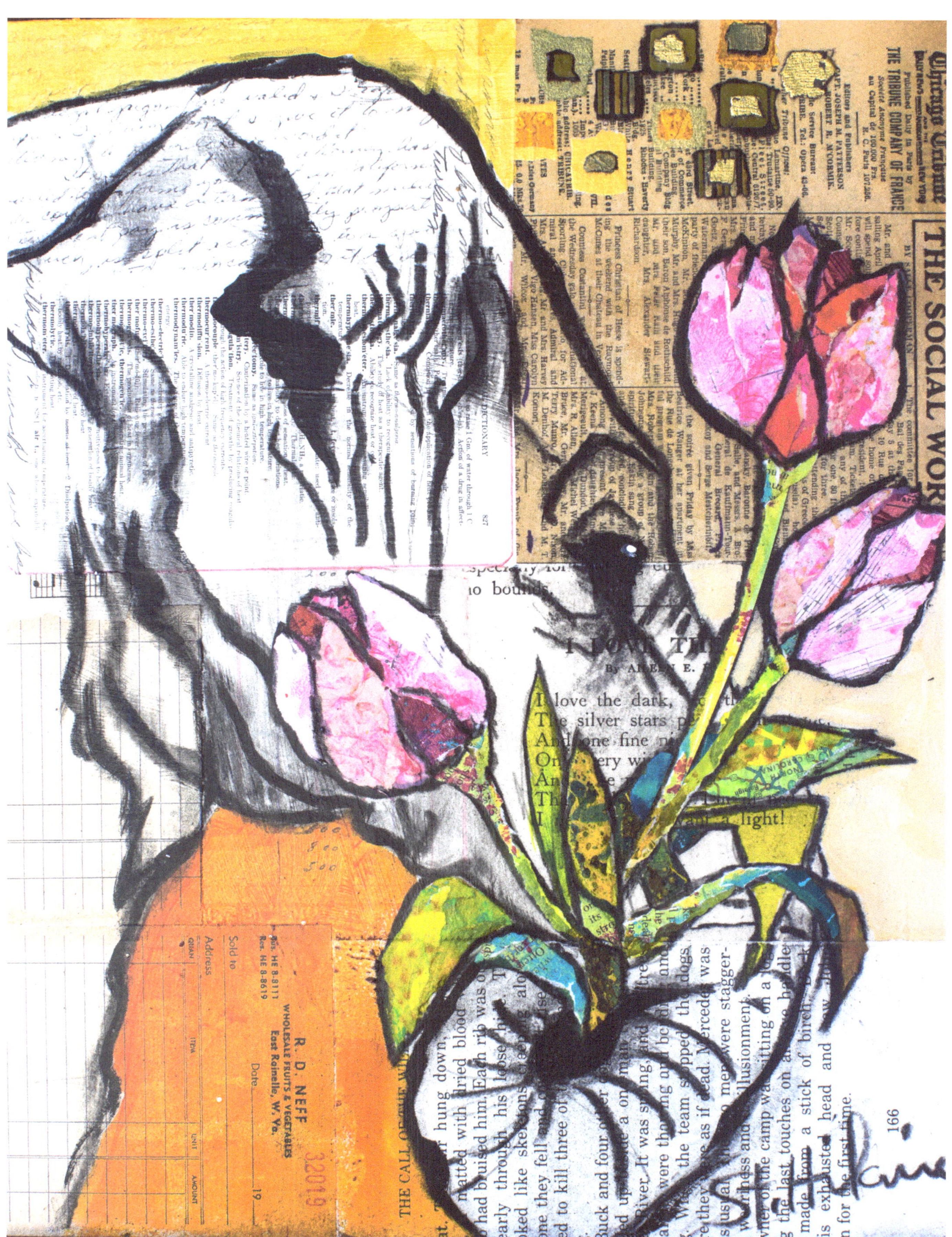

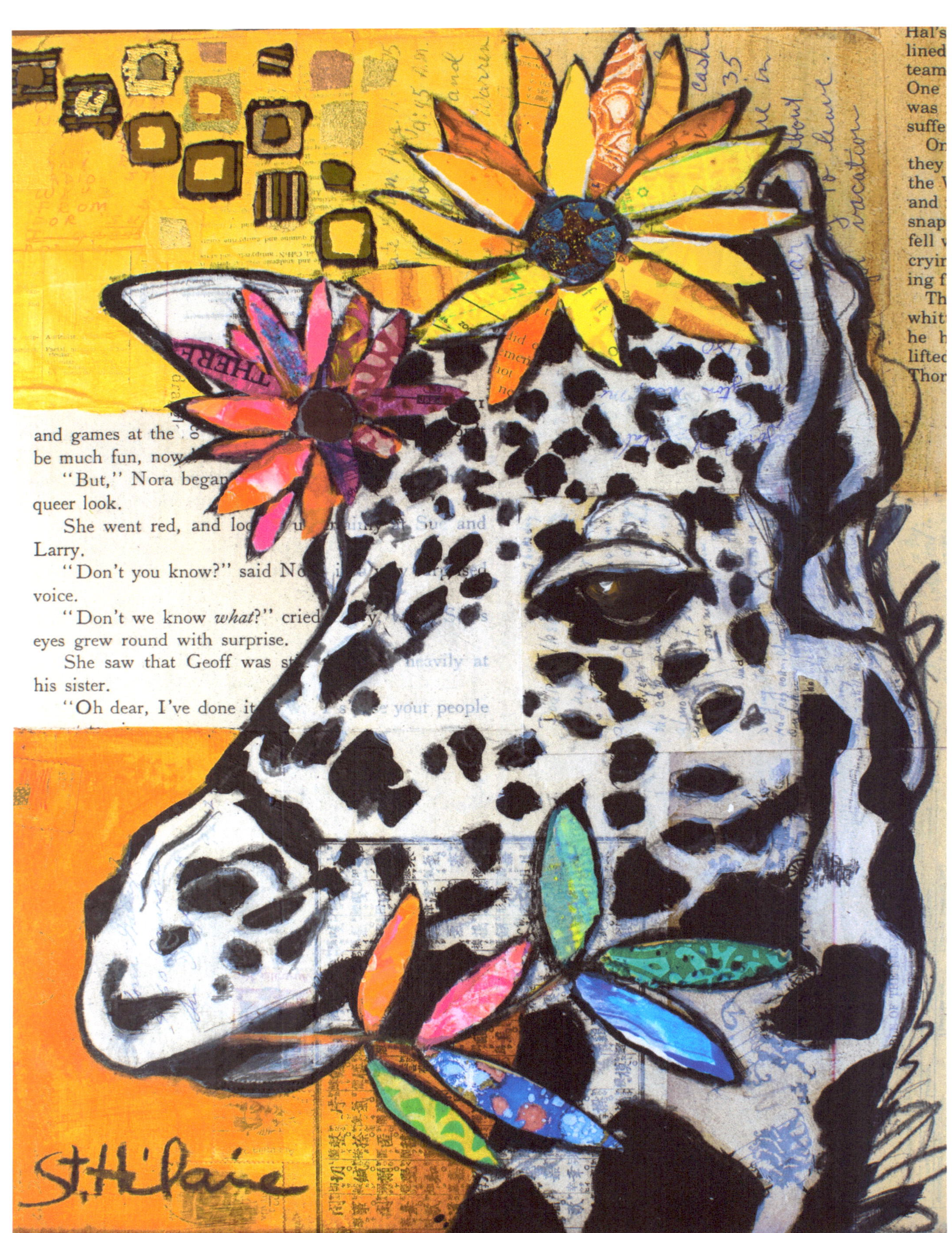
and games at the
be much fun, now
"But," Nora began
queer look.
She went red, and lo
Larry.
"Don't you know?" said N
voice.
"Don't we know what?" cried
eyes grew round with surprise.
She saw that Geoff was s
his sister.
"Oh dear, I've done it
St.Hilaire

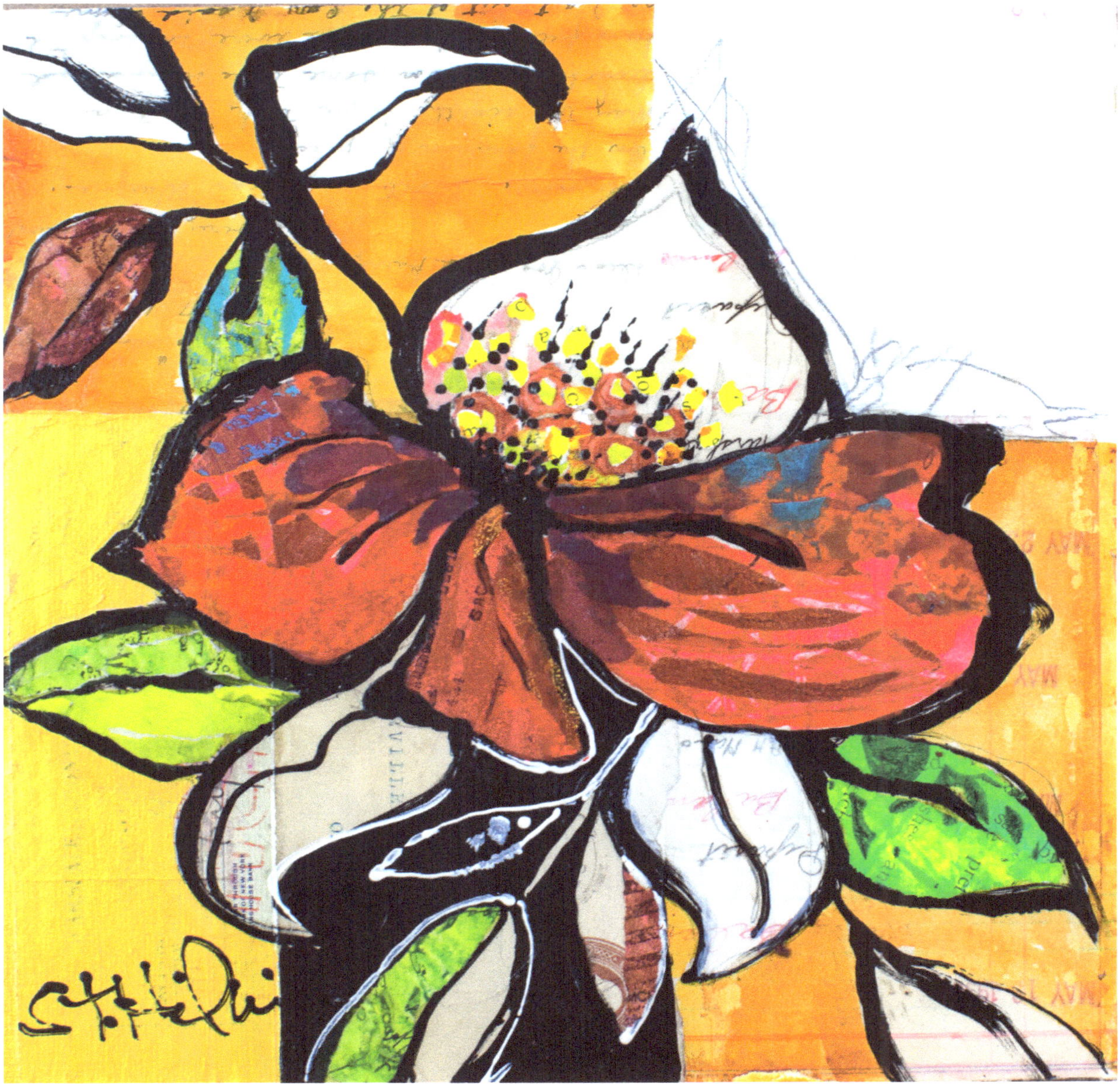

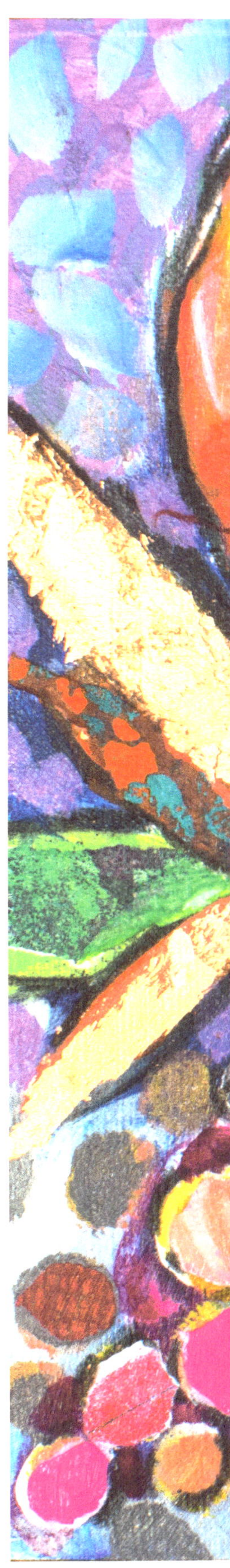

Black Outlines

Above: **Red Floral Study** *(10x10) features a background of various
ephemera glued down to the substrate. Black gesso outline, graphite,
and acrylic paint, combined with collage on top.*

Right: **Floral Study #2** *incorporates soft vine
charcoal in order to yield heavy black outlines in
the under-painting layer as well as added on top
of the collage. Copper metallic leaf works well in
combination with the hand-painted collage papers.
Metallic leaf is applied with an adhesive, I use
Mona Lisa brand for both products.*

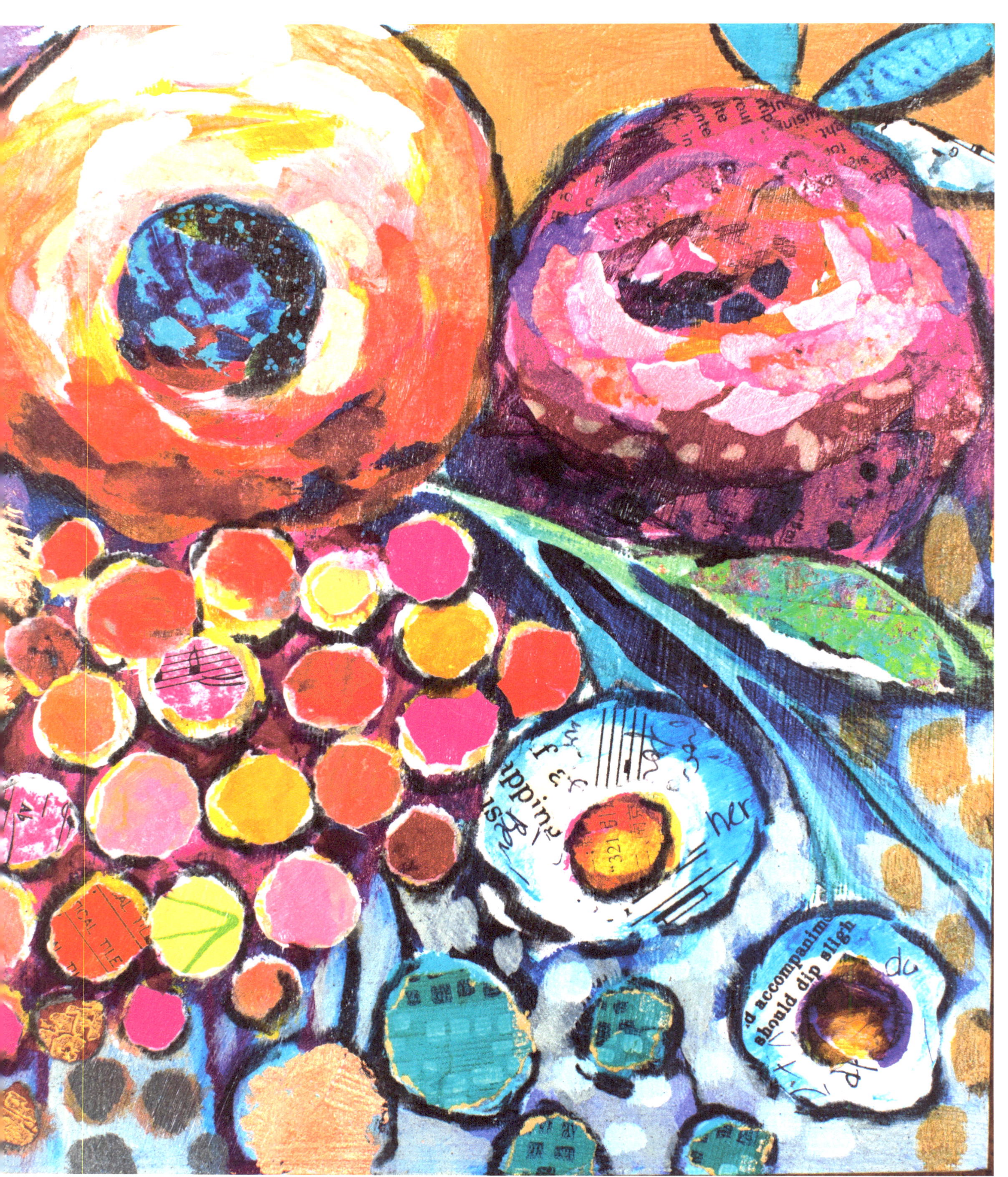

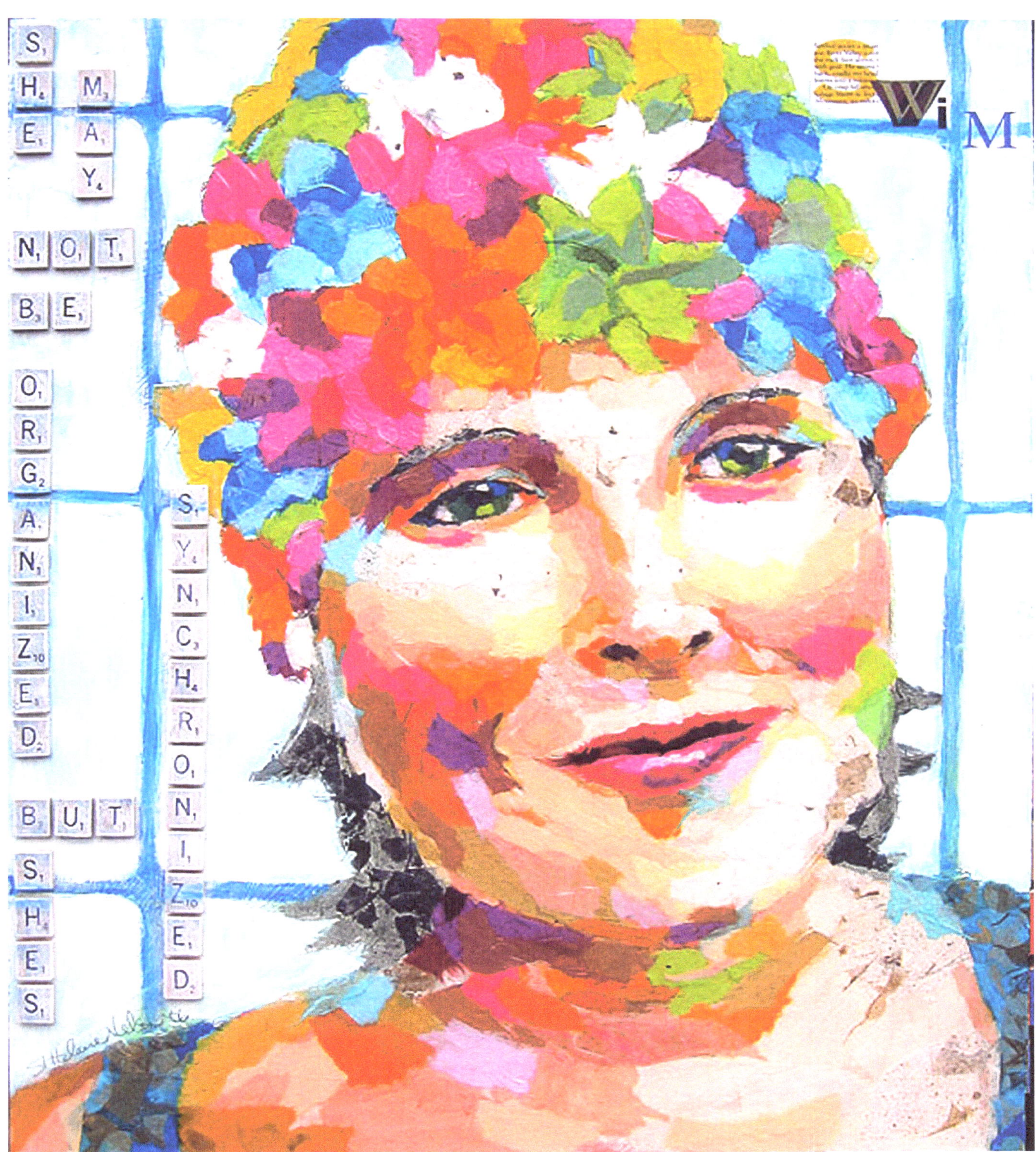

Game Tiles

Water Ballet (24X24) *incorporates lettering from game tiles and magazine print. In order to subdue the letter tiles, they were washed with the background color. All 3-D objects are applied on top of the final varnish coat to avoid puddling around them when applied.*

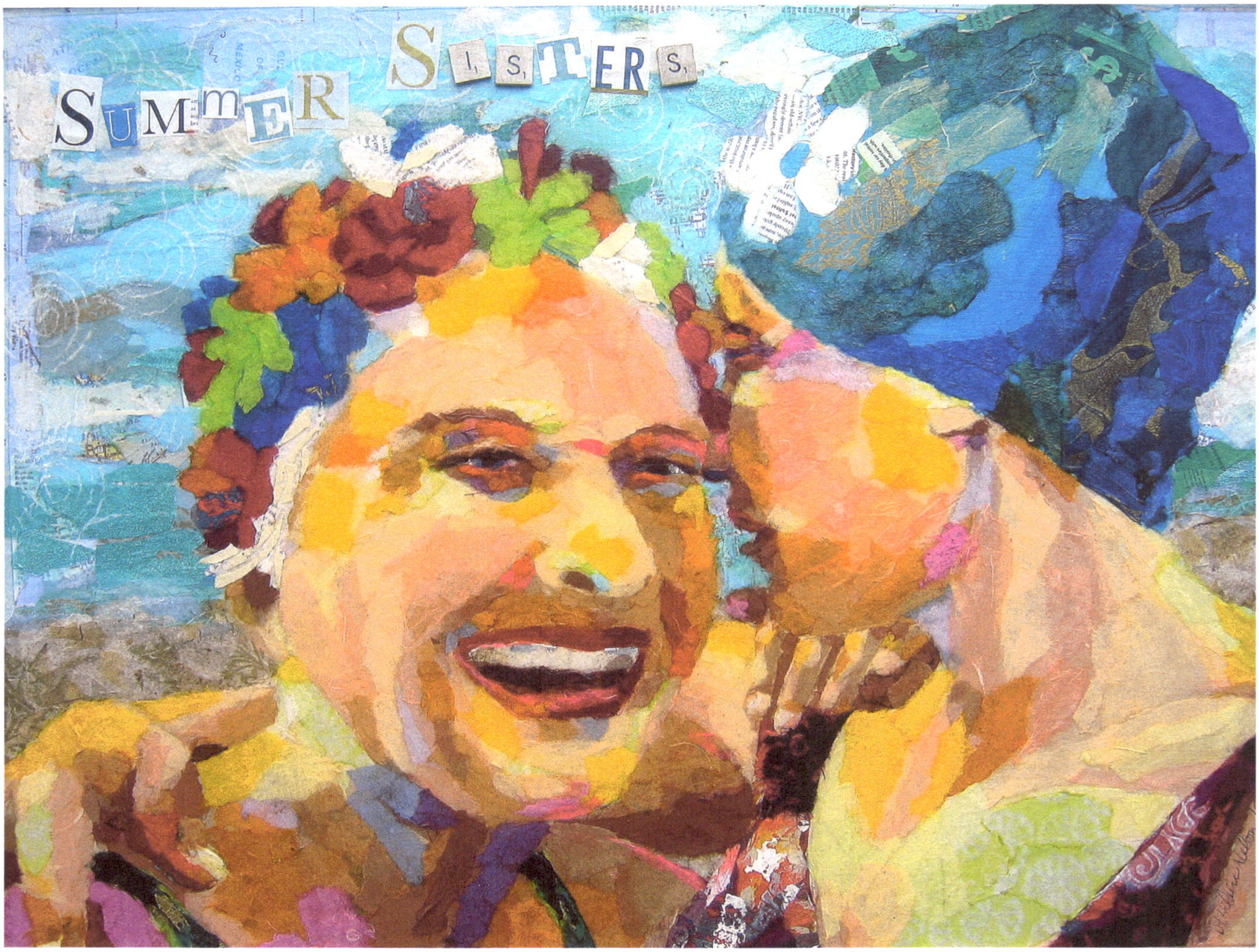

Game Tiles

Top: **Summer Sisters** (*24x20*) *lettering from game tiles and magazine print. In order to subdue the letter tiles, they were washed with the background color.*

Right: **Tweet** (*12x9*) *one of my earliest collages. This piece utilizes game tiles that have been tinted with yellow acrylic to be more harmonious with the color palette.*

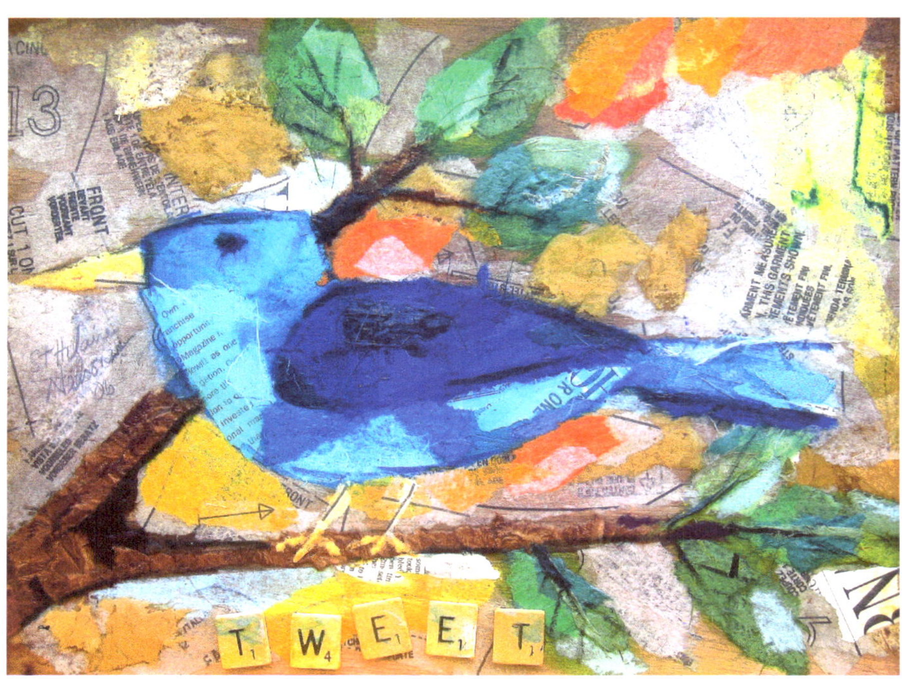

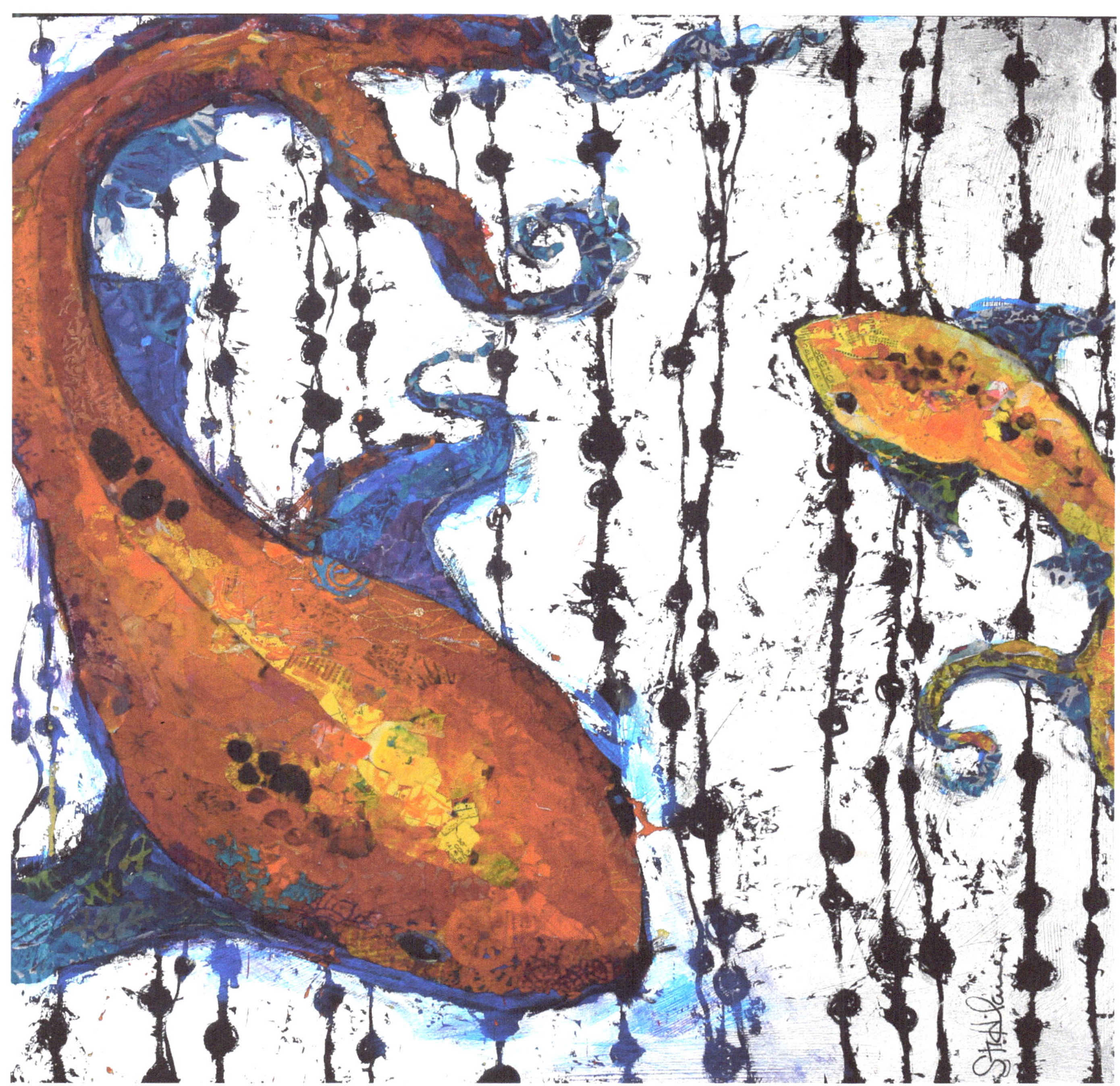

Metallic Leaf

Coy Koi *(24X24) has a full backdrop of silver metallic leaf applied over black gesso. The seaweed line and circle pattern was left without adhesive, allowing it to show through as positive shape after the silver metallic leaf was applied. I prefer Mona Lisa Simple Leaf, This transfer-style leaf is easier to handle and apply than traditional leaf, but delivers the same shimmering results. To apply the leaf, I use Mona Lisa's water-based brush-on adhesive, following the product instructions.*

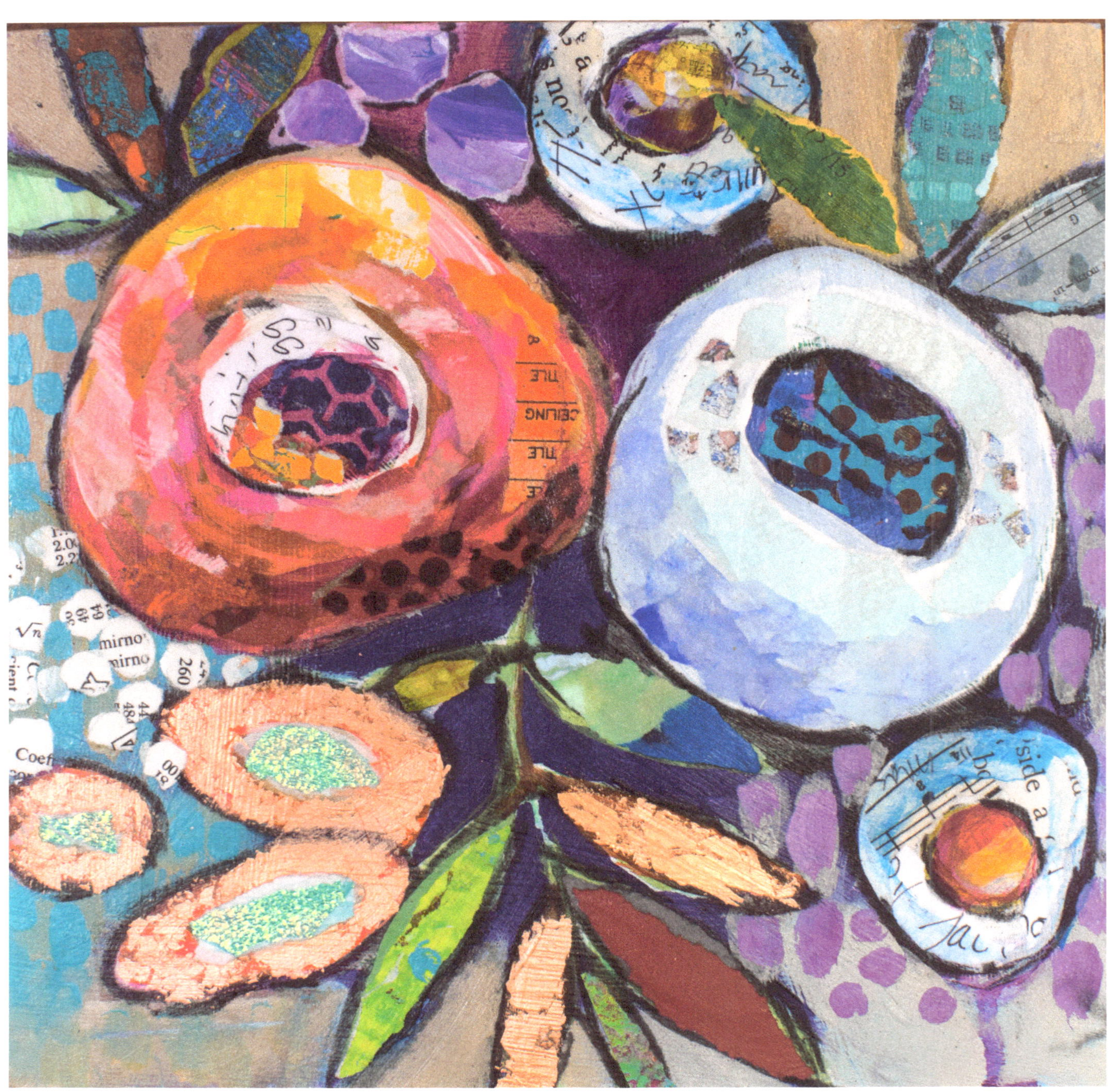

Metallic Leaf

Floral Study #1 (8x8) *incorporates copper metallic leaf accents that work well in combination with the hand-painted collage papers.*

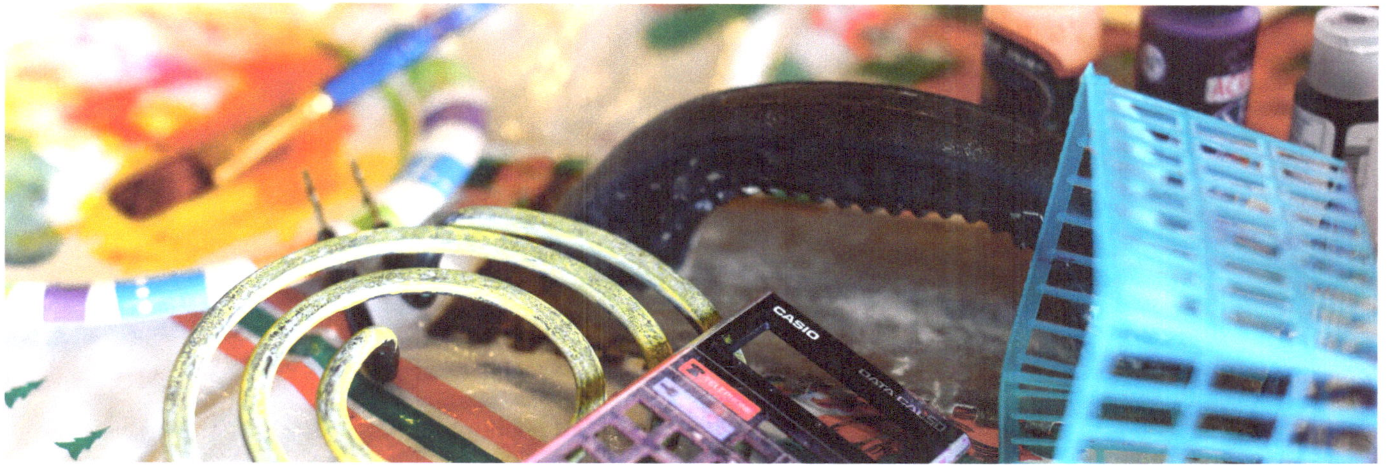

unexpected

IMPLEMENTING THE UNEXPECTED and unusual plays a huge part in the success of mixed media art. When you are not limited to any one material, you have the whole world at your disposal. Sometimes it's important to think outside the art supply store box and consider the hardware store, the kitchen supply or home goods store, the craft store... I pull supplies, tools and inspiration from everywhere.

The tools I use for mark-making, or the materials I apply to the surface, can come from unexpected places; such is the joy of mixed media!

Recently I took an abstract painting workshop in Orlando; the supply list asked us to bring small house paint samples from the Home Depot, a deli tray from the grocery store for paint mixing, hardware store chip brushes and putty knives. How fun and freeing it was to work with such non traditional media outside my comfort zone!

Last year I took a welding workshop, the instructor taught us how to use a blow torch and an arc welder—how to cut and combine metal in an artistic manner. Over the course of the weekend we combined mixed metals from a junk heap to create beautiful art sculptures.

Taking a class or workshop in a media that you normally do not work with is a great way to jump-start your creativity. If you are looking to be inspired and motivated, try something artistically different. Having to work at new techniques exercises your creative muscles, not to mention you never know where it will take you in your artistic journey.

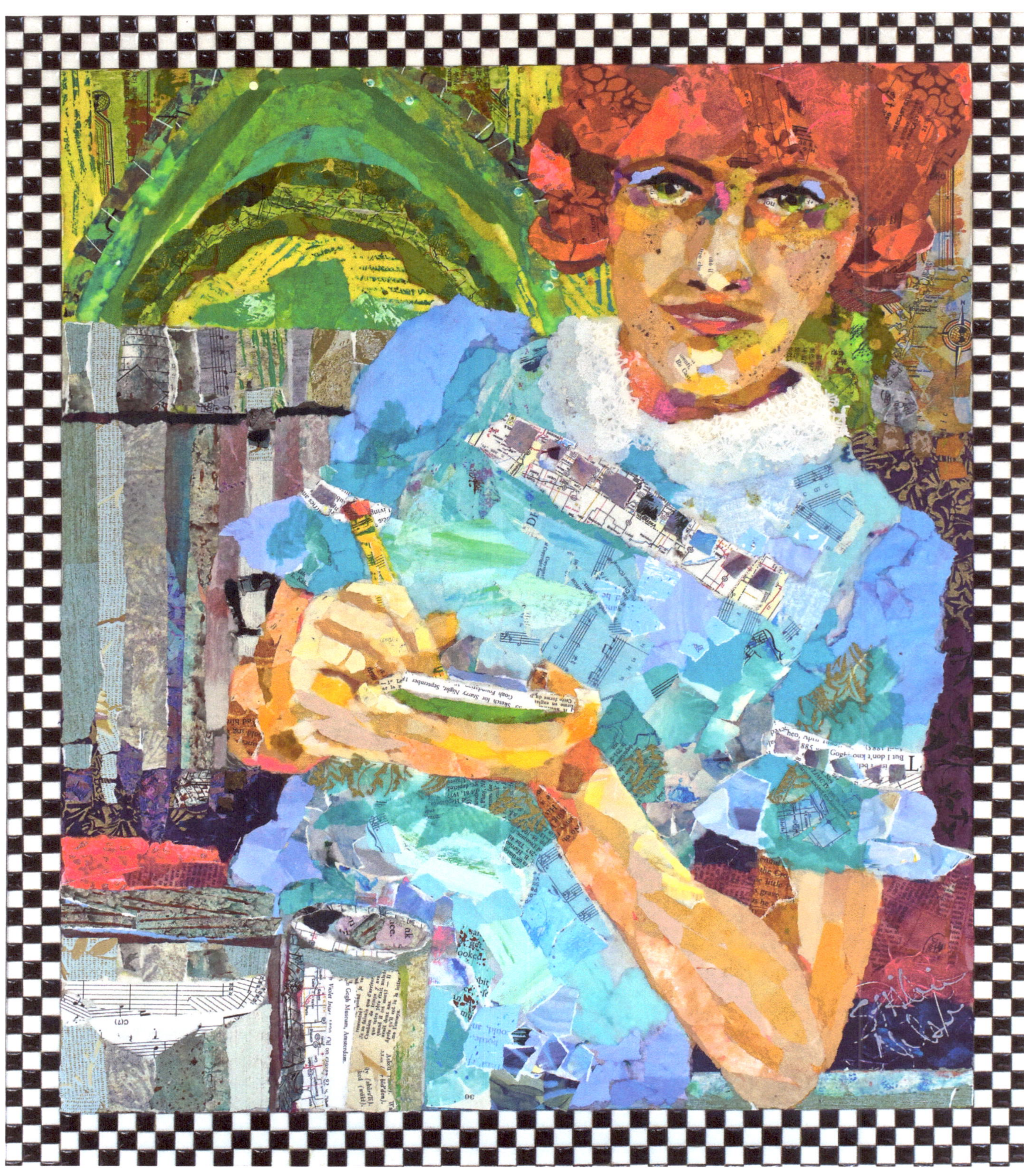

At Your Service #1 *(20x24) features a glass tile border, applied one-at-a-time with construction adhesive. The effect I was going for here was a 50's diner feel with black and white tile; the piece is framed in silver metallic molding.*

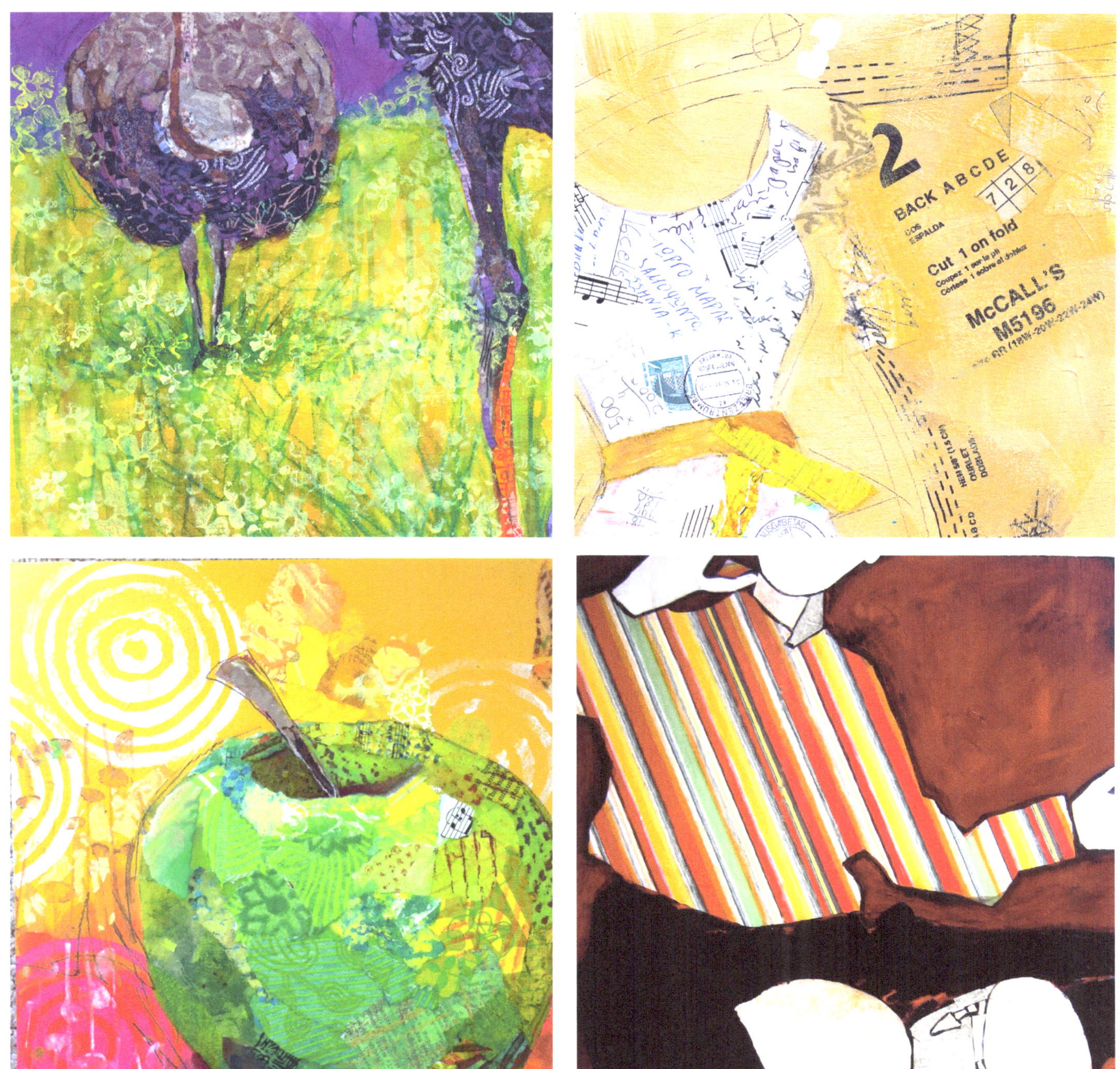

Household Inspiration

EXPERIMENTING WITH FOUND ITEMS can keep your work fresh. **Top left:** stamping with non-slip silicone bath mat directly onto the background. **Top right:** sewing pattern paper. **Bottom left:** hand carved stamp made from an oversized eraser, combined with a store bought rubber stamp. **Bottom right:** wallpaper sample book pages from Home Depot combined with acrylic paint and black gesso.

MIXED MEDIA COLLAGE INSPIRATION

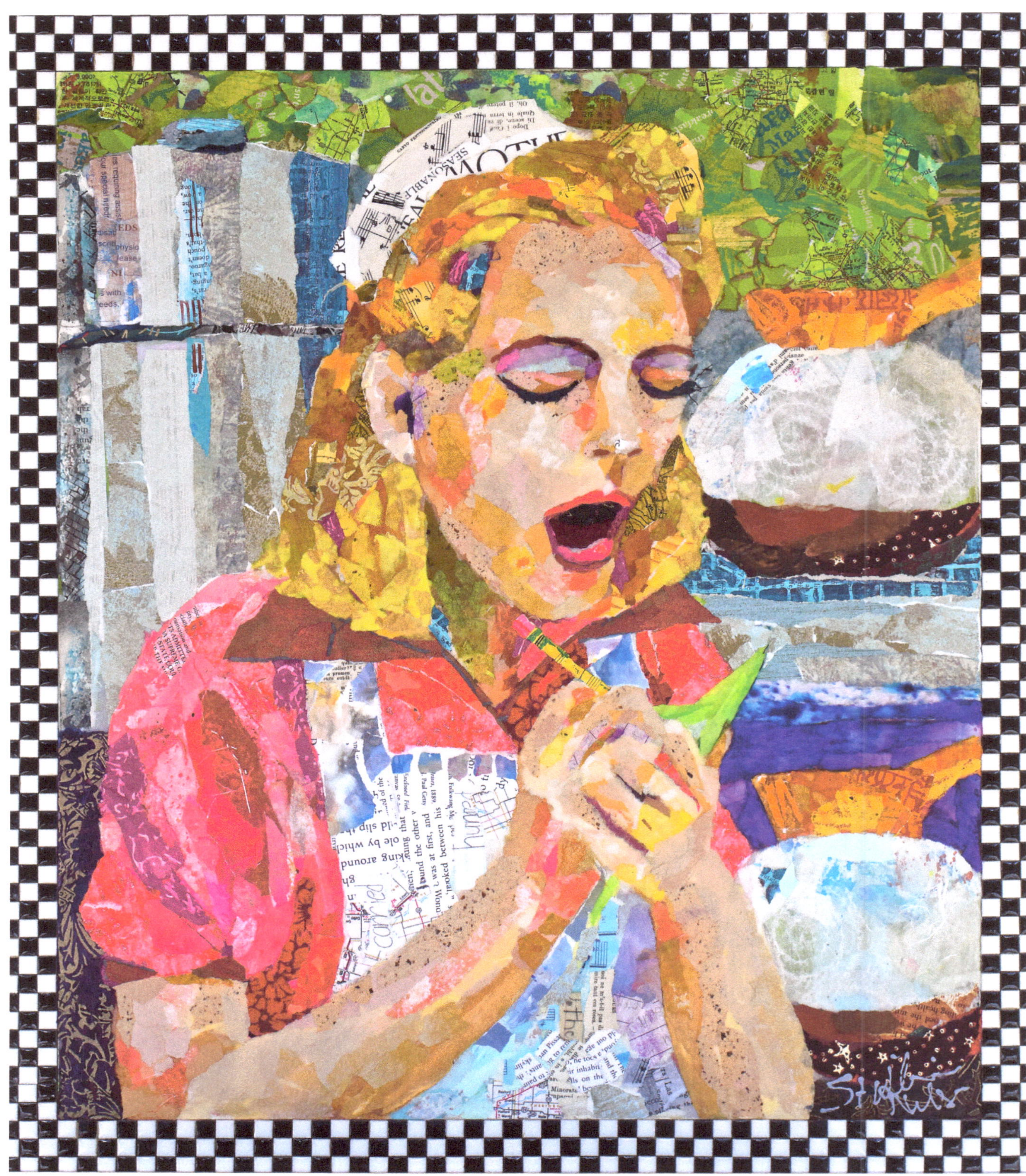

At Your Service #3 (20x24) *features a glass tile border, applied one-at-a-time with construction adhesive. The effect I was going for here was a 50's diner feel with black and white tile; the piece is framed in silver metallic molding.*

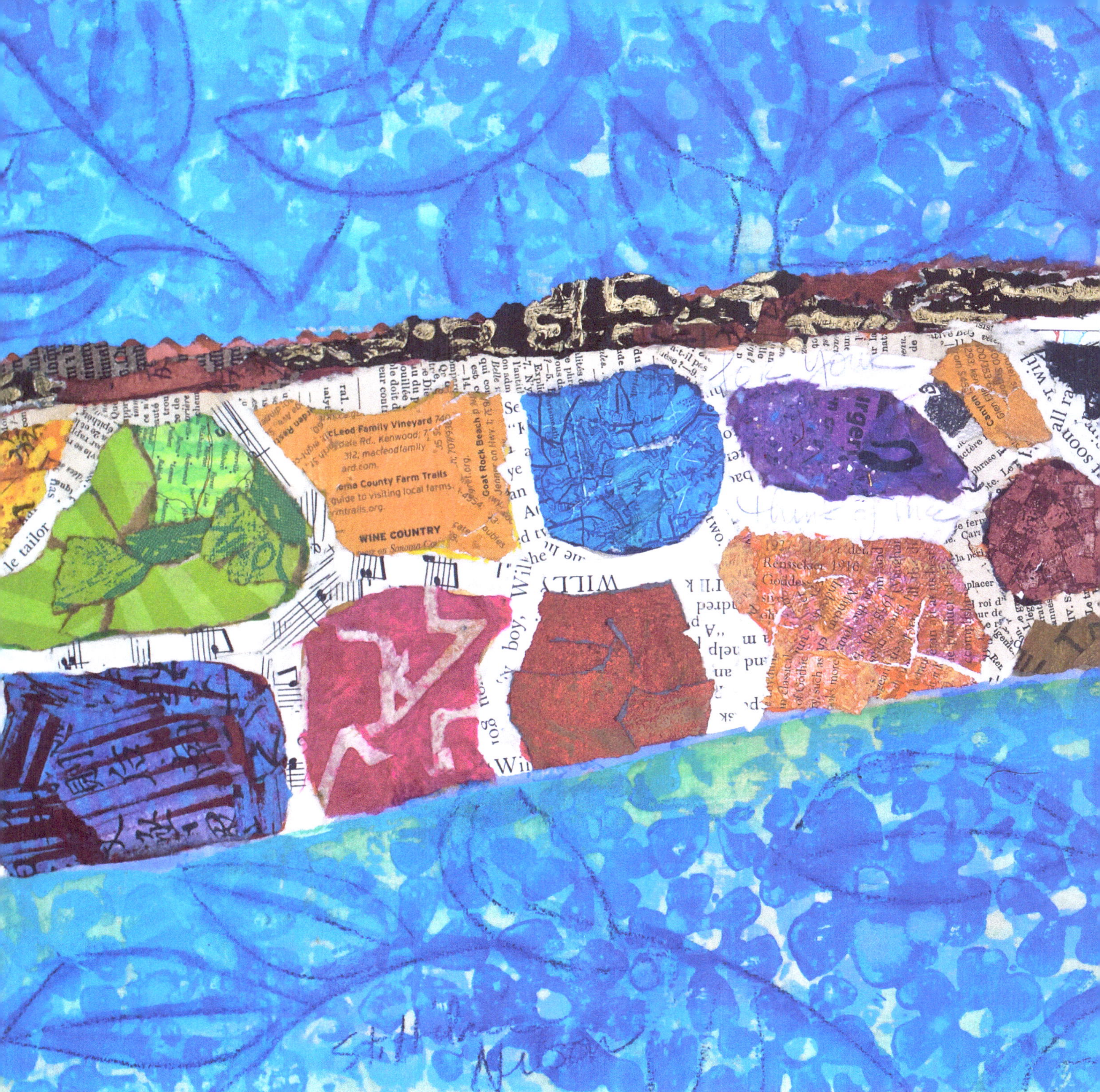

Bathtub Liner Stamping

George Giraffe (24X12) *makes use of stamping and drawing in the background. The first layer is full bodied blue paint applied with a non slip, floral patterned bathmat. On top of the stamped pattern, a leafy branch is illustrated with Derwent InkTense pencil, which bleed when water is applied, but are permanent once dry.*

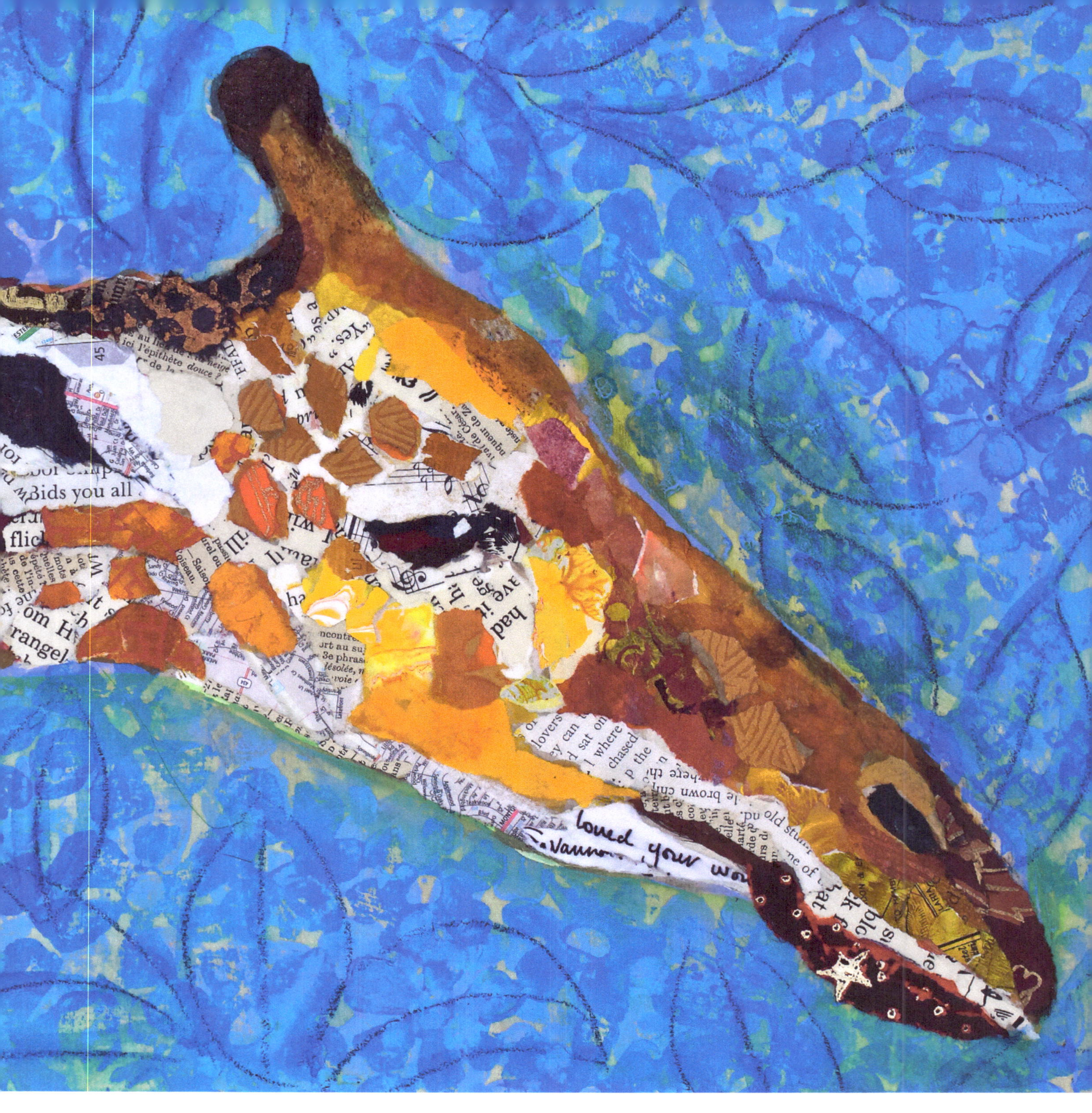

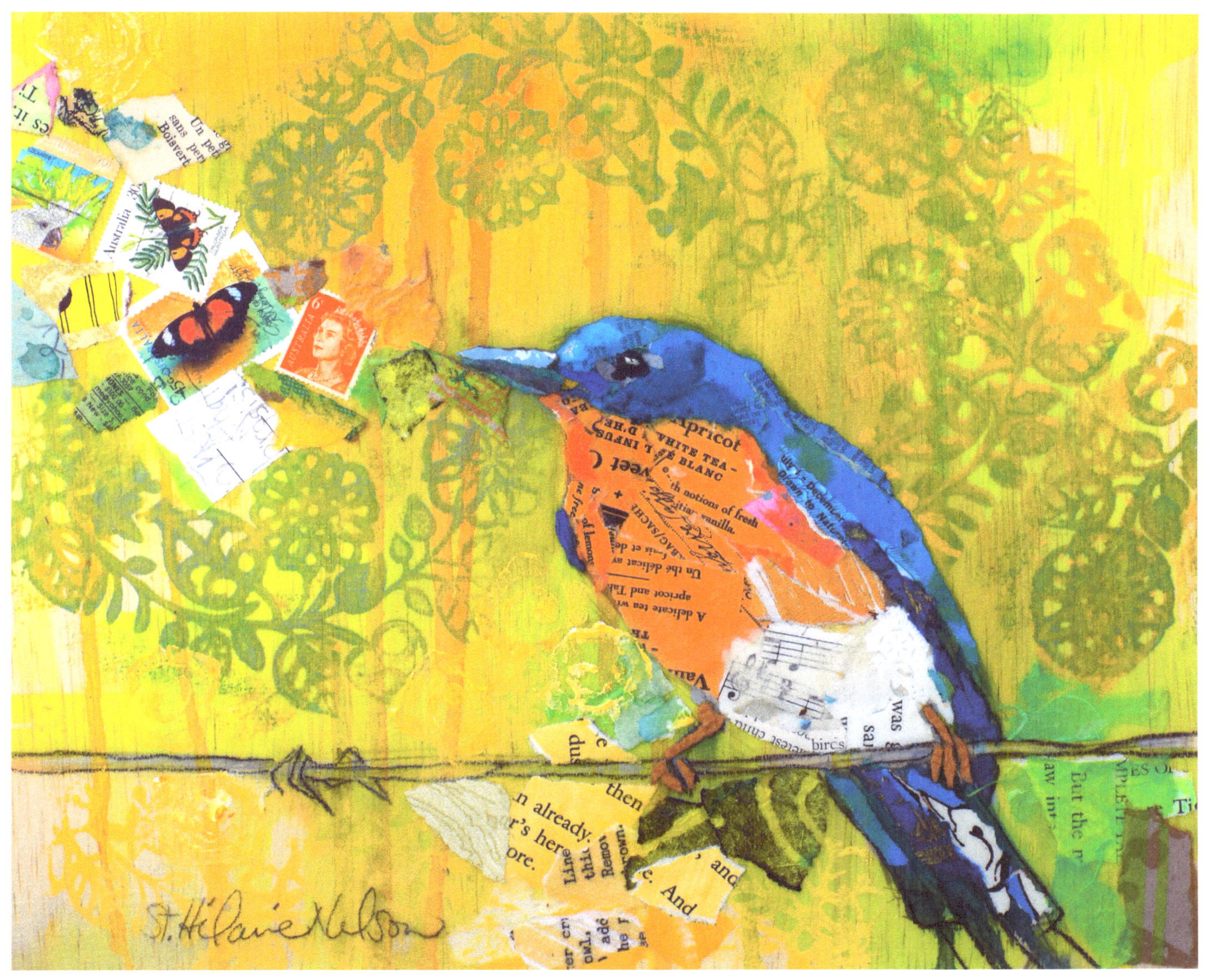

Greeting Card Stamping

Birds and Butterflies *(9X12) The floral pattern in the background of this piece was stamped from a greeting card. The birthday card had a soft embossed material on it that I thought would make a beautiful impression when pressed with paint. Although it couldn't be used too many times, it worked perfectly to create the patterned background in this piece. Postal stamps make up the butterfly component, the barbed wire is illustrated in graphite.*

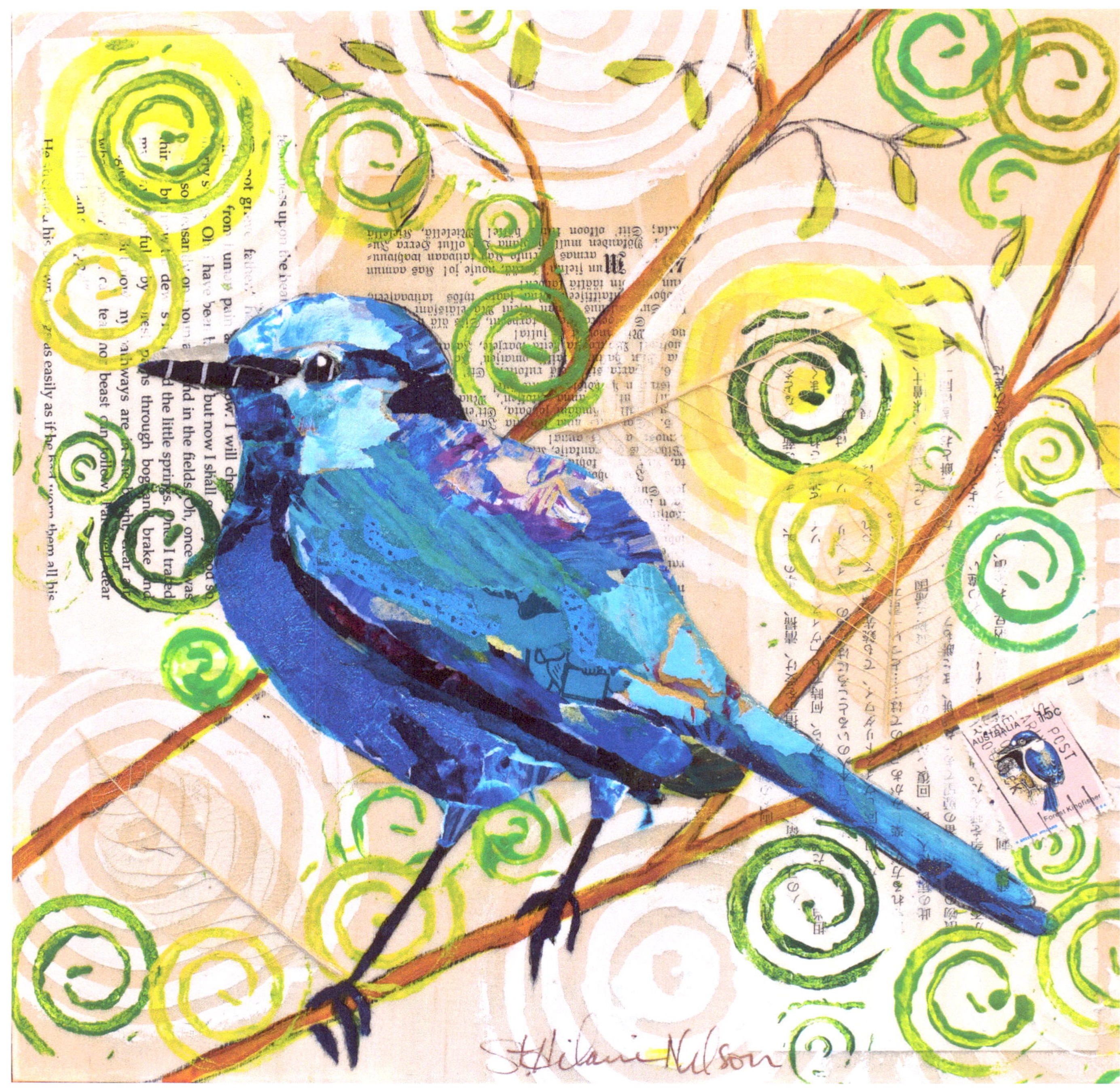

Carved Eraser Stamping

Blue Bird of Happiness *(12X12) The spiral pattern in the background of this piece was stamped from two different materials. The yellow and green are from an off-the-shelf stamp that I found in the scrap-booking section of JoAnn Etc. I am always drawn to spirals and concentric circles, and so this tool spoke to me. The white spiral underneath is one that I carved by hand, out of an oversized eraser in Target's $1 bin at the front of the store during Back to School Days. I use a Speedball carving tool: plastic handle with interchangeable nibs. Acrylic paint is applied to the stamp and applied it over a clear primed wood panel.*

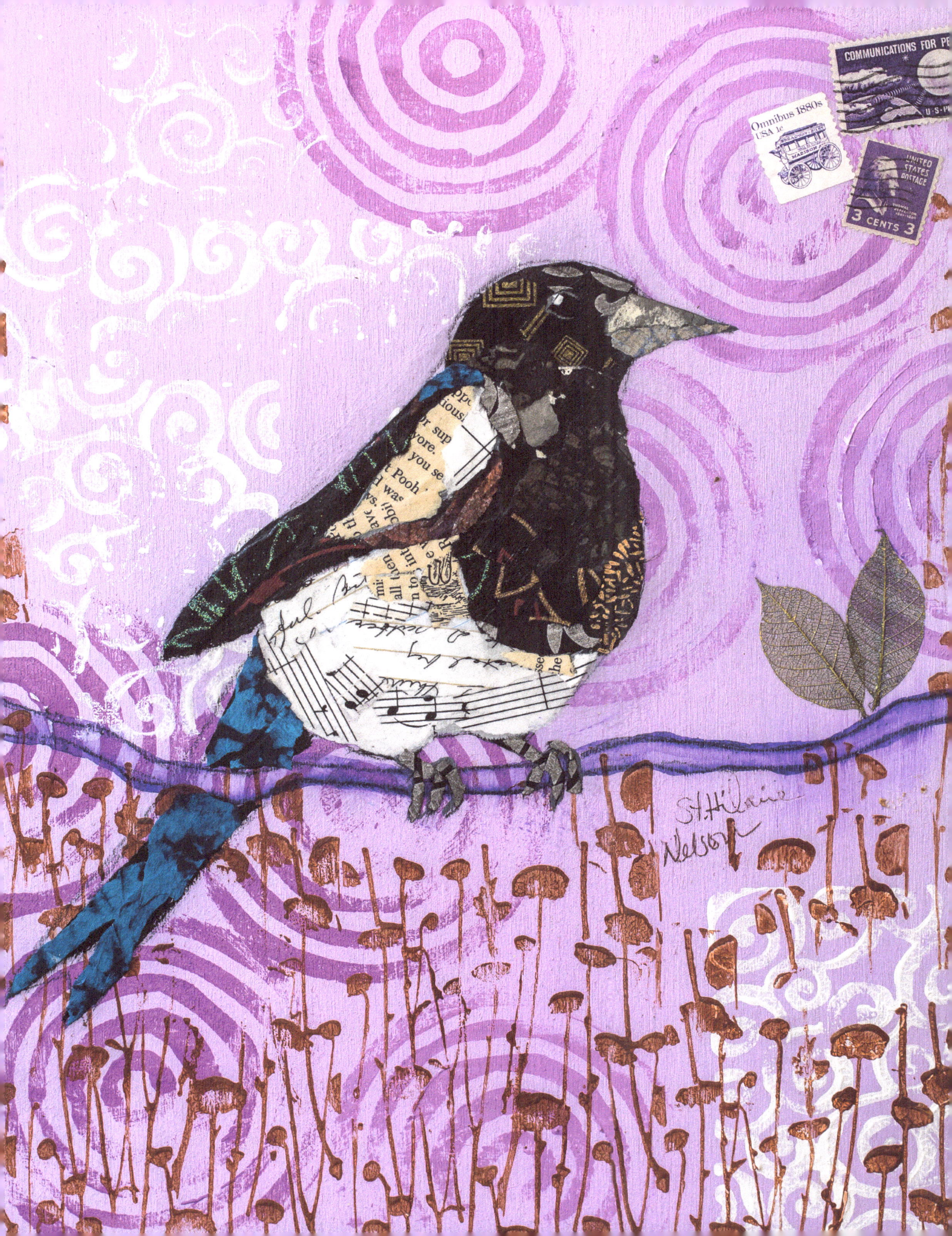

COMMUNICATIONS FOR PE
U.S.P
Omnibus 1880s
USA 1c
UNITED STATES POSTAGE
3 CENTS 3

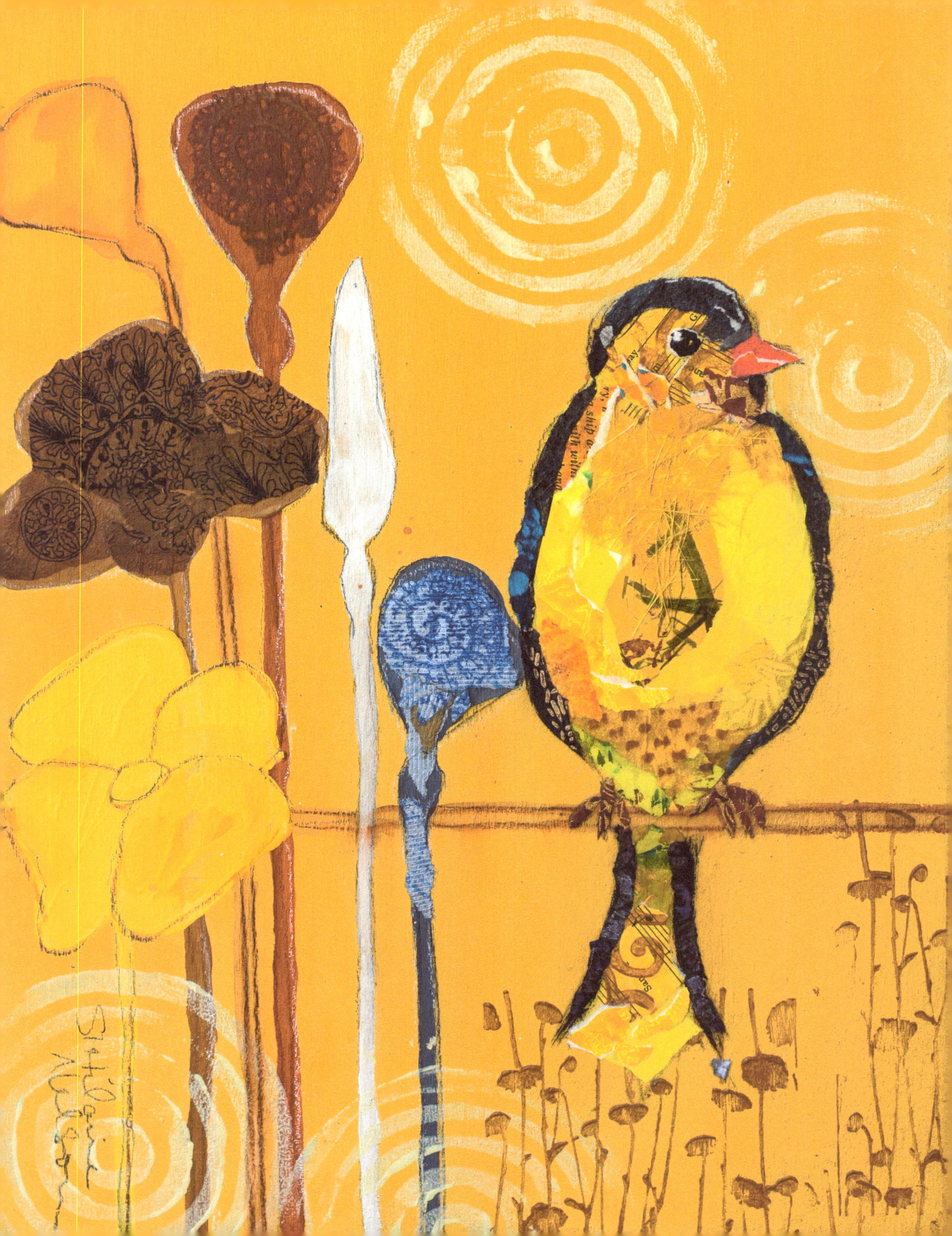

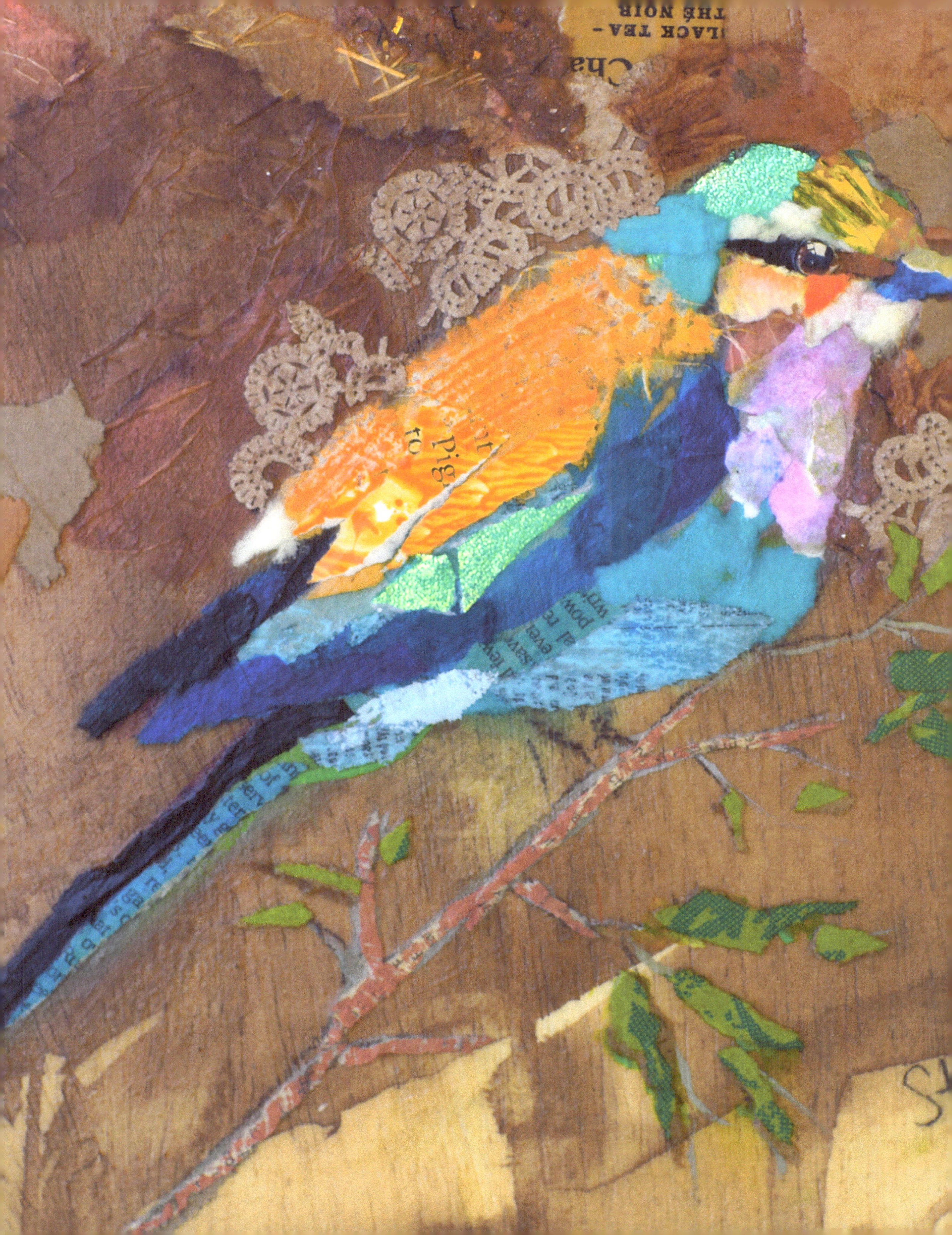
BLACK TEA -
THÉ NOIR
Cha

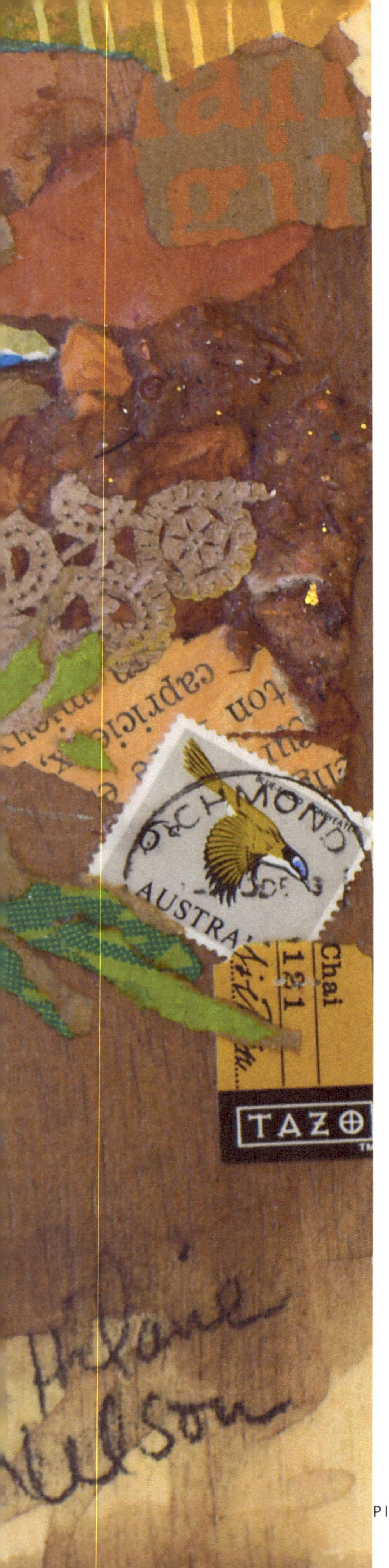

Found Papers

Left: **Contemplation** *(8X8) This bird has interesting materials in the background, to include paper doilies, tea bag tag and sachet, Starbucks paper bags (in the leaves), and iridescent bits of plastic. The single Australian postage stamp brings in a second bird image to the composition.*

Below: **Chai Tea** *(10X10) This piece is one of a series that was created for an exhibition at Orlando's Dandelion Communitea Café. The background makes use of Orlando maps and subject related laser prints, as well as tea bag tags and sachets, and a Chinese fortune. The teapot is cut from the page of an old wallpaper sample book, obtained from the Home Depot.*

Overleaf: **DRESS SERIES** *(12X16)* **Red Dress** *and* **White Dress**. *This series featured vintage sewing patterns which were the inspiration for dress imagery. In addition to the patterns, the pieces feature sheet music, paper doilies, vintage letters and other found papers.*

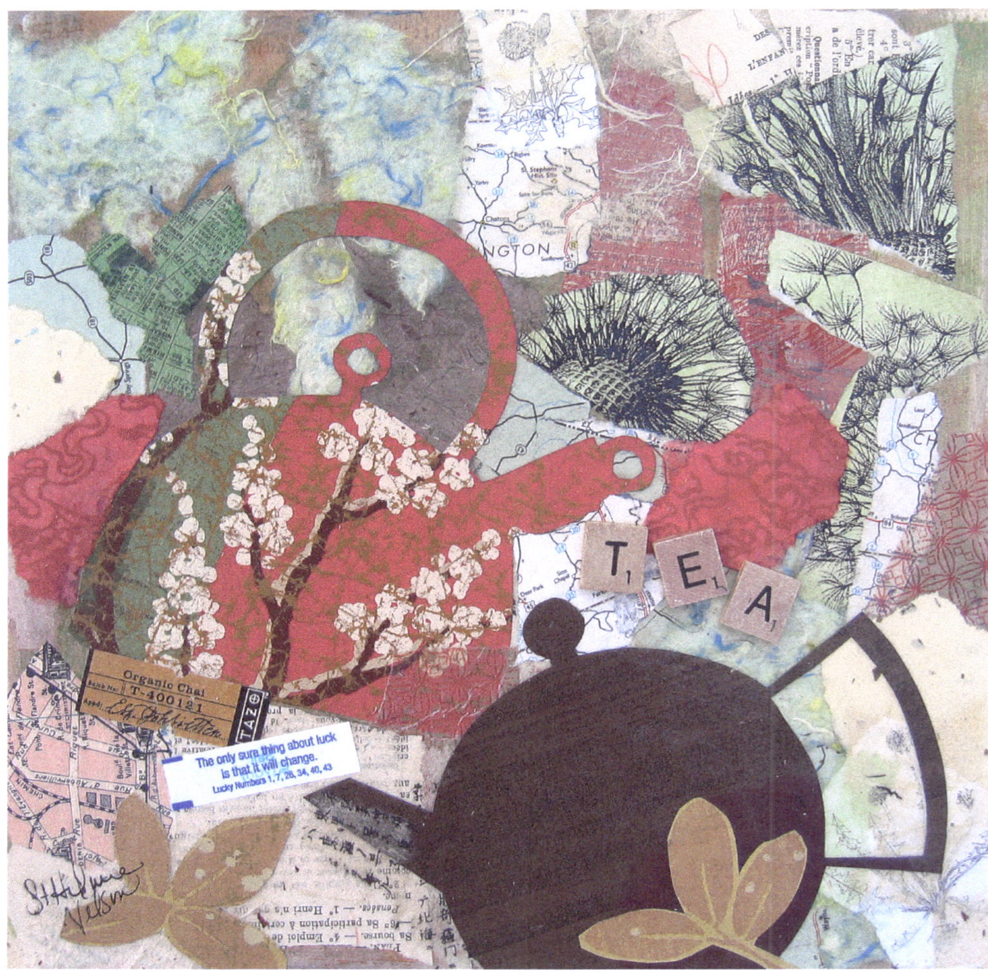

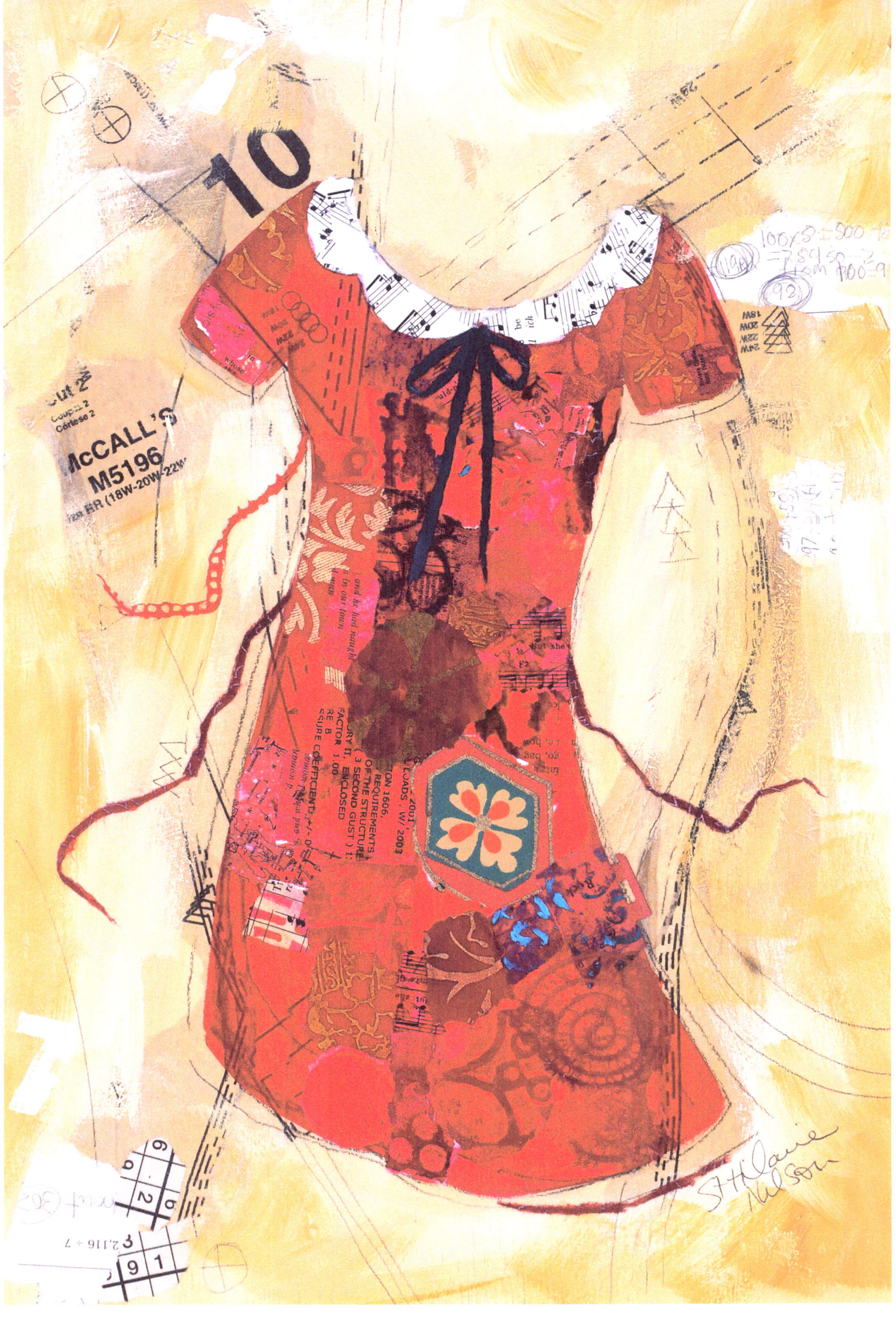
10
McCALL'S
M5196
Cut 2
Coup. 2
Córtese 2
92

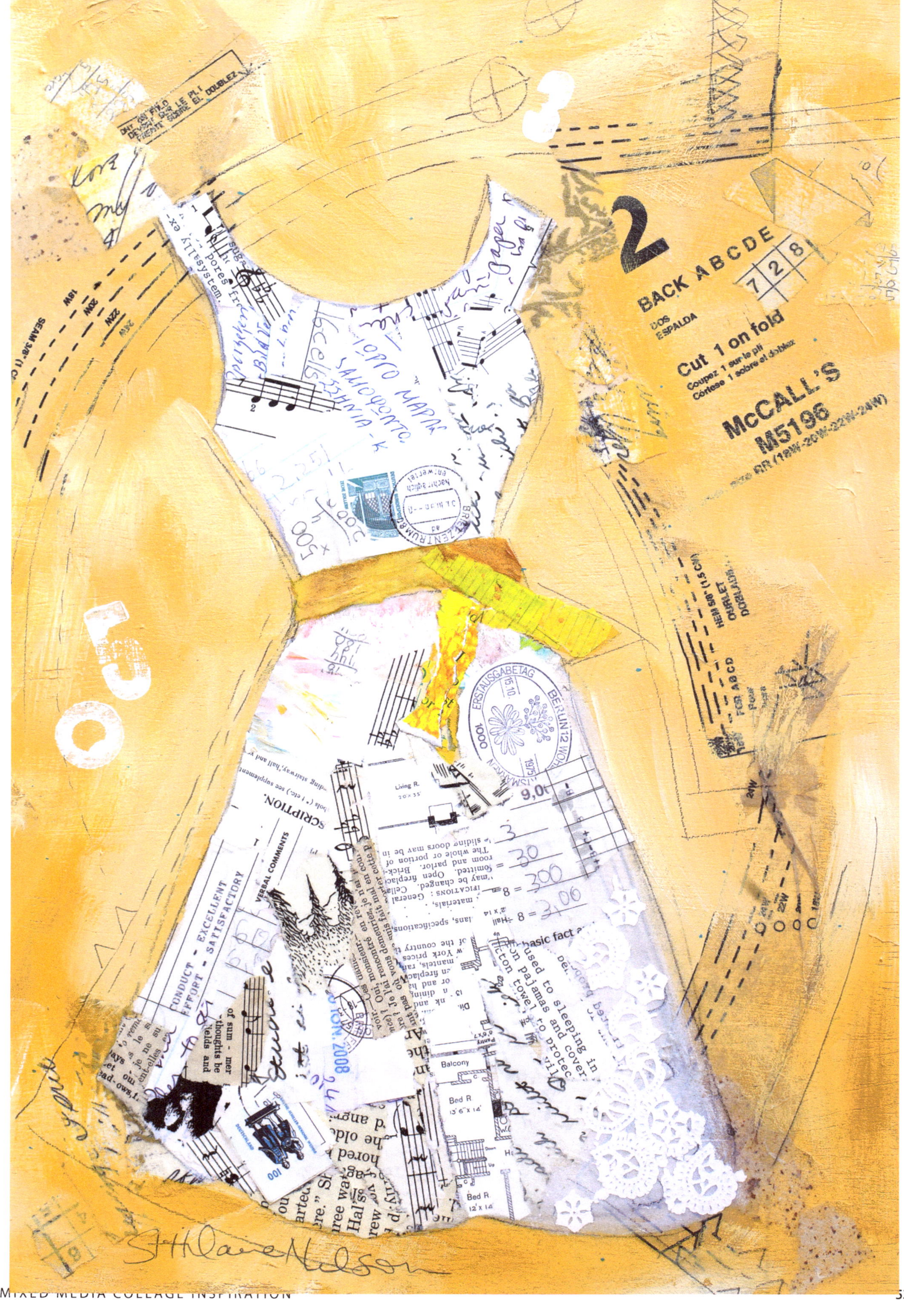

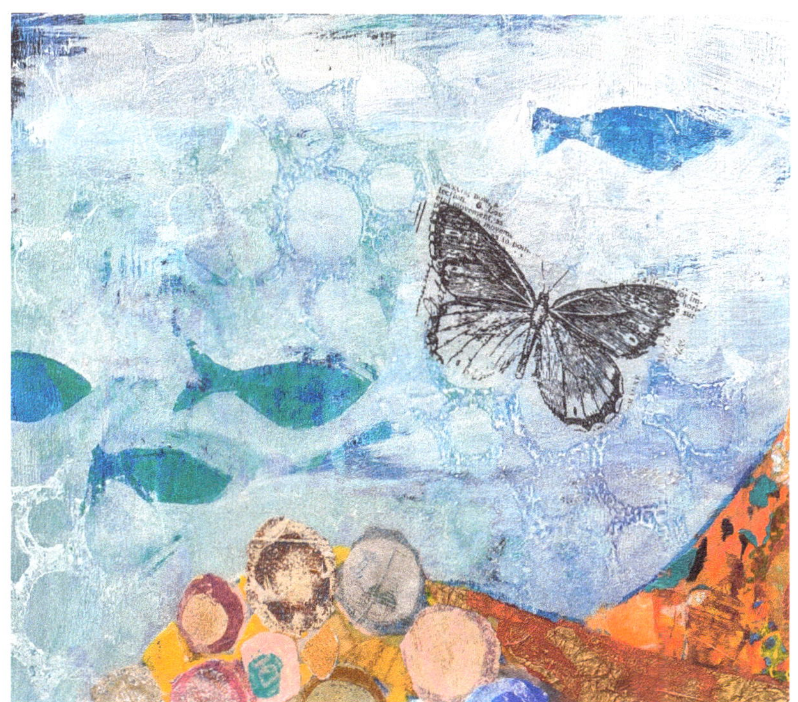

backgrounds

I HAVE BEEN ENCOURAGED to teach a course simply on background treatments. I believe the success of my backgrounds has been inspired by the concept of creating a successful supporting role for what has always been my leading lady; collage.

From stencils and place-mats for masking and marking, to drips and splattered drops for suggesting texture, noting is off limits when you work with mixed media. Since good drawing is the foundation of successful painting, there was a period of time where I featured a significant amount of line work in my backgrounds. I wanted to bring drawing back into my work, and what better way than to employ it in subtly suggesting background imagery— setting the stage for some of my animal portraits. Several of the portraits featured here were part of my 2011 *Noah's Ark Series* of 50 paintings that were exhibited at the Thrasher Horne Center for the Arts in Jacksonville, FL.

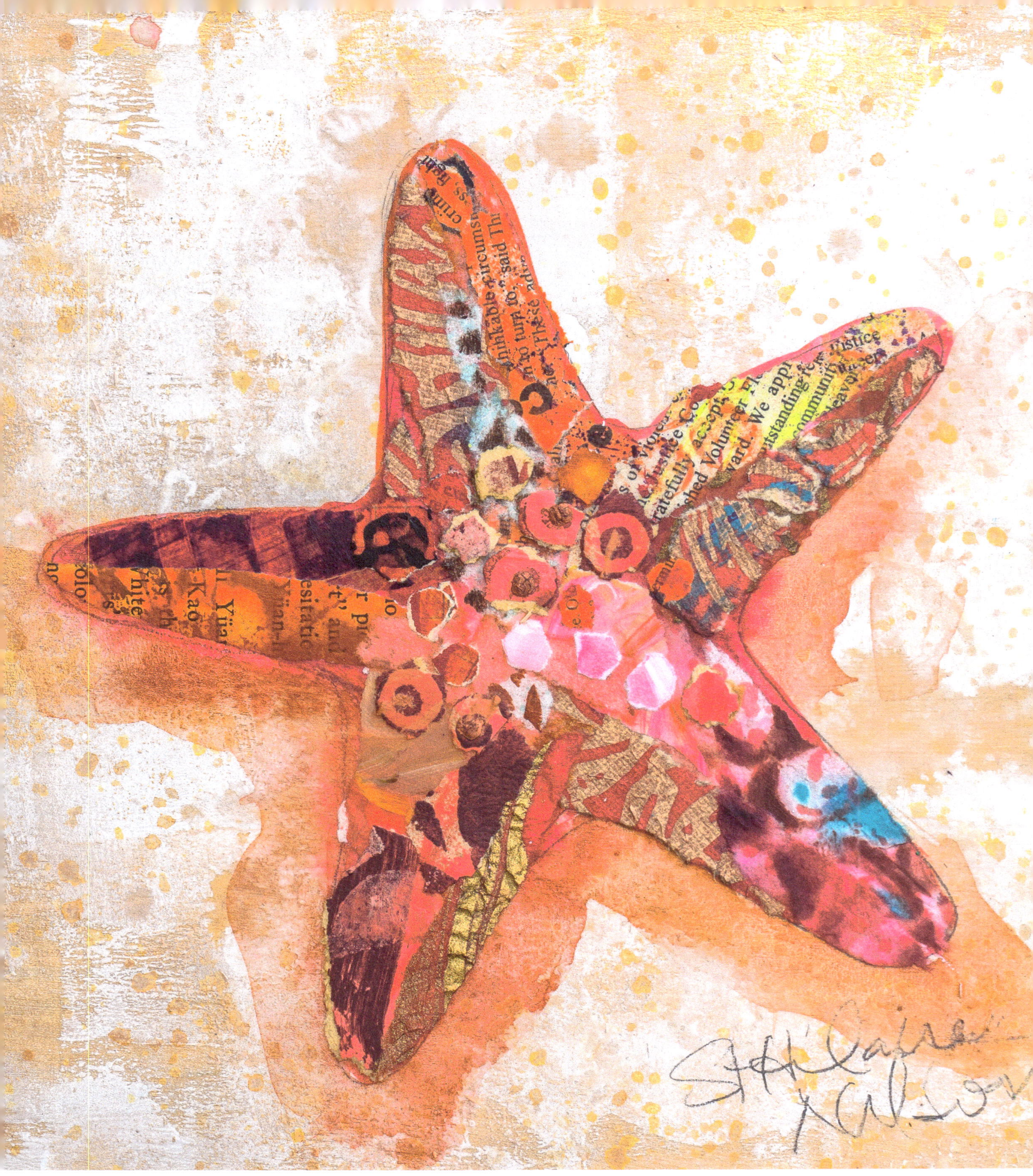

Starfish *(8x8) cradled wood panel primed with clear gesso. A secondary partial coat of white gesso is added sparingly, allowing the wood to show through. Splattered, watered down fluid acrylic is added on top of the white gesso coat, followed by painting the drop shadow. The collaged starfish is the final step, once all paint layers are dry.*

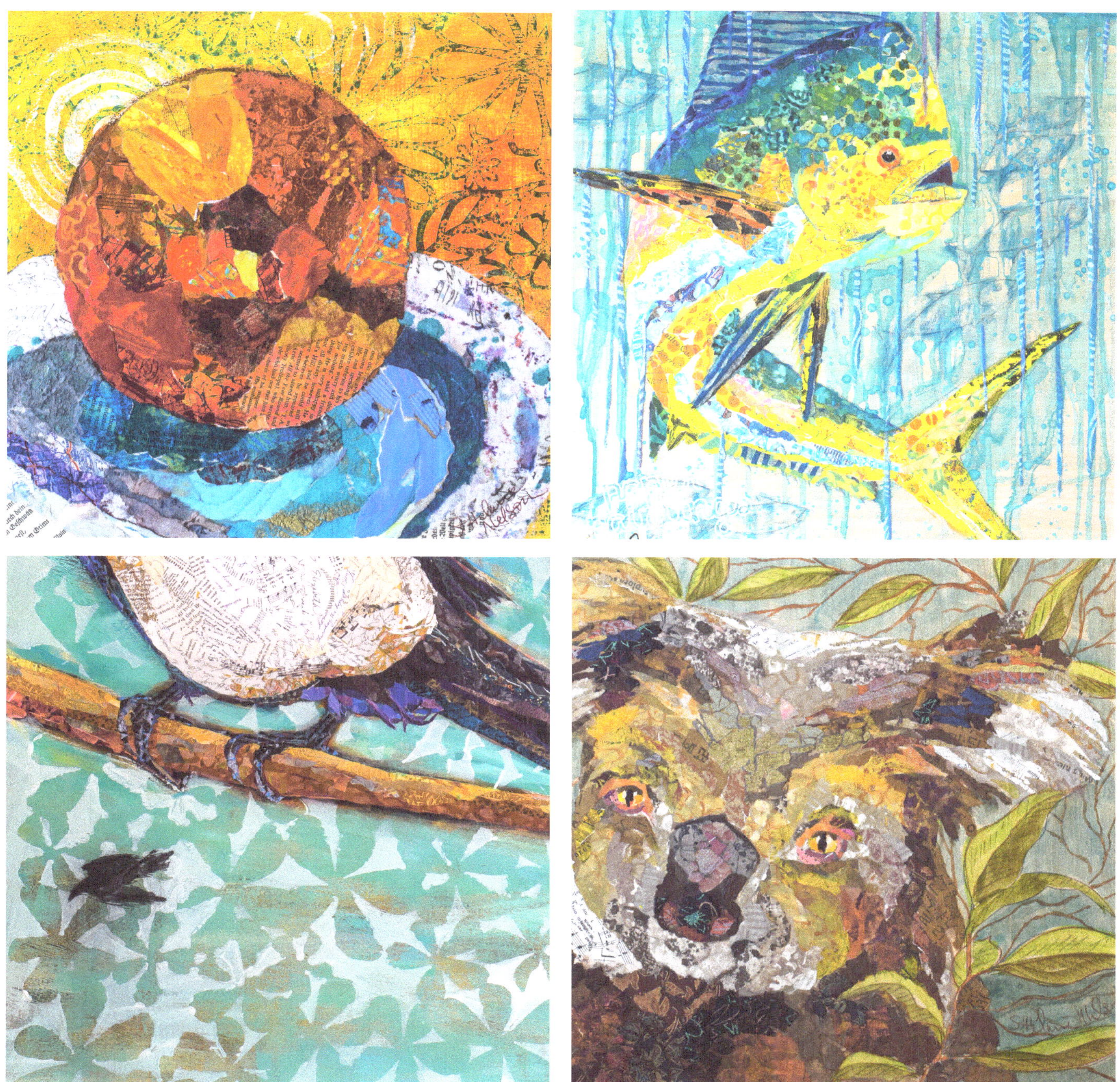

Background Inspiration

MIXED MEDIA BACKGROUNDS set the stage for your collaged subject. **Top left:** commercial stencils over painted background. **Top right:** drippy, watered down paint. **Bottom left:** using a plastic Dollare Store place-mat as a mask. **Bottom right:** drawing with graphite, colored, and InkTense pencils.

Right: **Darcy Dove** *(20x24) The background features graphite pencil drawing with paint washes*

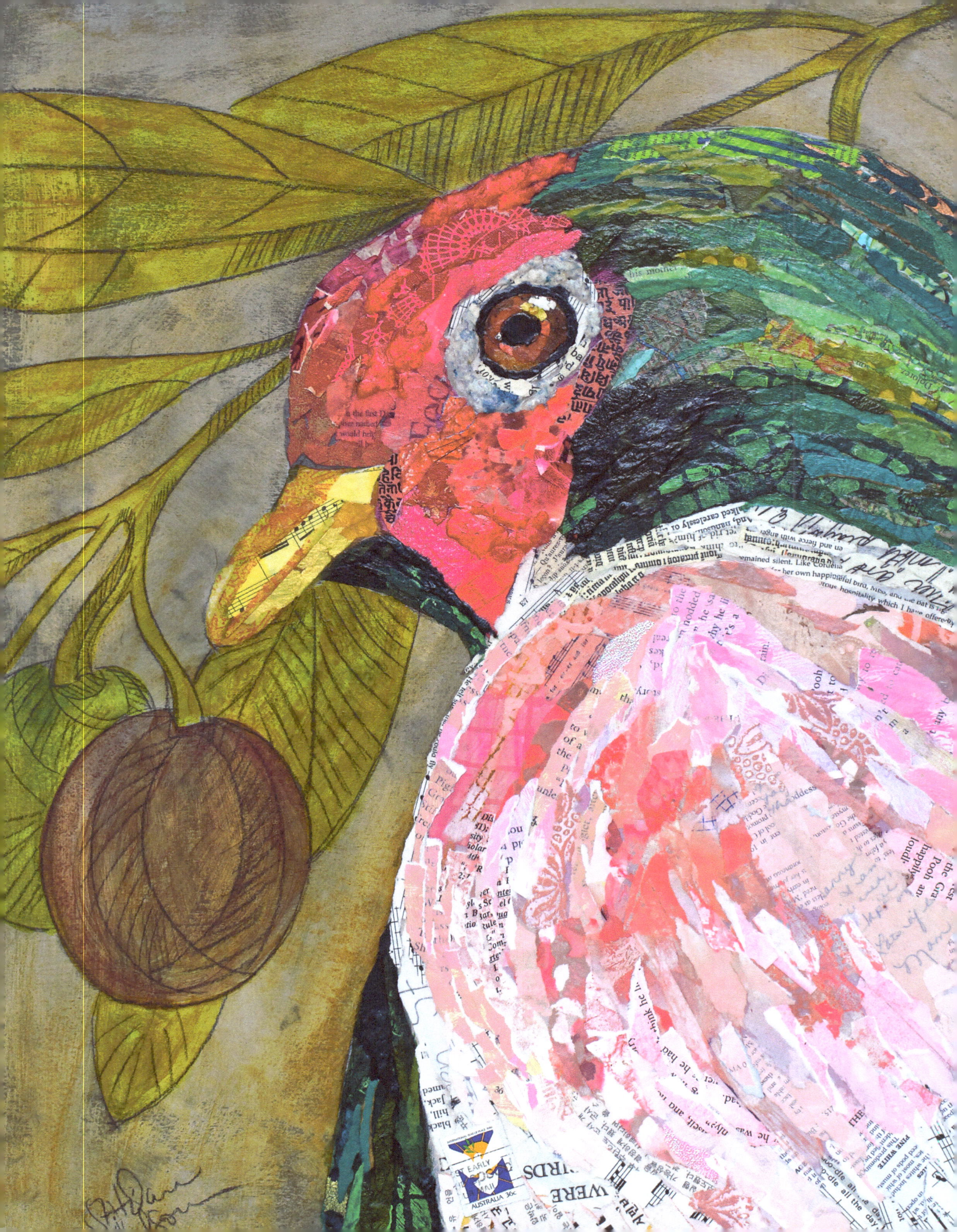

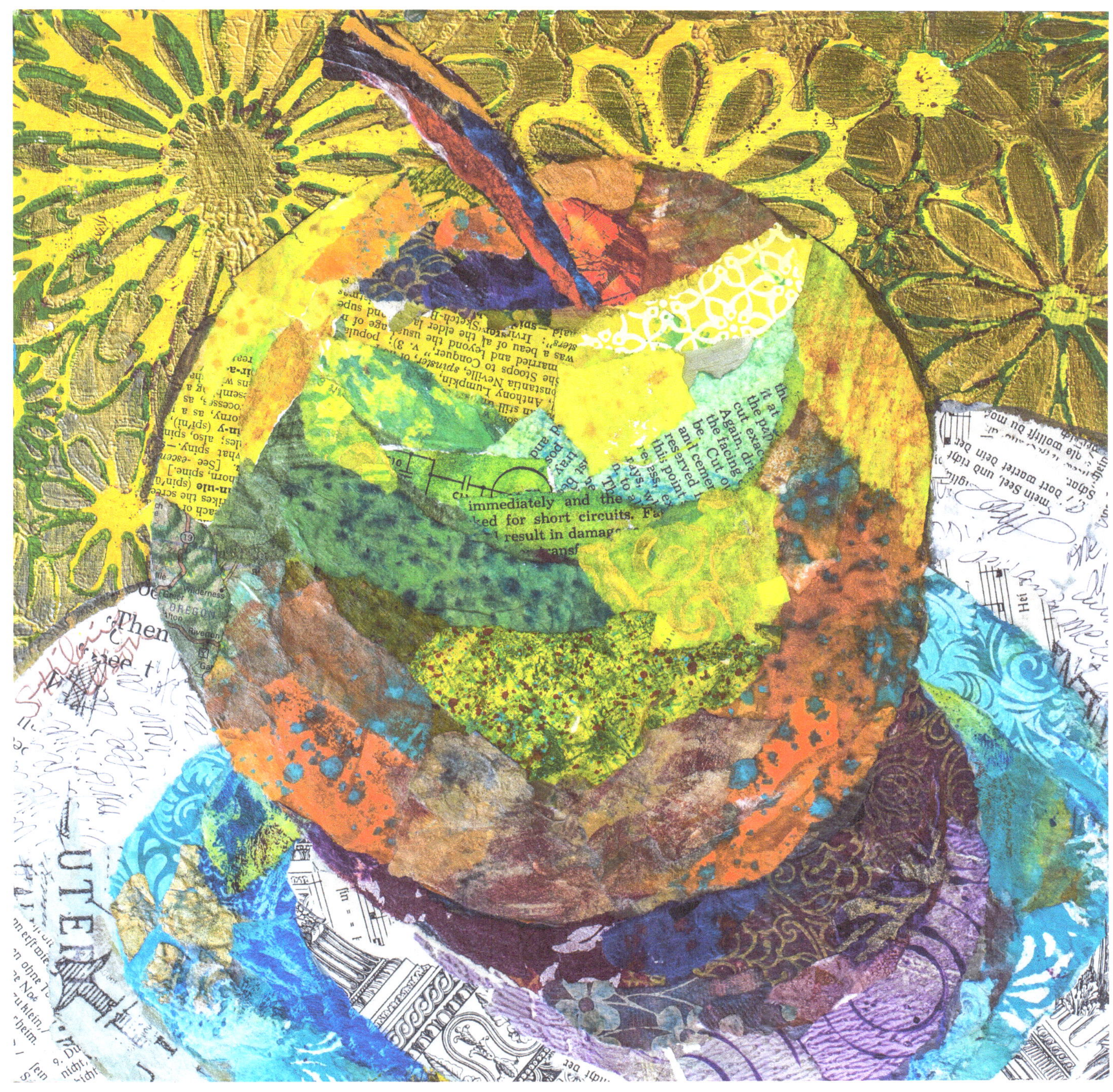

Stencils

Grannie Smith Apple (12X12) *The floral pattern in the background of this piece was created by applying two separate layers of paint (yellow, then green) through a stencil, over a solid painted background.*

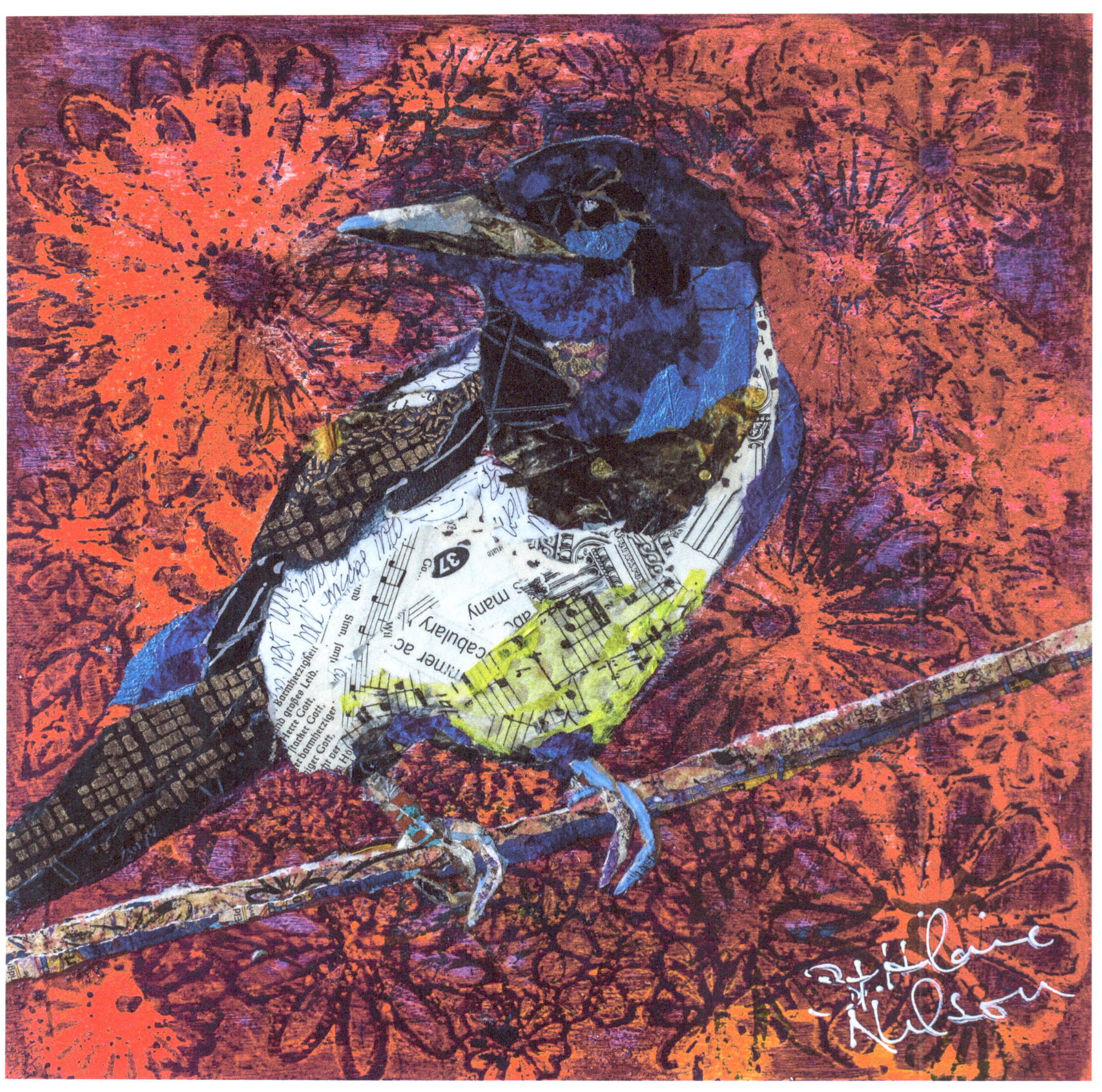

Stencils

Mischievous Magpie *(12X12) The floral pattern in the background of this piece was created by applying blue paint through a stencil, over a solid painted background.*

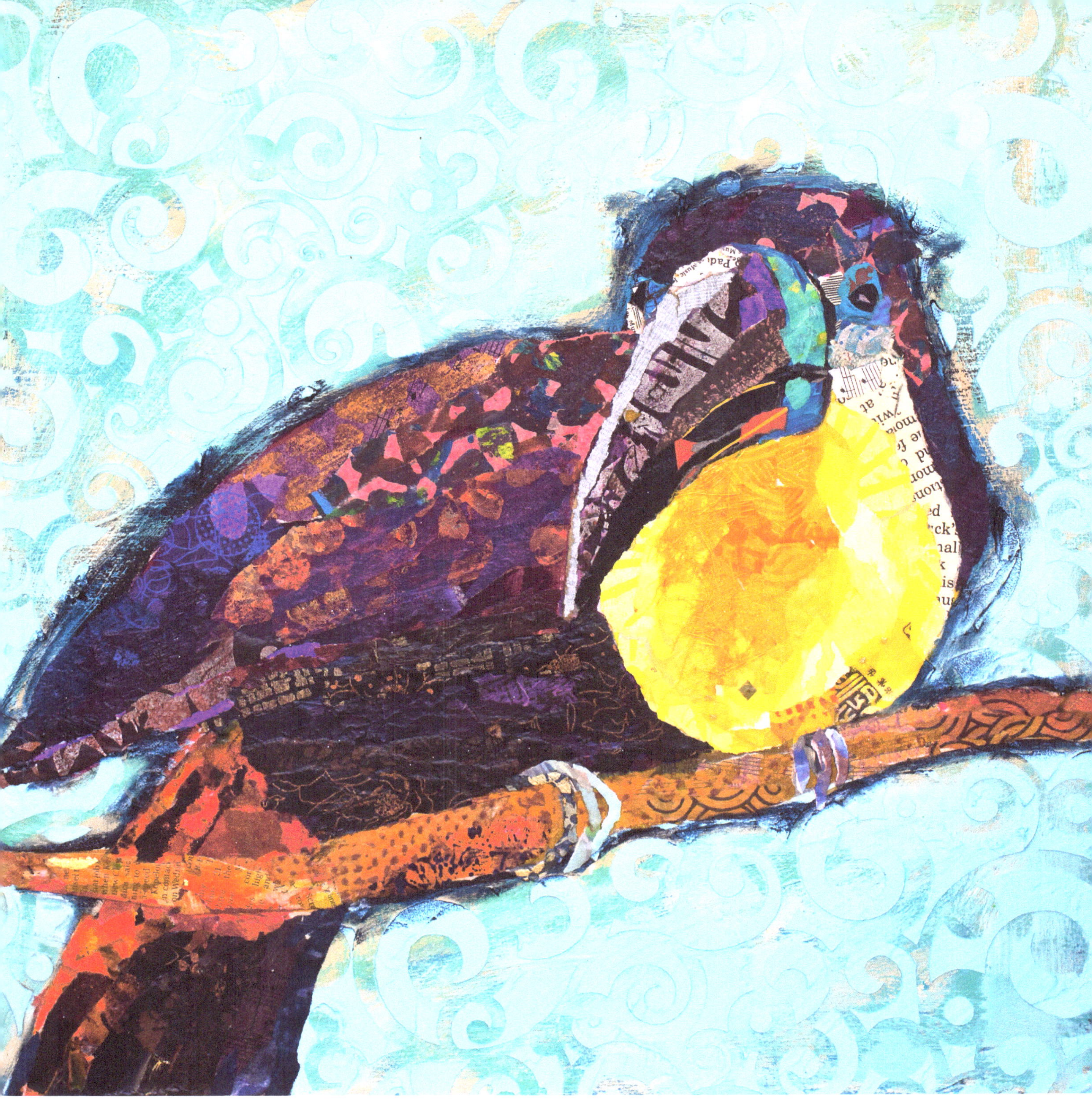

Stencils

Birds on a Wire *(18X36) The swirl pattern in the background of this piece was achieved by pushing Golden Light Molding Paste, tinted with fluid acrylic paint, through a stencil with a palette knife. The result is a raised swirl pattern over a base of blue brush work on clear primed birch panel, the collage is then applied on top.*

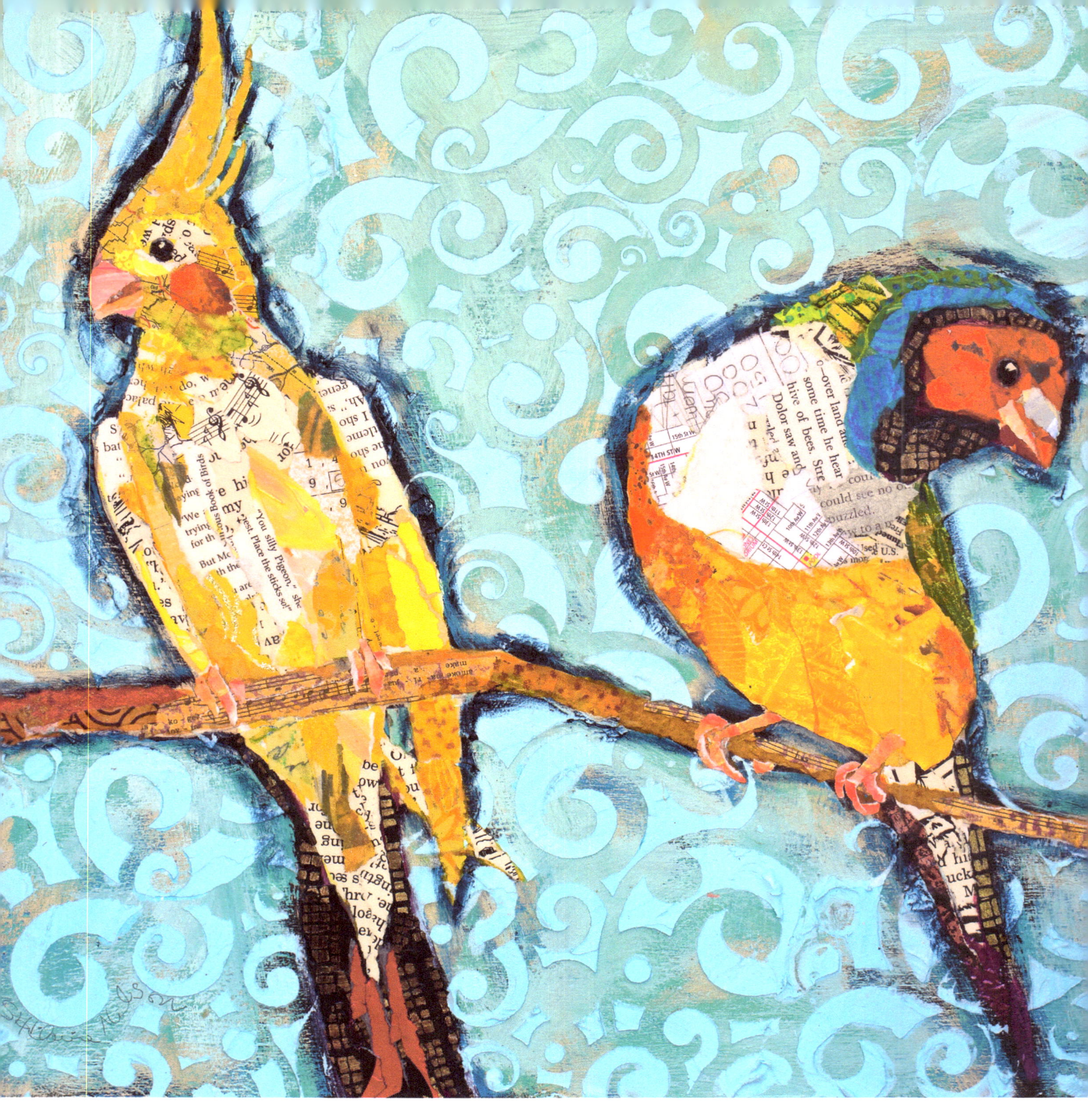

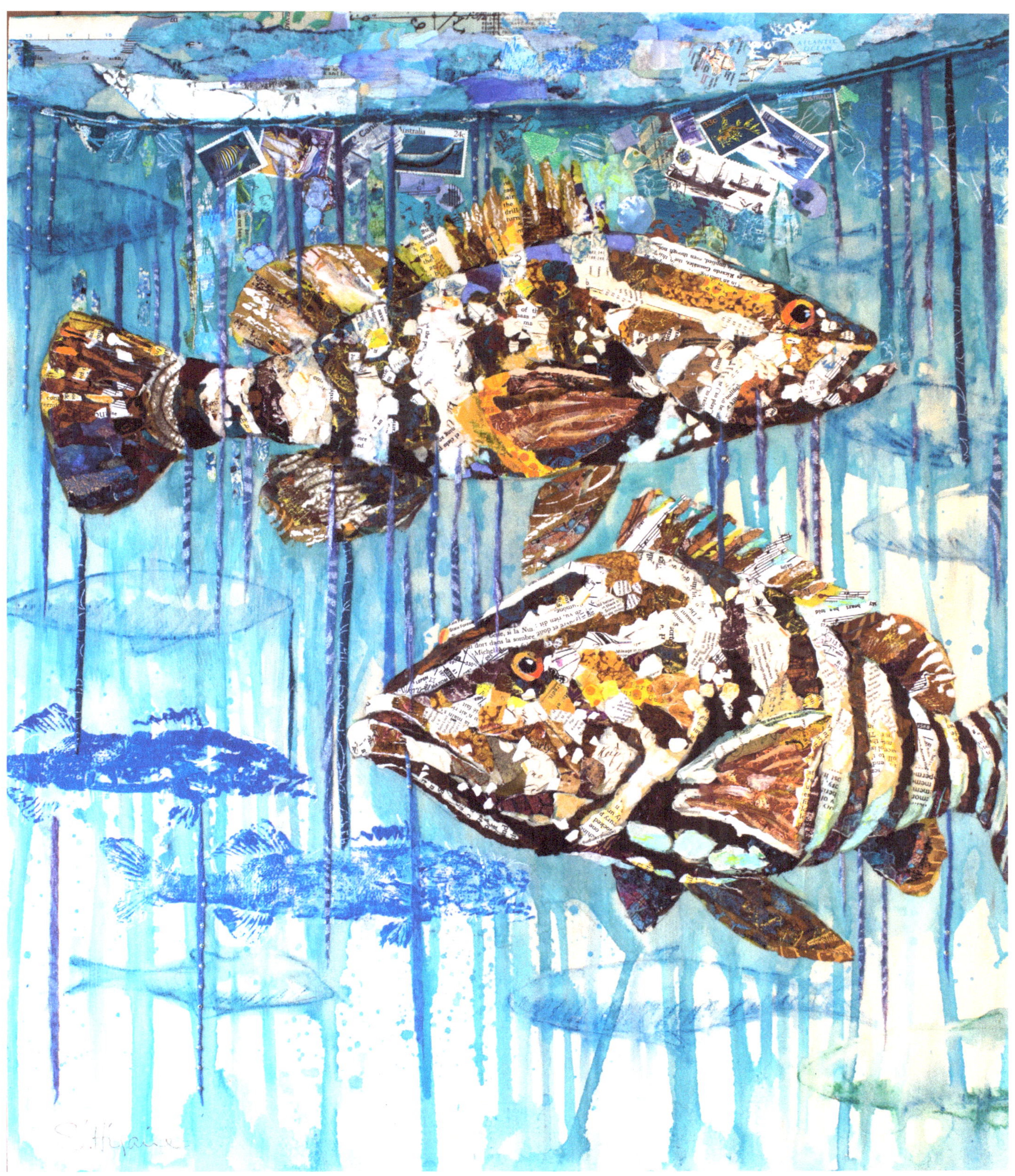

Drips

Grouper (20X24) Watered down paint is dripped and splattered and allowed to run down a clear primed wood panel in the background under-painting. The drip lines are re-enforced with thin slivers of collage papers.

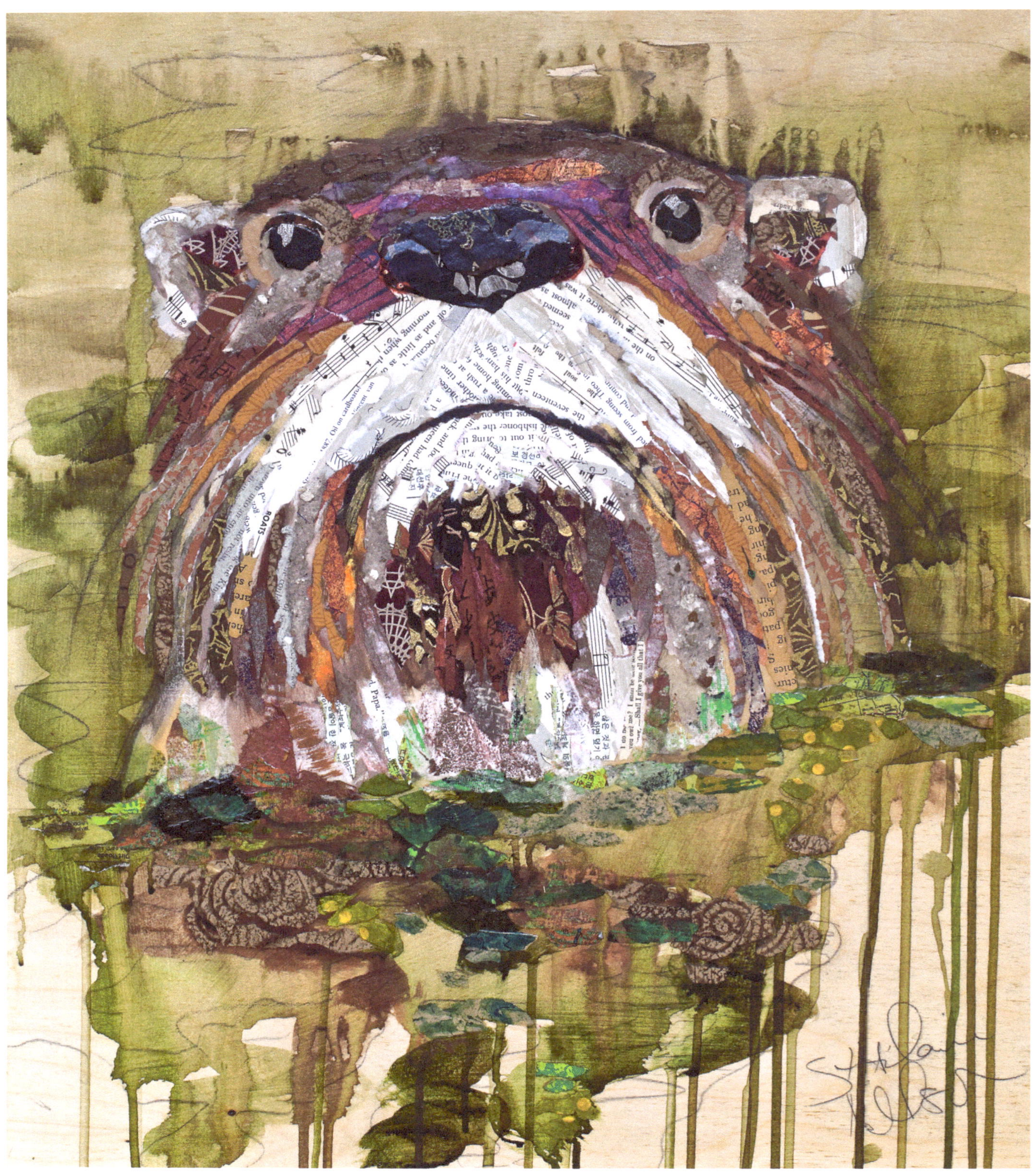

Drips

Ollie Otter (20X24) *Watered down paint is dripped and splattered and allowed to run down a clear primed wood panel, as part of the background under-painting. The translucency of the paint allow the original sketch to show.*

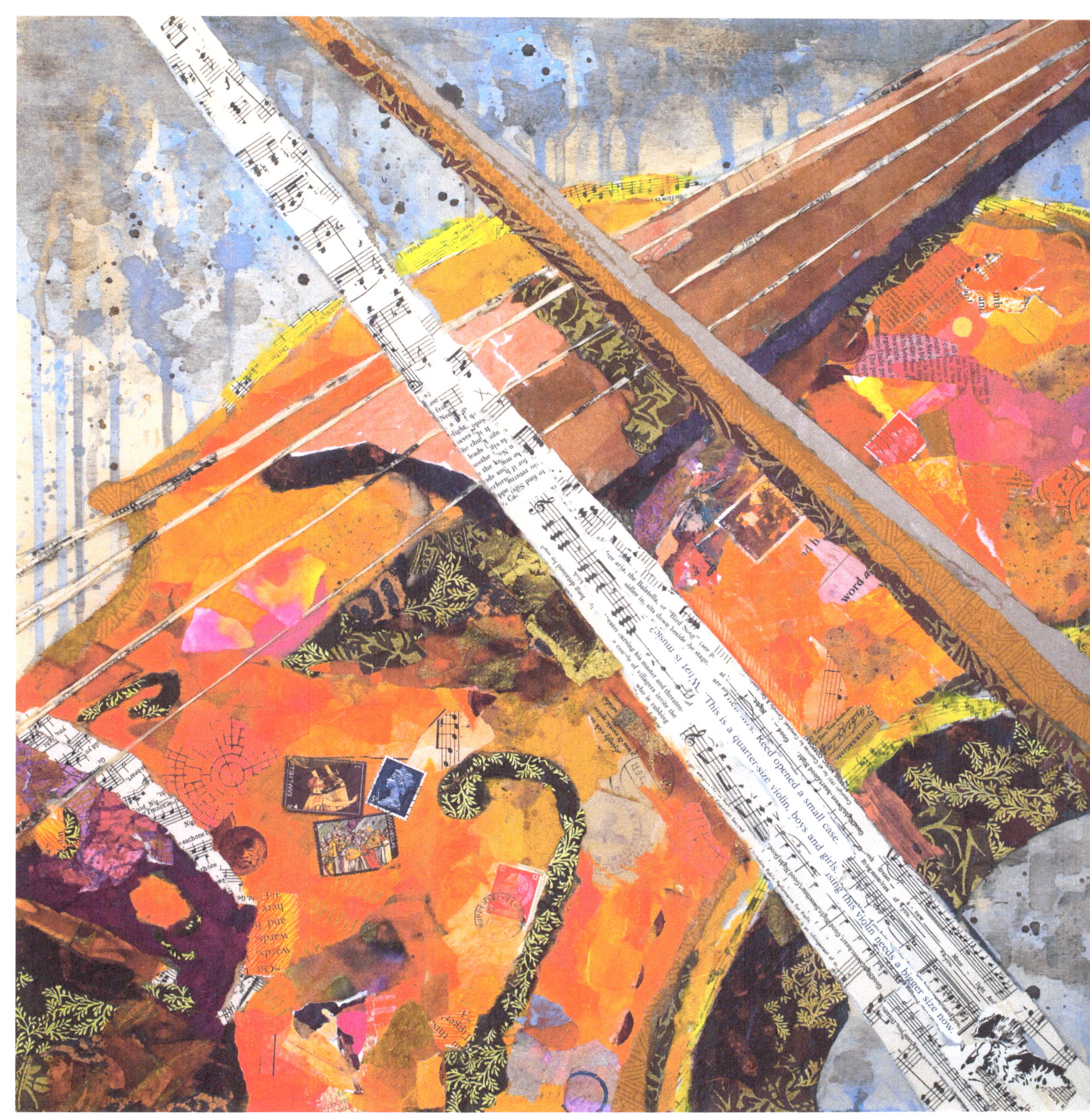

Drips

Sul Tasto (24X20) *Watered down paint is dripped and splattered and allowed to run down a clear primed wood panel, as part of the background under-painting – collage papers are applied on top.*

 MIXED MEDIA COLLAGE INSPIRATION

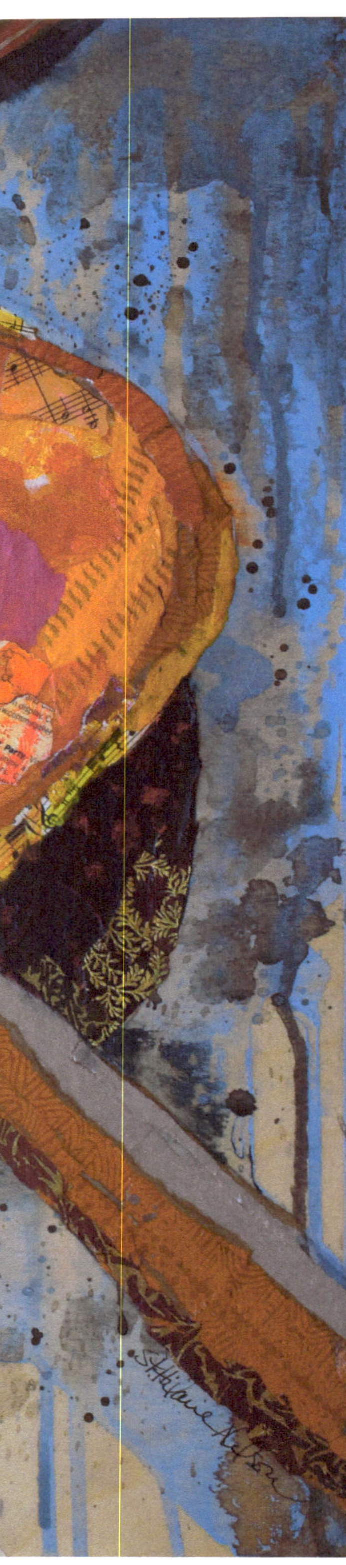

Drips

Indian Paint Brush #2 *(16X20) Watered down paint is dripped and splattered and allowed to run down a clear primed wood panel, as part of the background under-painting. The blue area behind the flowers is then re-enforced with collage papers of the same hue.*

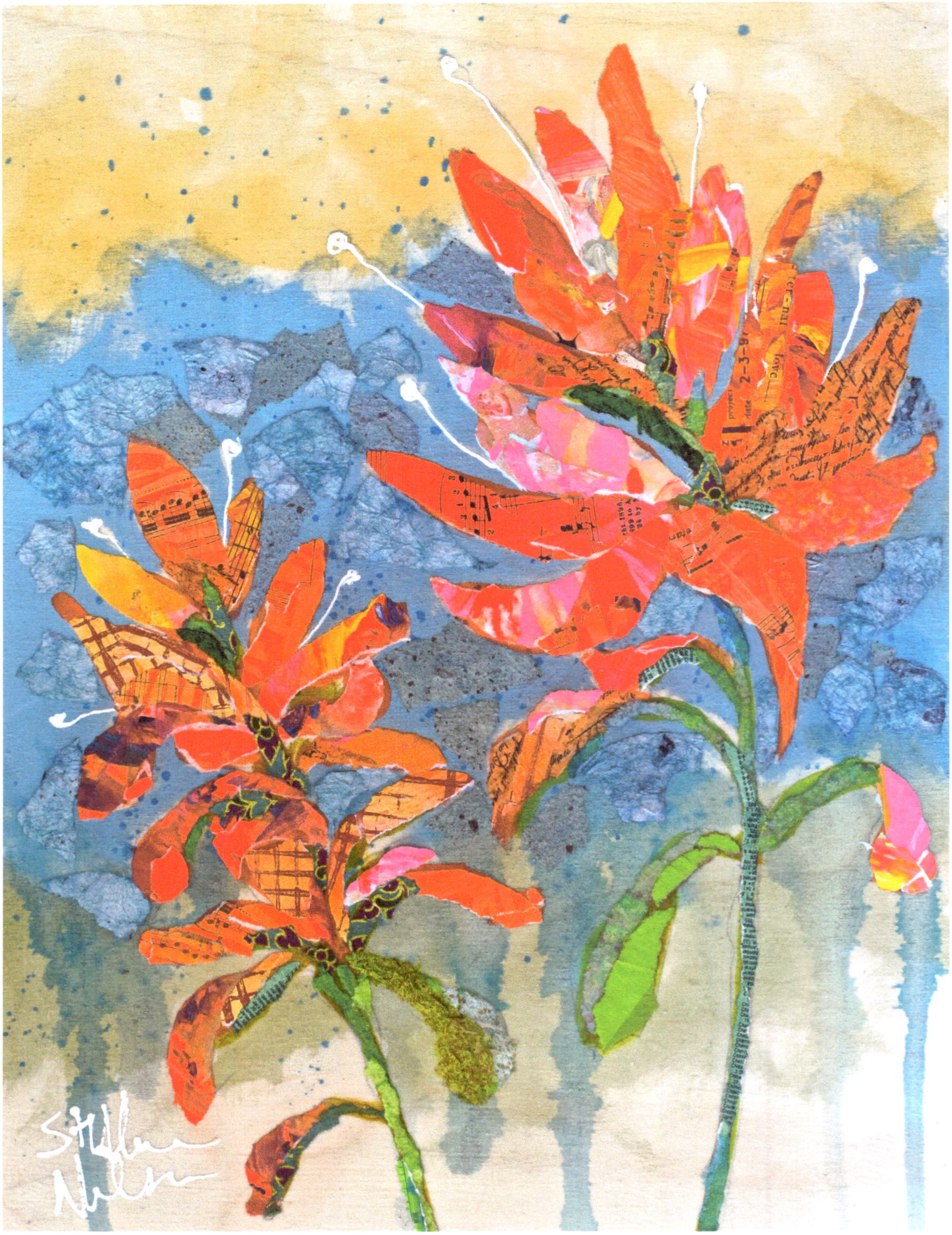

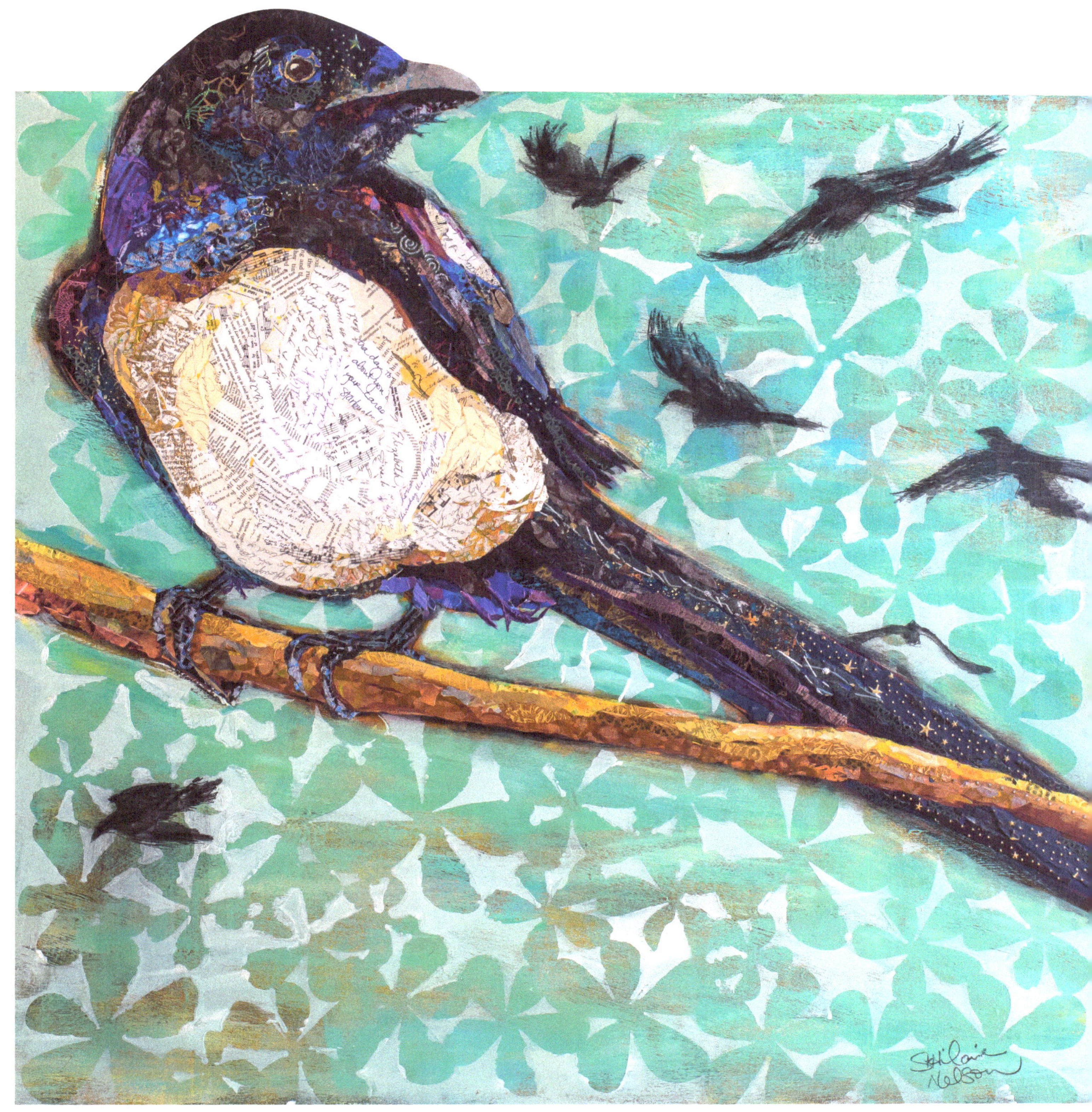

Place Mat Mask

Counting Crows *(36X36) The floral pattern in the background of this piece was created by painting white gesso, over a multi colored background, into the negative spacess of a Dollar Store plastic place-mat. Collage is then applied on top.*

Place Mat Mask

Rooster and Rollers (30X30) *The floral pattern in the background of this piece was created by painting white gesso, over a multi colored background, through the negative spaces of a Dollar Store plastic place-mat. The floral shapes were then re-enforced with colored pencil drawing in pale blue and violet; The collage was applied on top.*

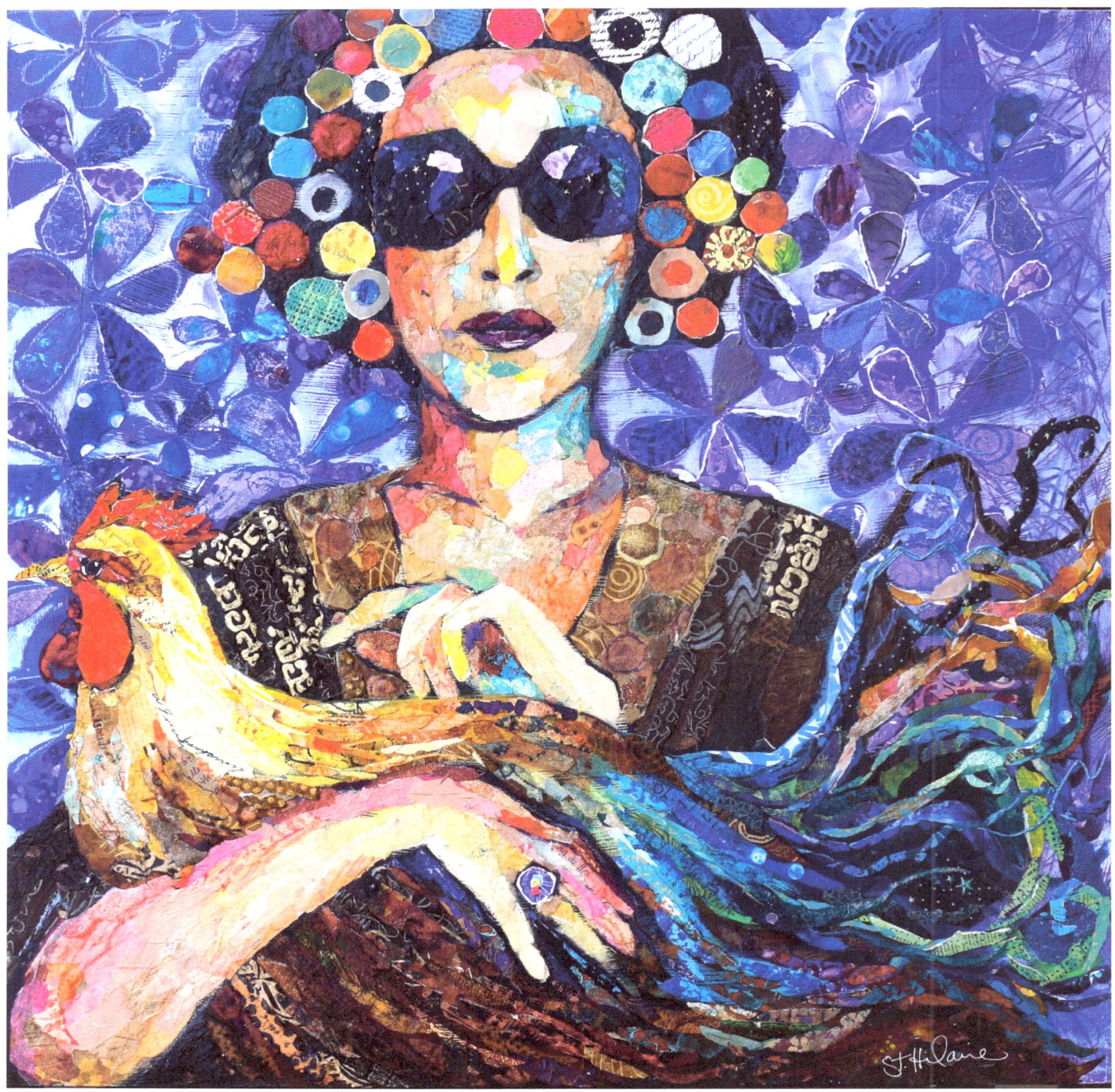

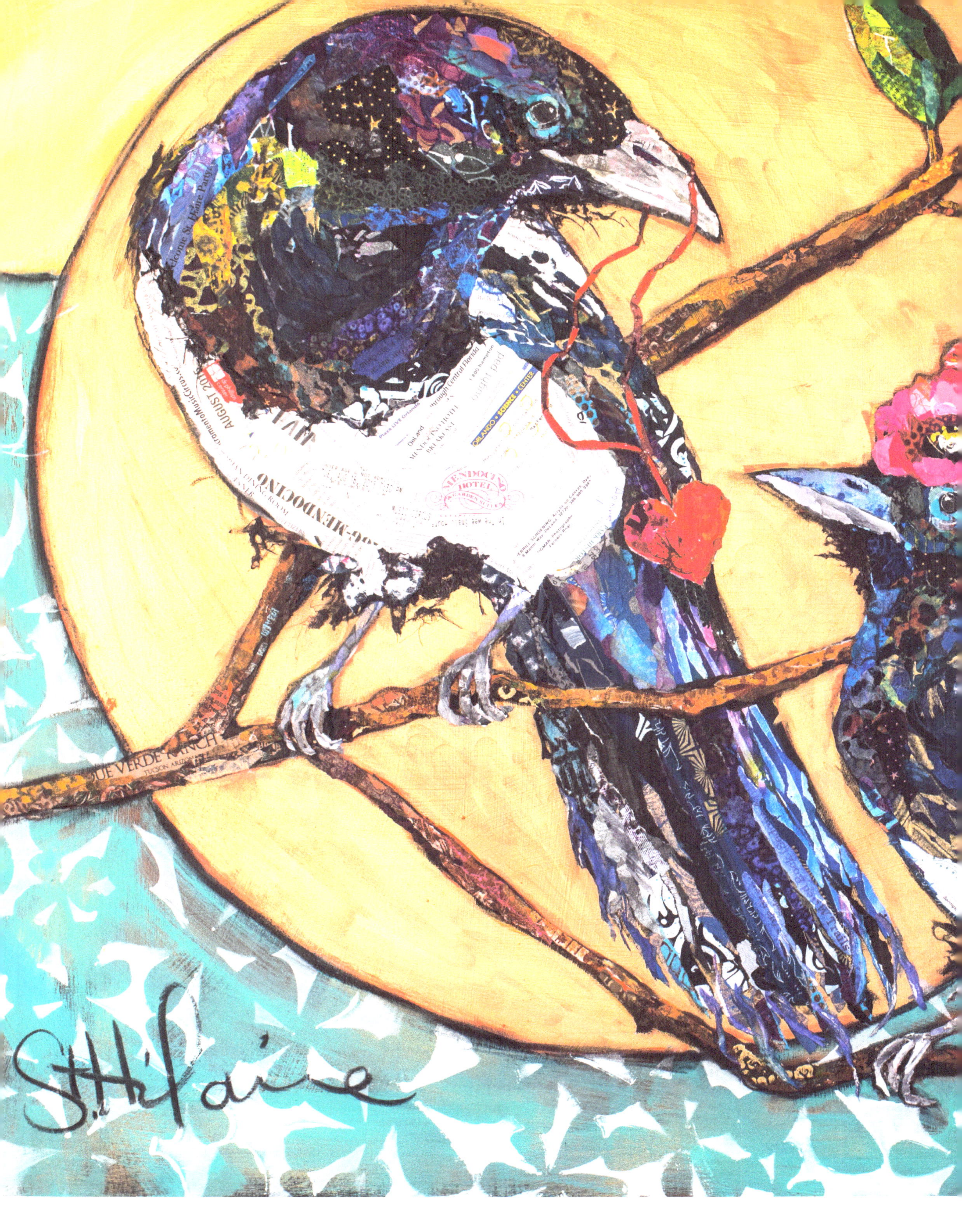

St.Hilaire

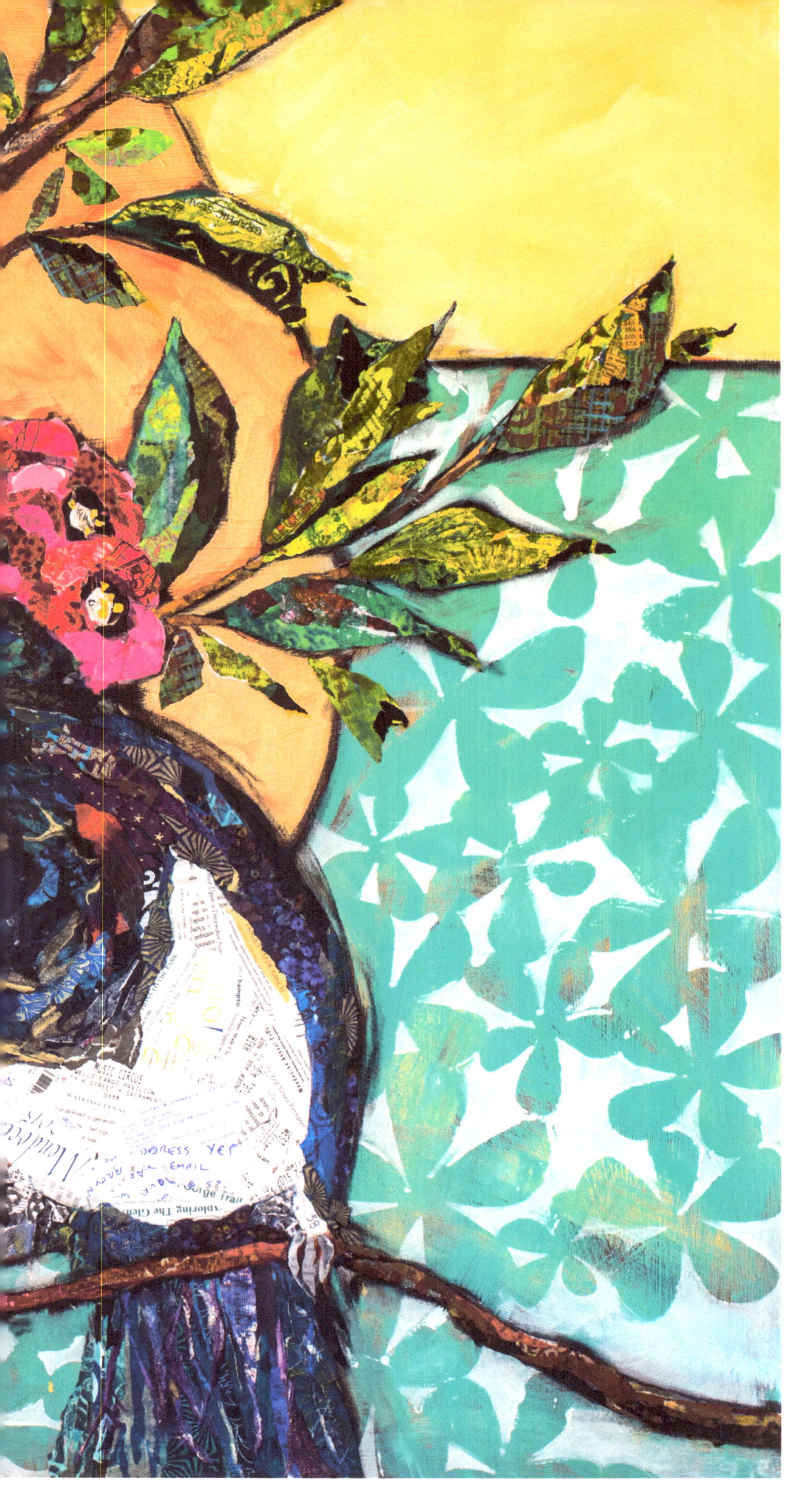

Place Mat Mask

Two For Joy (36X48) *The floral pattern in the background of this piece was created by painting white gesso, over a multi colored background, into the negative spaces of a Dollar Store plastic place-mat. Collage is applied on top. Black lines are a result of soft vine charcoal, the metallic moon is iridescent gold paint. This being a commissioned piece, all the white papers in the bellies of the birds is personal ephemera of the patron.*

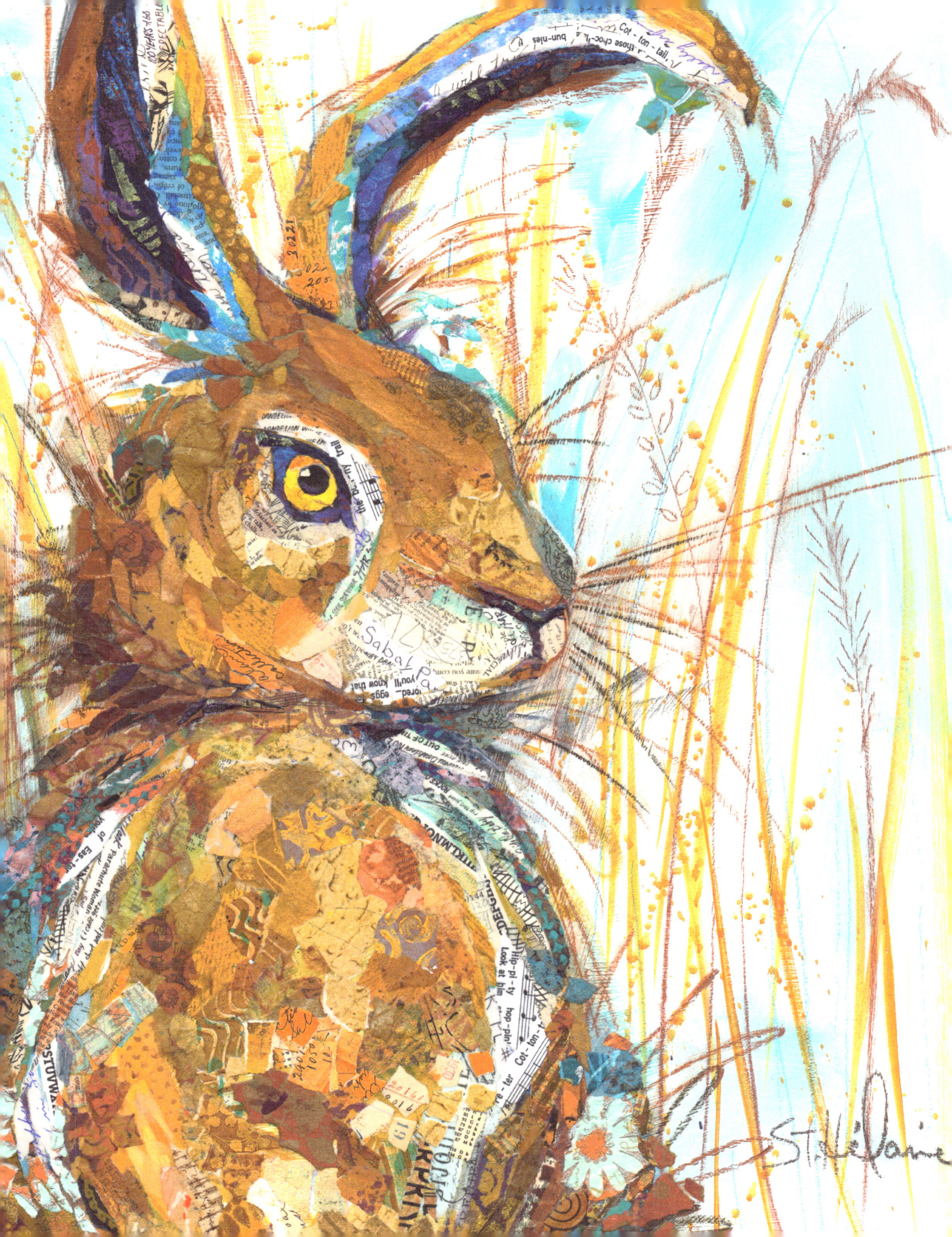

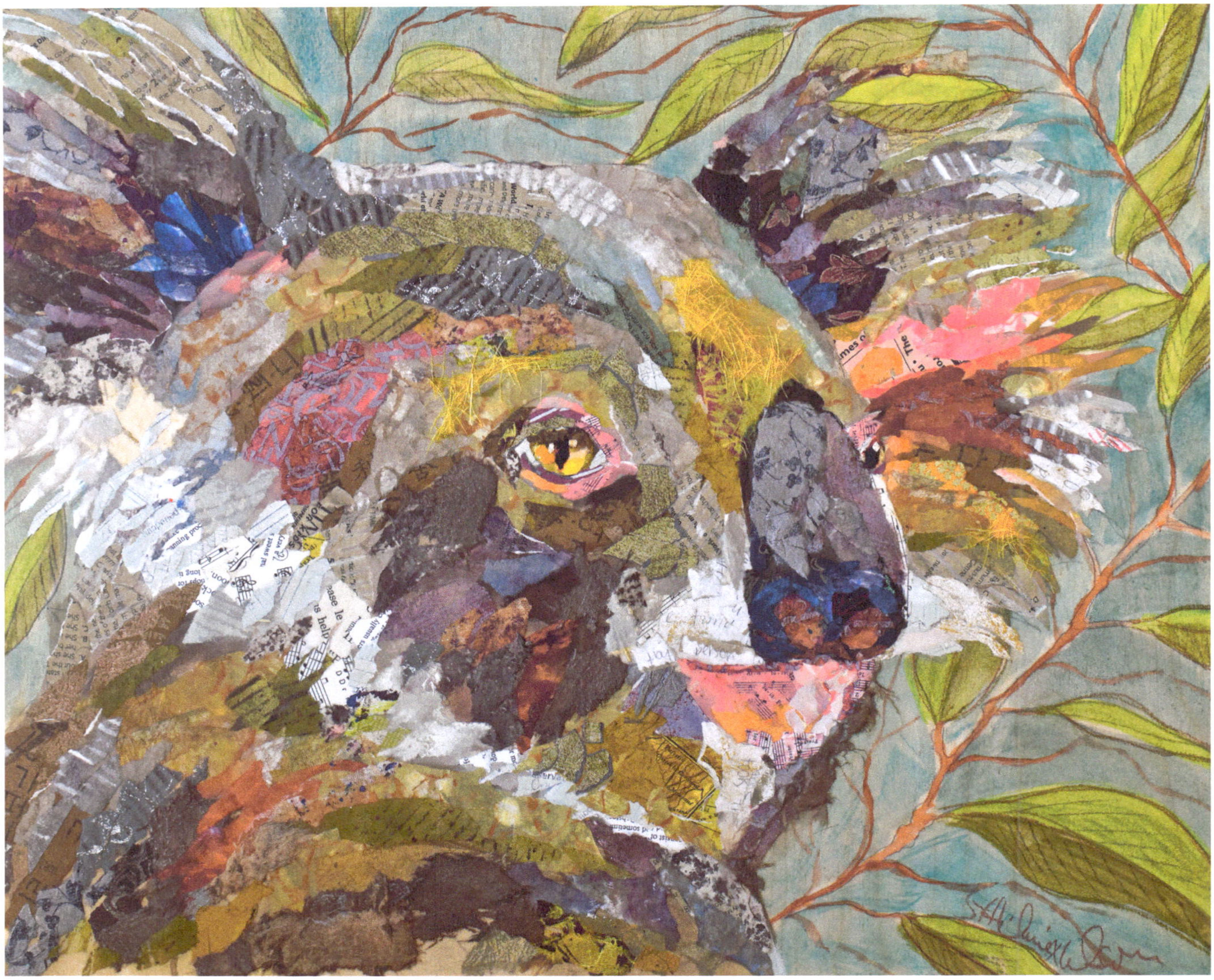

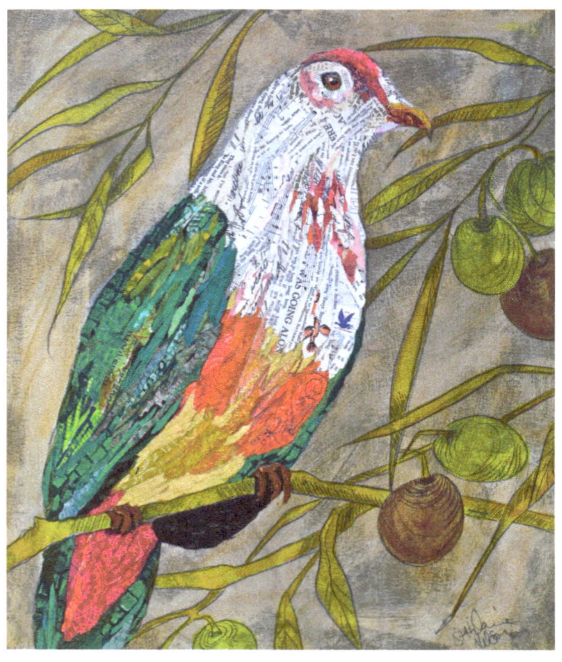

Drawing and Mark Making

Left: **Brown Hare** *(20X24) The grassy pattern in the background under-painting of this piece was created with Derwent InkTense pencils. The marks from this medium can be washed with water to create bleeding and blending, much like watercolor pencils. InkTense are permanent when dry and will not smudge when collage glue or varnish is applied.*

Top: **Katy Koala** *(24x20) the eucalyptus branches in the background are created with a combination of graphite and InkTense pencils, washed with paint.*

Left: **Darwin Dove** *(24x20) the olive leaves and branches in the background are created with a combination of graphite and InkTense pencils, washed with paint.*

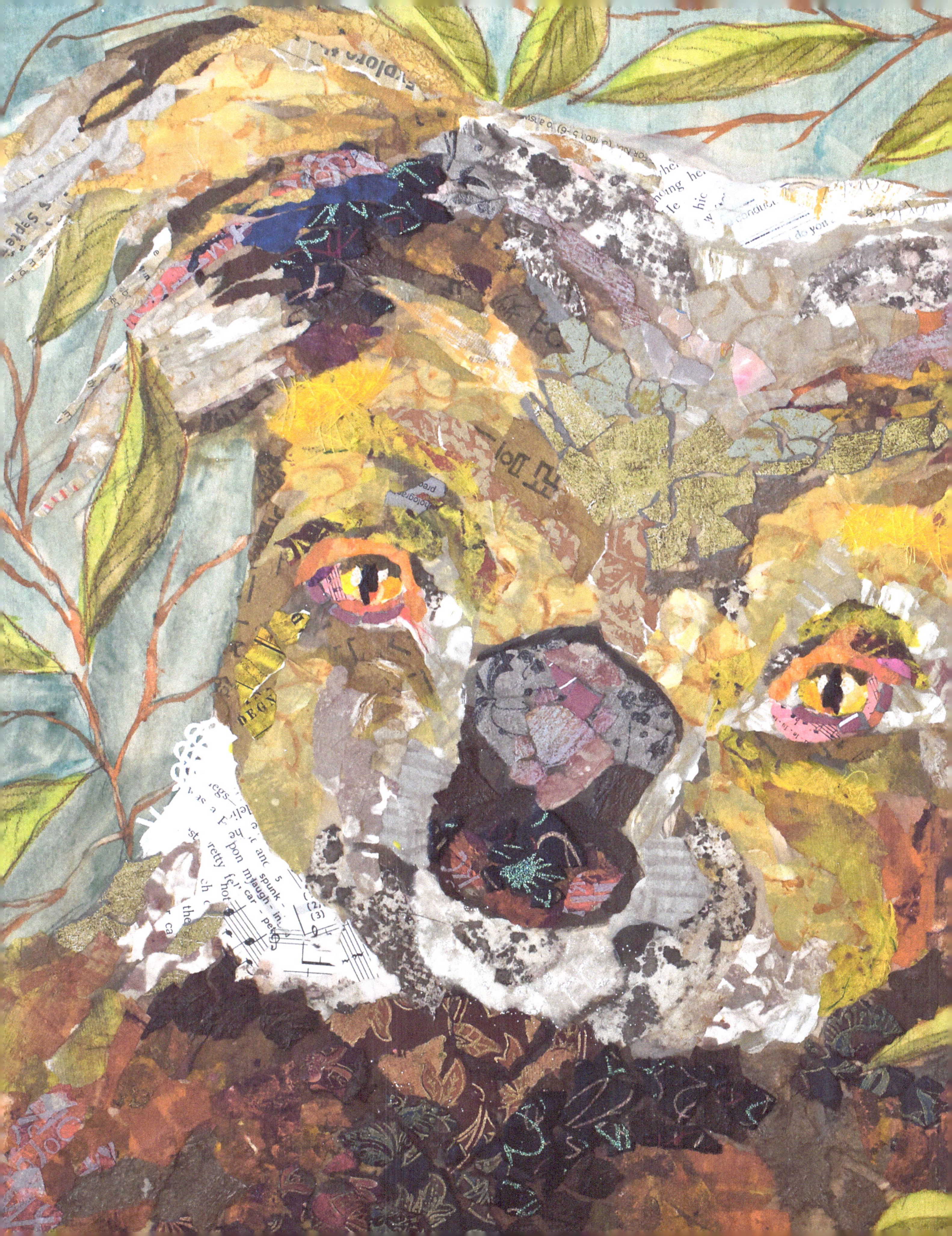

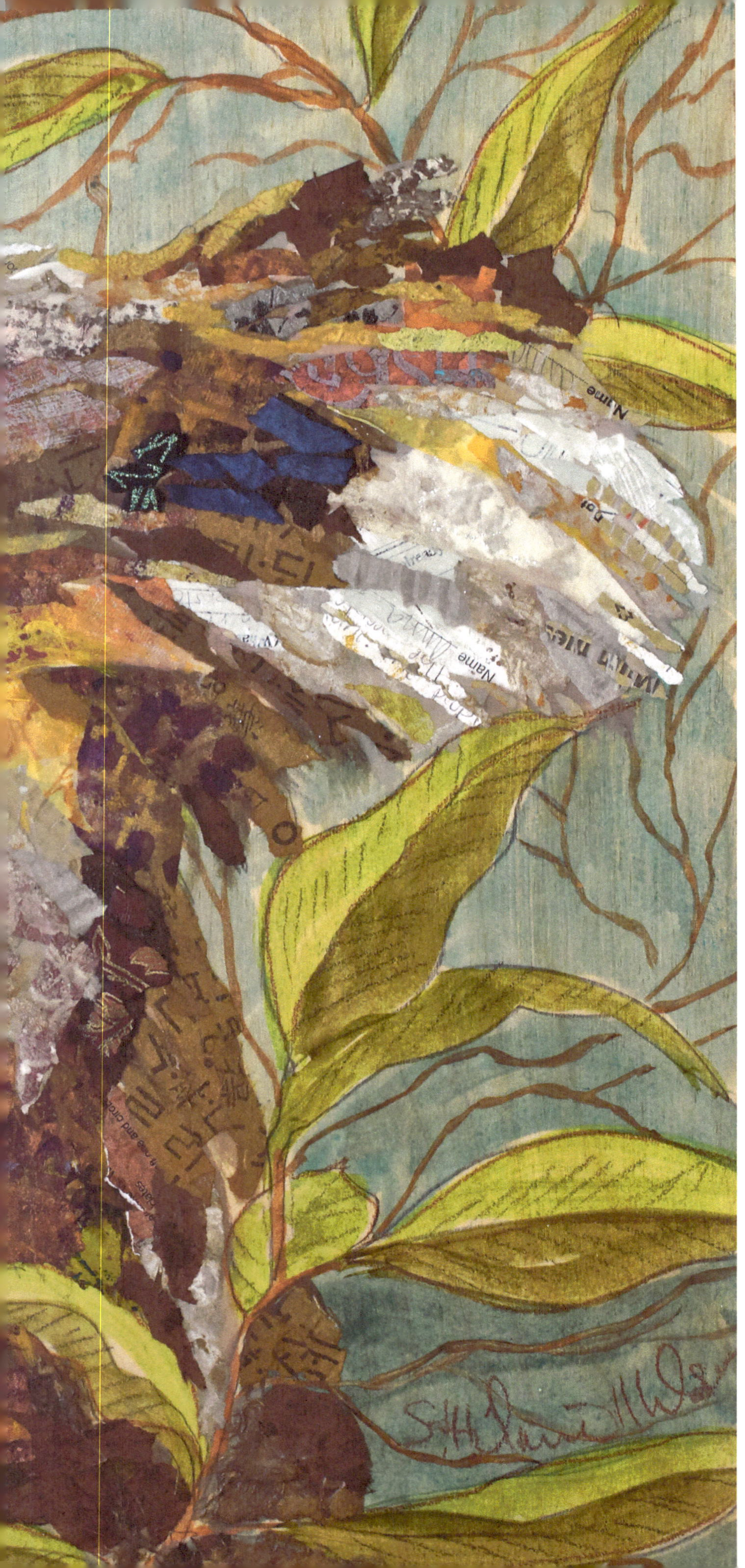

Drawing and Mark Making

Karl Koala *(24x20) The background of this piece (the companion to Katy Koala) features eucalyptus branches created with a combination of graphite and InkTense pencils, washed with paint.*

Derwent Ink Tense pencils lay down like colored pencil, and blend like watercolor pencil when water is applied. The benefit to this product is that it is permanent once blended, and will not re-constitute when glue or varnish is applied.

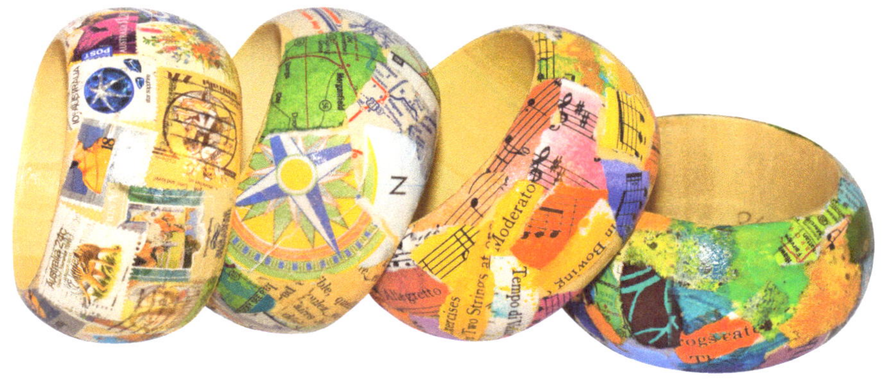

substrates

I AM OFTEN INSPIRED BY different substrate materials for my collage work. In the beginning of my career I worked primarily on white gesso primed wood panel, soon after I discovered clear gesso, which allows the wood grain to show through. When you work larger format, having wood panels built is more economical than purchasing them on-line and inuring oversized shipping fees.

Having my panels fabricated locally allowed me to experiment with various substrate materials. I dabbled in cabinet grade birch veneer, then fell in love with OSB (oriented strand board) which has a flake-like texture that is very visually similar to that of the collage papers I would apply on top.

Recently I have discovered Ampersand's Aquabord, a Masonite panel with a white clay surface that takes paint like paper; this paved the way for my watercolor backgrounds.

I branched out from the confines of the picture plane and experimented with 3-Dimensional wood bracelets. My LOVE LETTER wearable art series (*above*) featured collaged postage stamps. I am not a fan of wrapping paper around 3-D forms, due to the level of difficulty. But you may love it, so why not give it a try!

You never know.

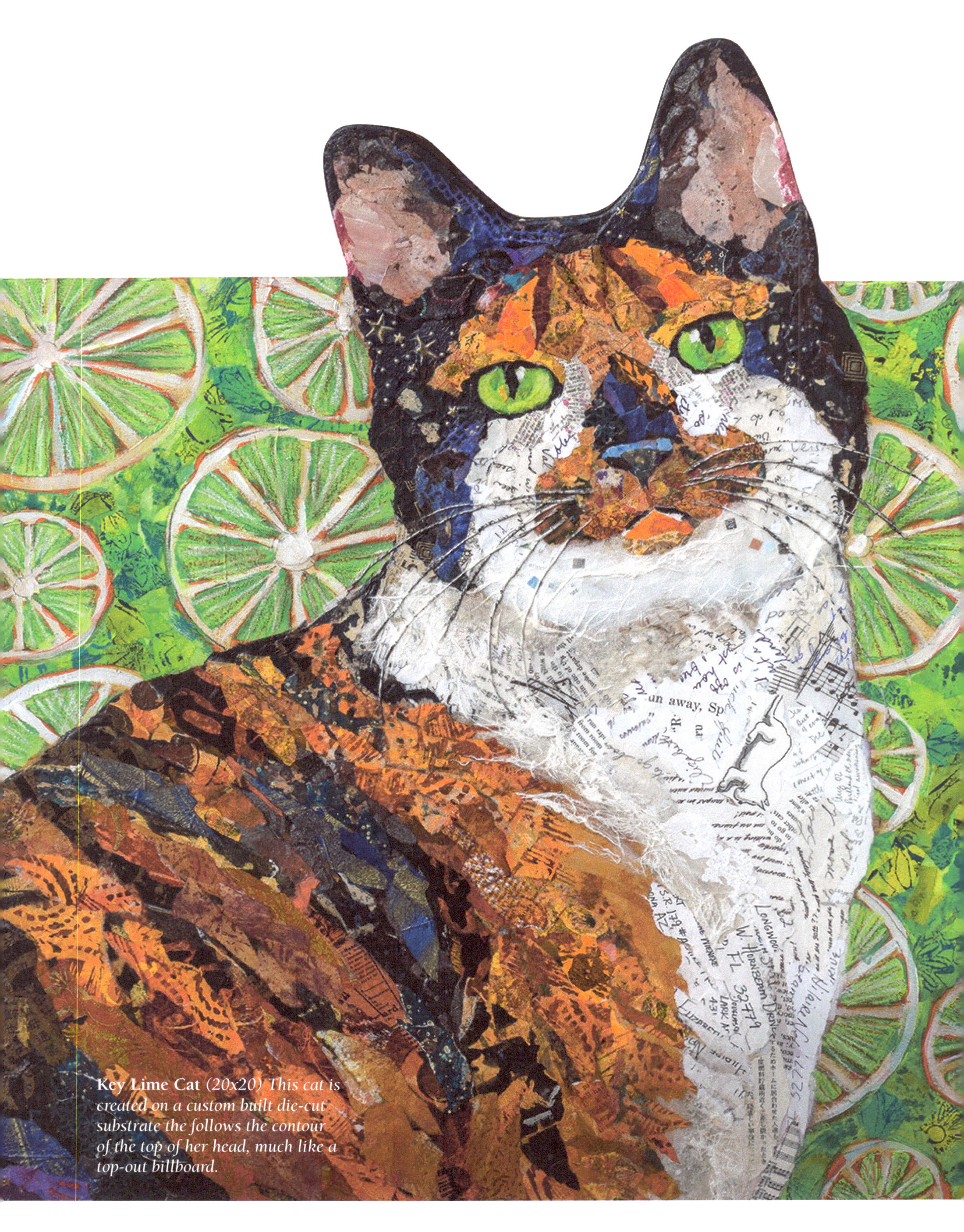

Key Lime Cat (20x20) *This cat is created on a custom built die-cut substrate the follows the contour of the top of her head, much like a top-out billboard.*

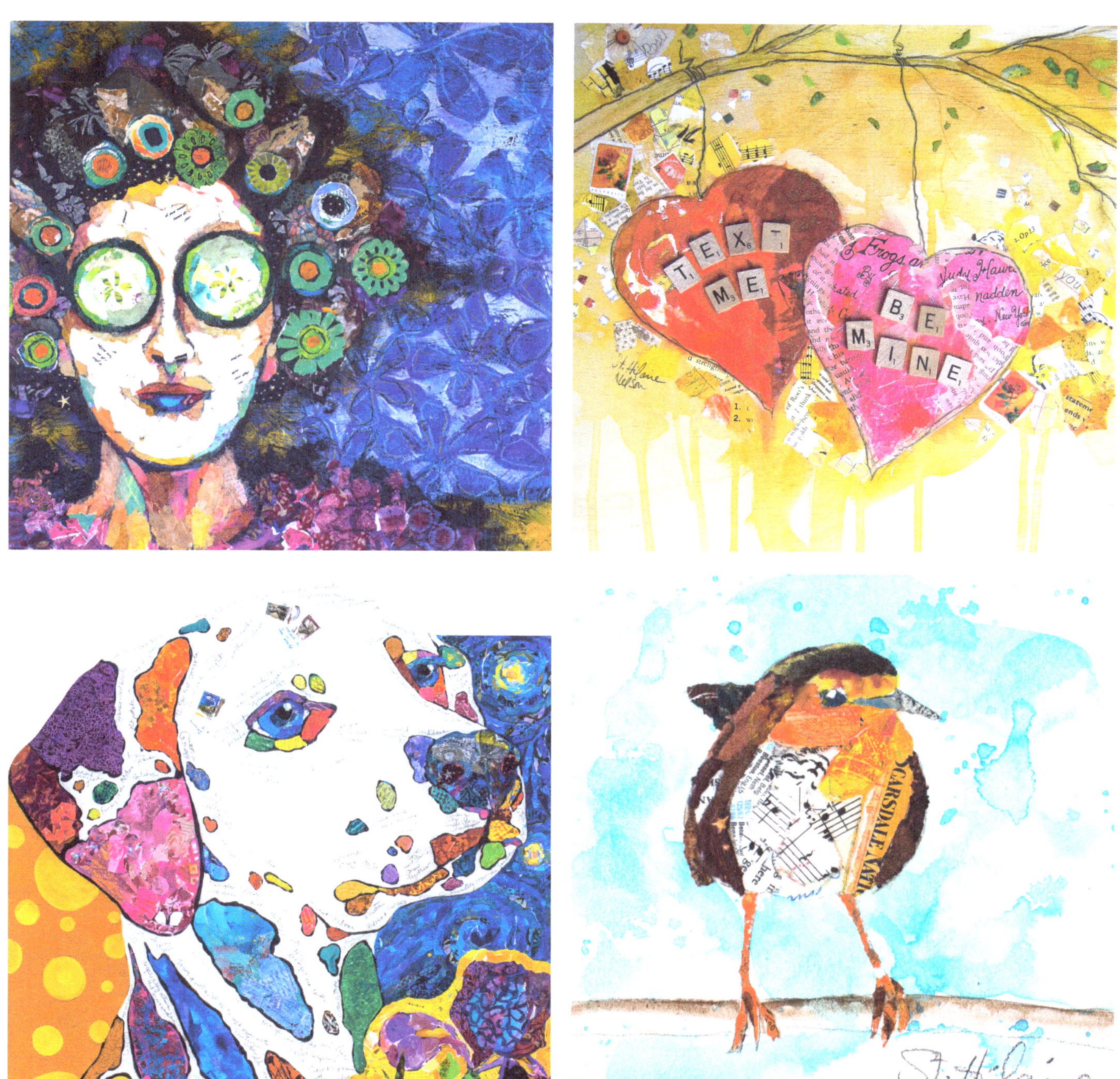

Substrate Inspiration

COLLAGE CAN BE APPLIED TO ANY SURFACE so why limit yourself? Top left: oriented strand board offers a highly textured surface to paint and collage upon. Top right: clear primed birch panel with the grain showing through. Lower left: custom made die cut wood panel. Bottom right: Aquabord panel by Ampersand.

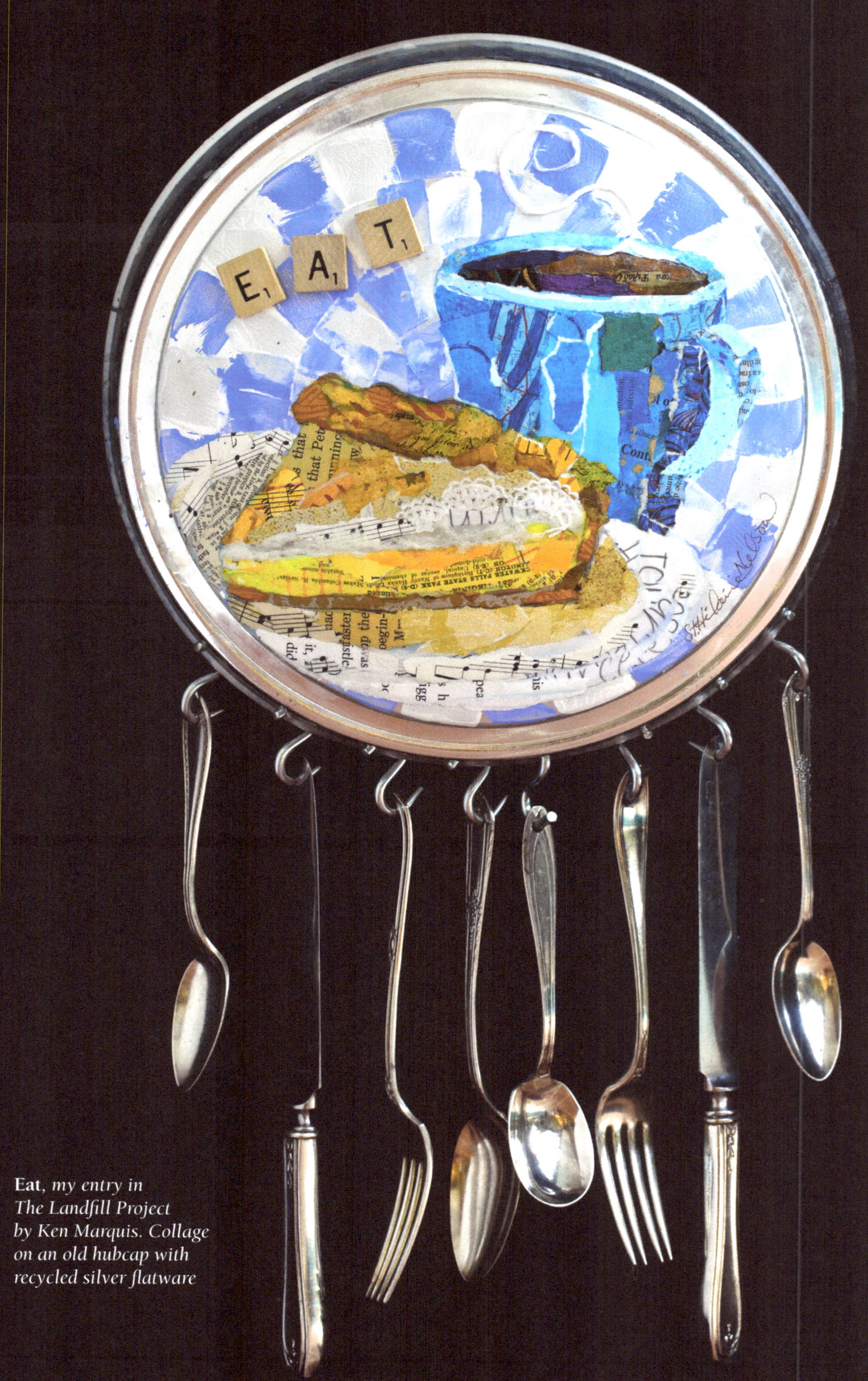

Eat, *my entry in The Landfill Project by Ken Marquis. Collage on an old hubcap with recycled silver flatware*

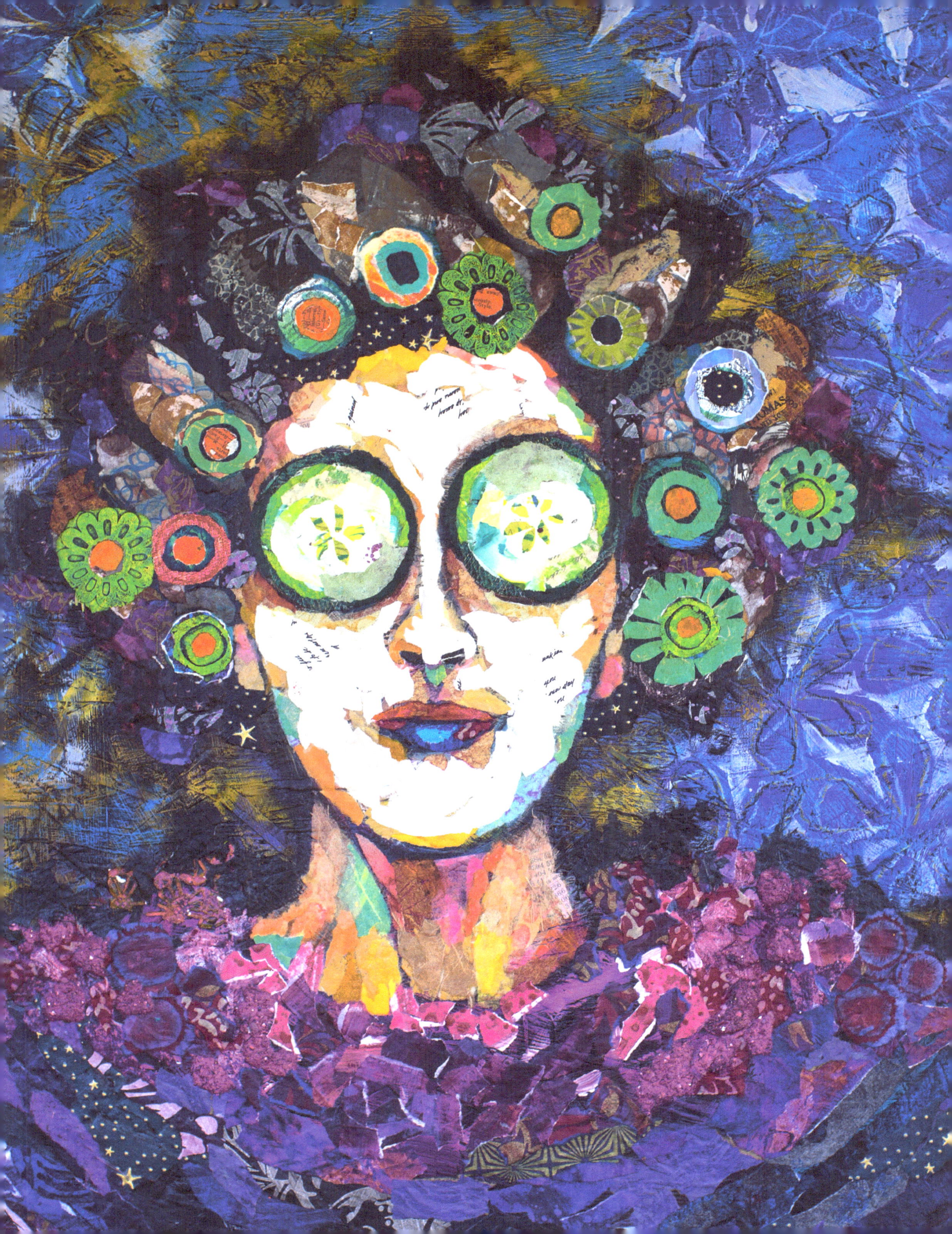

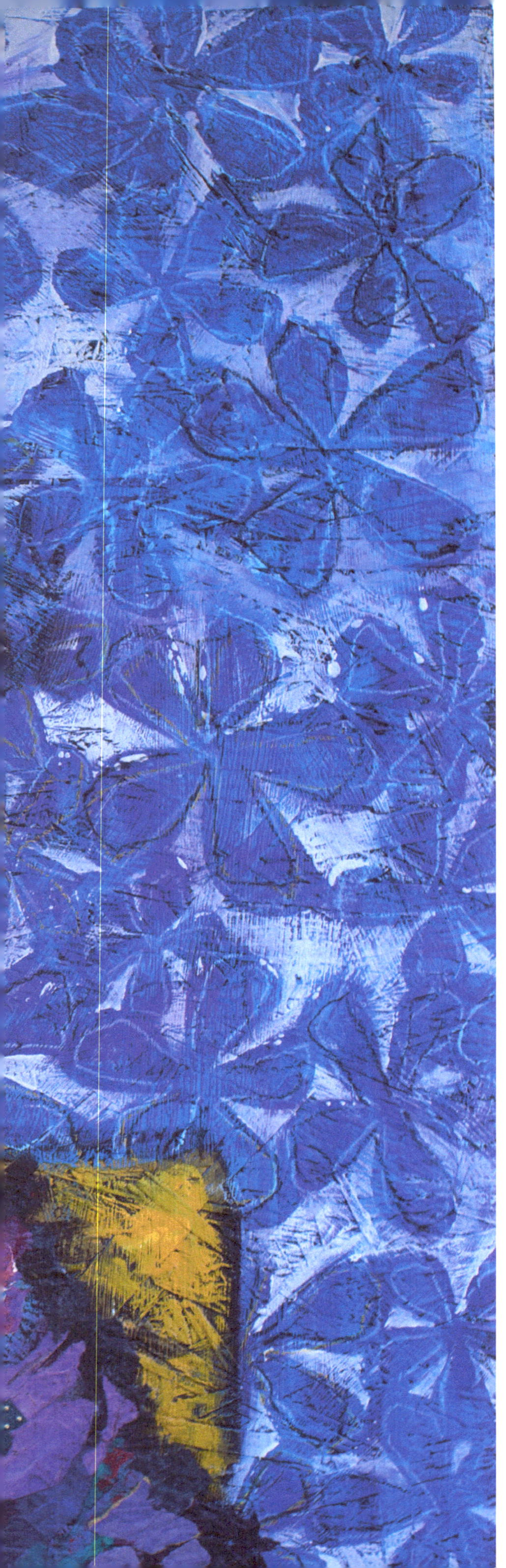

Oriented Strand Board - OSB

Cucumbers, Curlers, and Cold Cream *(30X30) This piece was created on a custom built cradled panel made of a highly textured surface is also known as flake-board, or oriented strand board (OSB). This product is a type of engineered lumber similar to particle board, formed by adding adhesives and then compressing layers of wood strands (flakes) in specific orientations. You can find OSB at the Home Depot, it comes in a variety of types and thicknesses.*

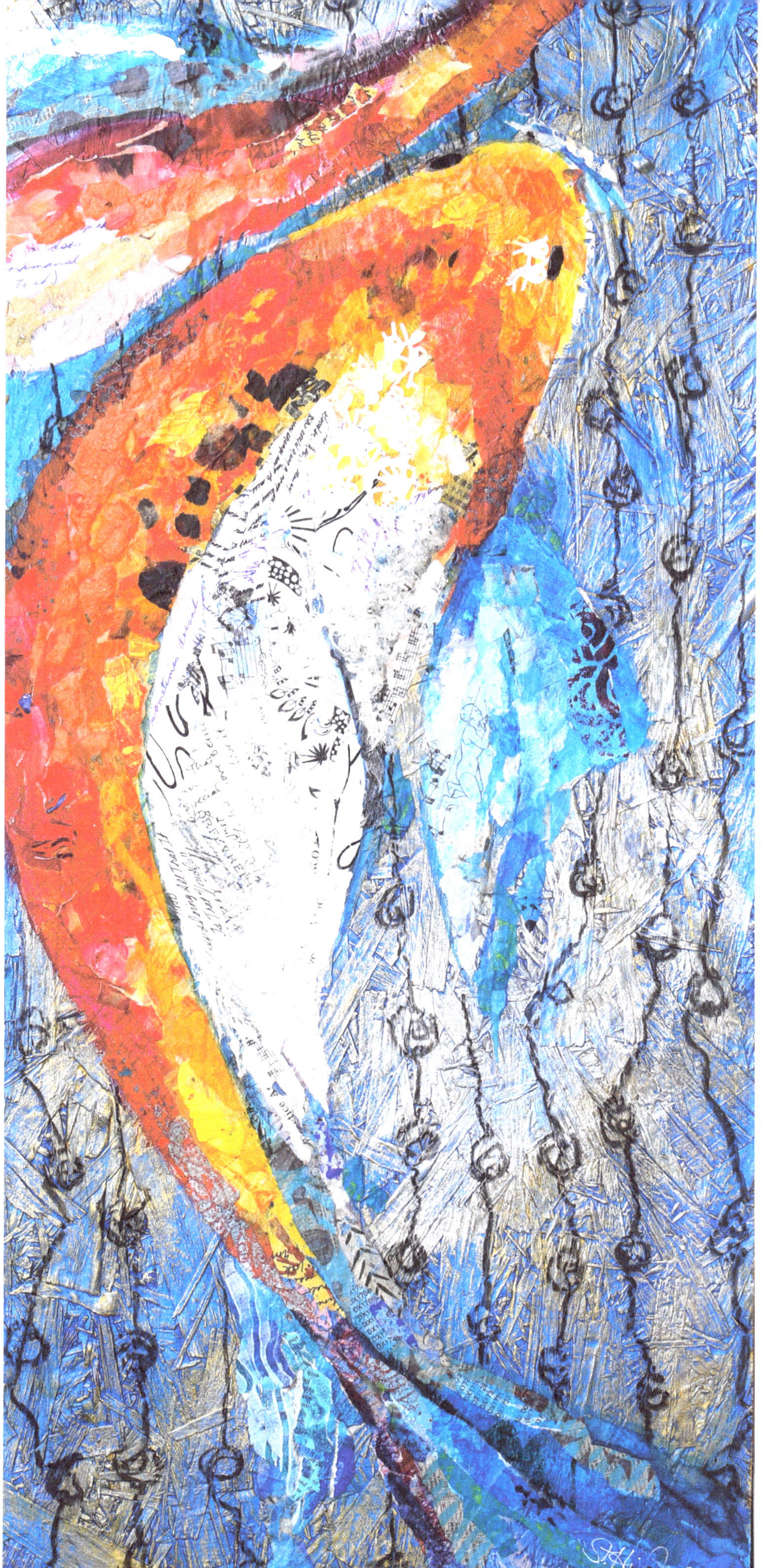

Entwined (16x36)
The highly textured OSB substrate provides a surface that is complimentary to the collage papers applied on top.

I heavily coated the wood with clear primer/sealer (back and front) in order to ensure that there were no loose pieces that would flake off.

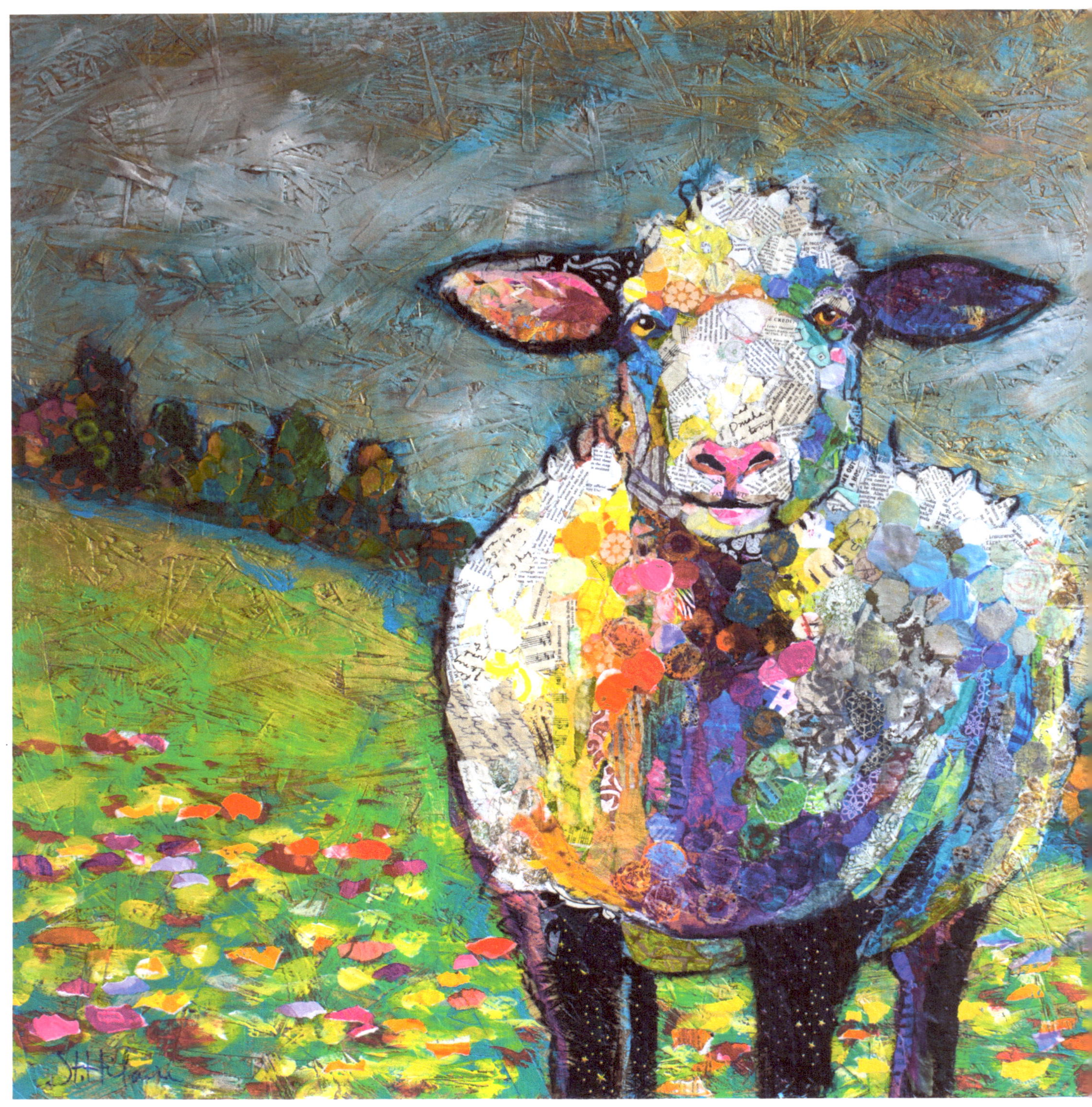

Field of Sweet Dreams (30x30) *The highly textured OSB substrate provides a surface that is complimentary to the collage papers of the sheep. In the background, both the tree-line and the flowers are collage elements while the sky and meadow are painted wood. The texture of the OSB has a collage feel (due to the multi-directional pieces) that marries well with the hand-painted paper adhered on top.*

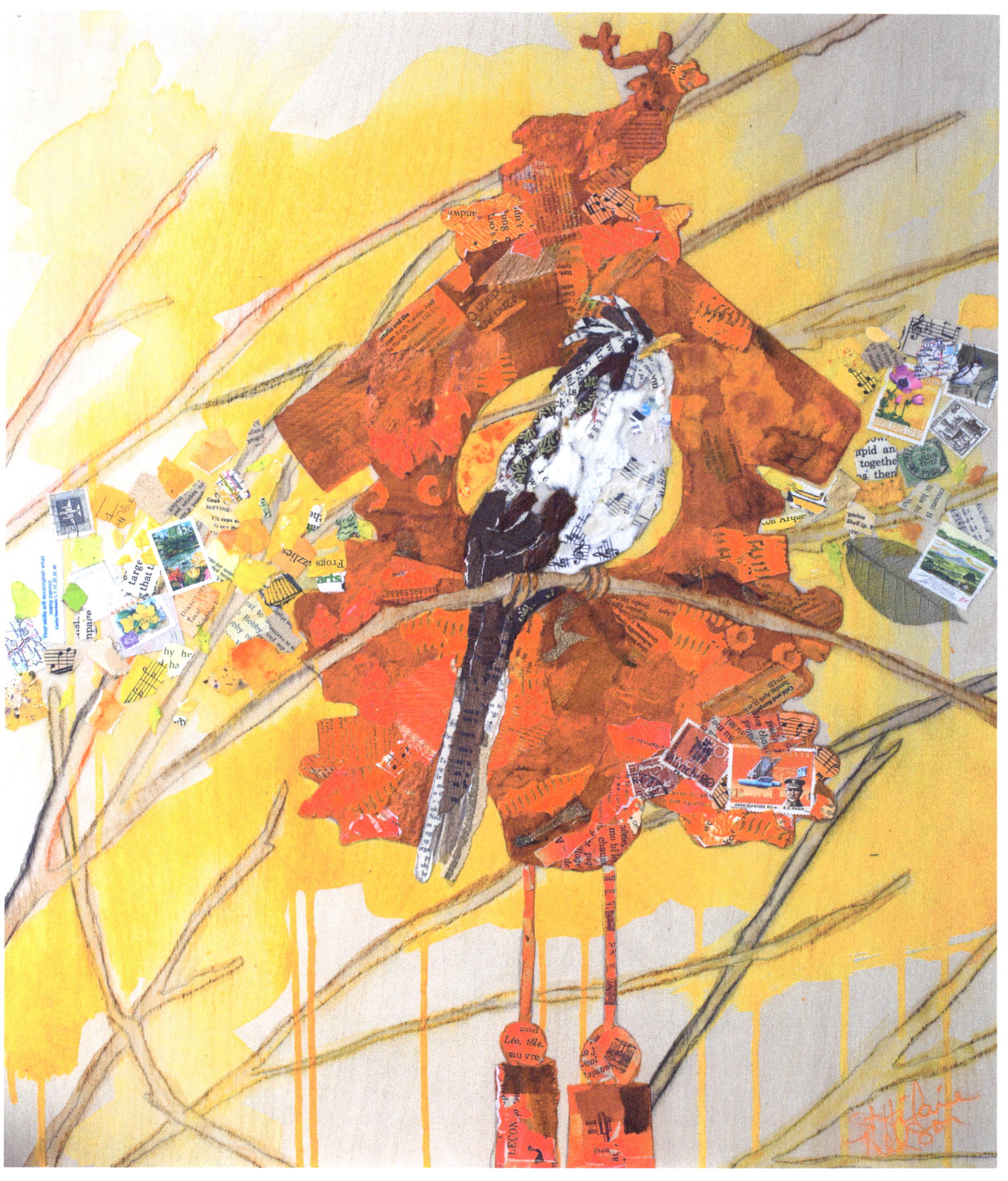

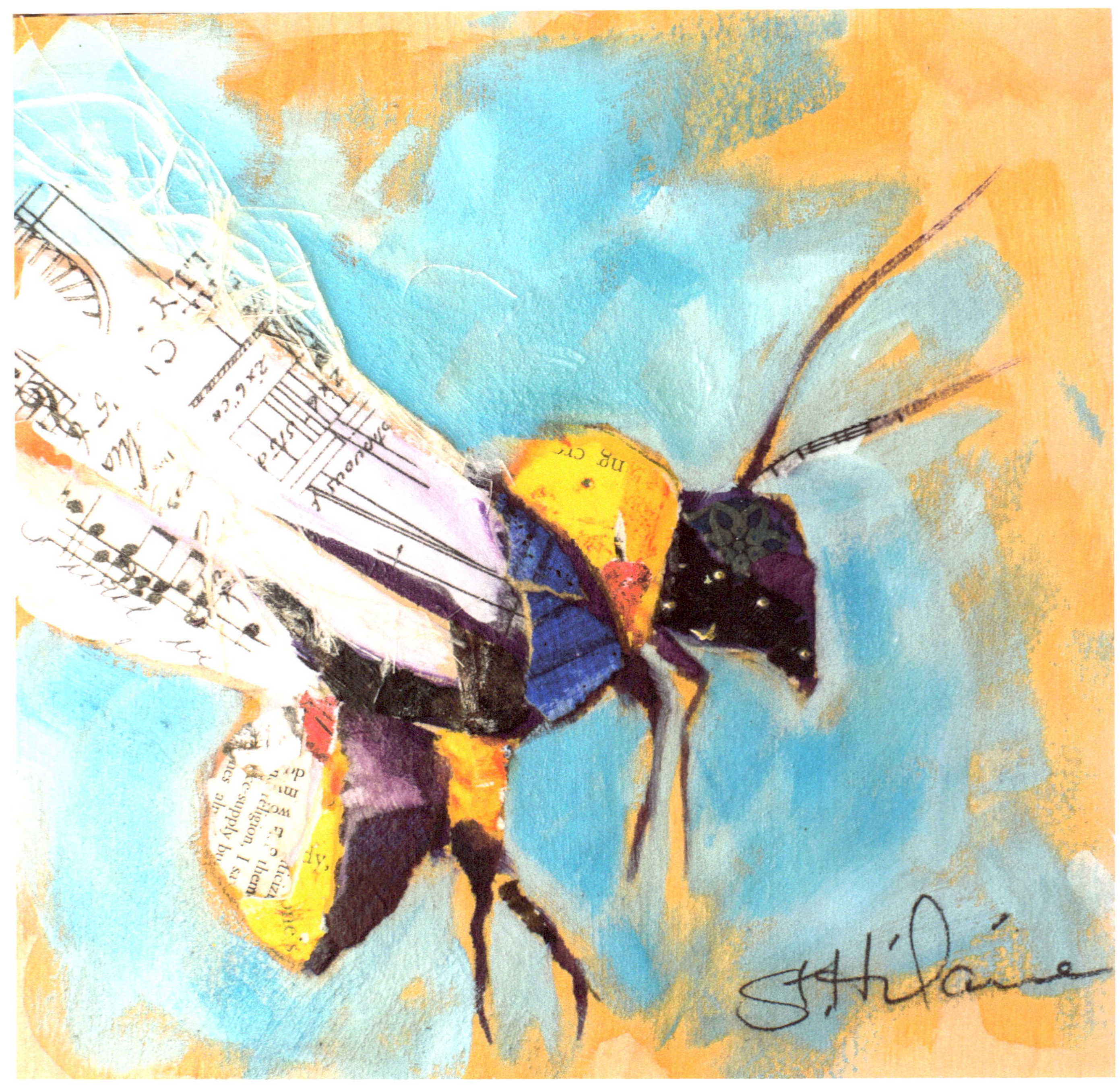

Clear Primed Wood

Left: **The Cuckoo** *(20X24) Above:* **Bees Knees** *(8x8) The substrate of these pieces is 2-inch deep cradled birch wood panel that has been primed with Golden's GAC-100 with a coat of Liquitex clear gesso on top of that. GAC seals the wood to prevent support induced discoloration; clear gesso gives a nice tooth that grabs and holds sketching and painting.*

Die-Cut Wood Panel

Blue Turtle Dream *(39X25) This turtle protrudes out of the traditional square format. The custom made birch wood panel is cradled with 1x2-inch wood all the way around, the turtle shape was cut out with a jigsaw. The format of these die-cut pieces is much that of a top-out billboard–inspired by the graphic designer in me.*

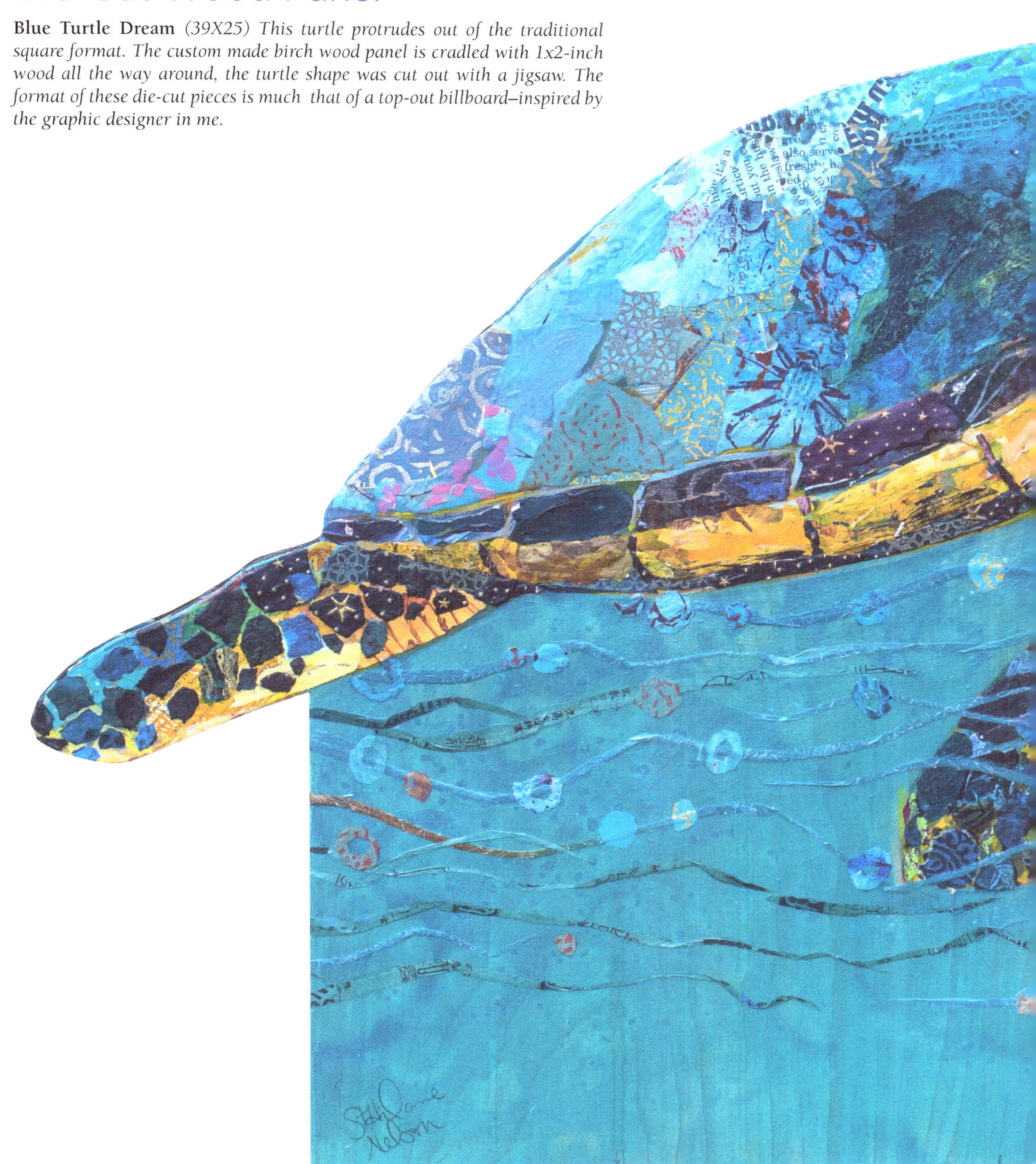

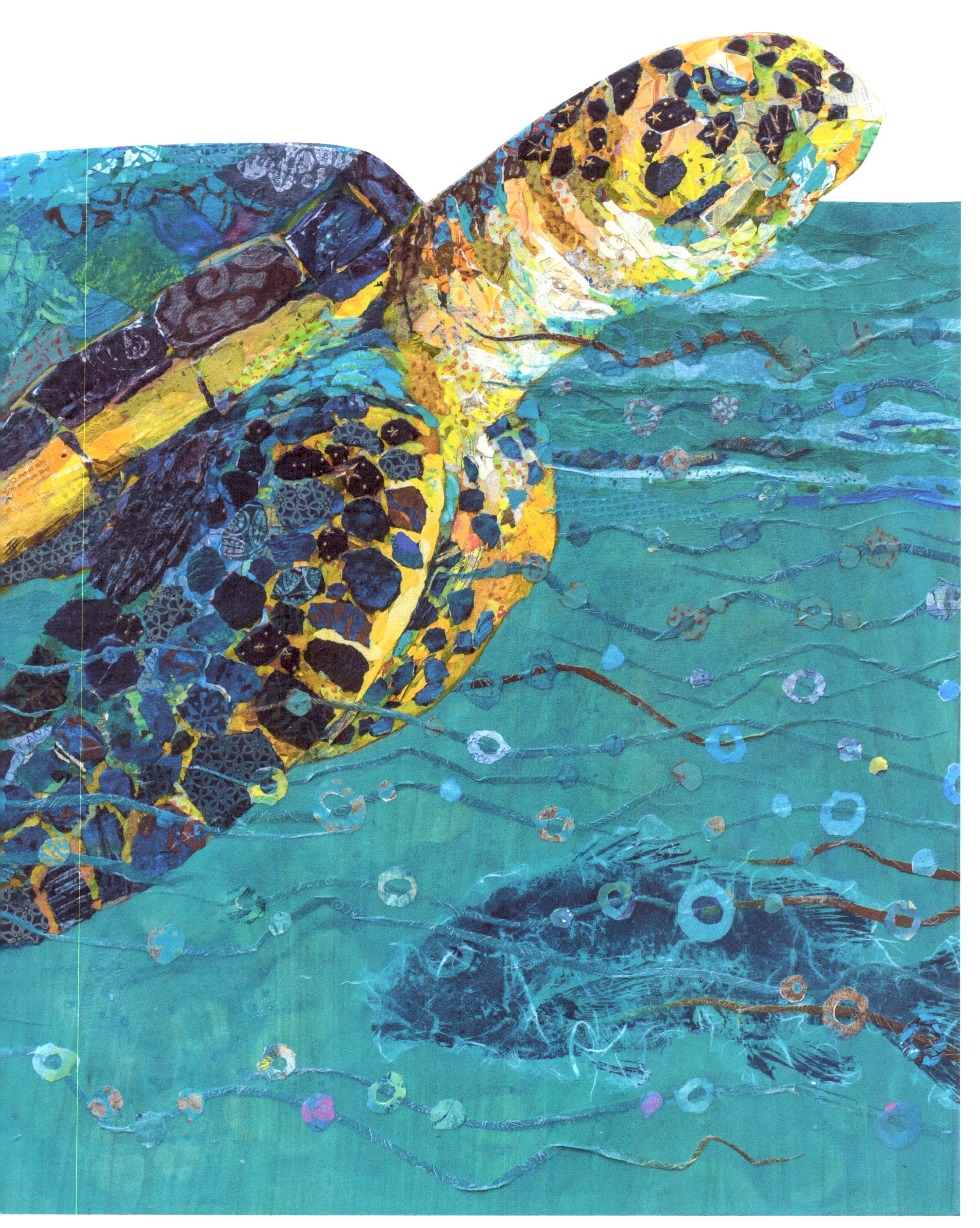

Die-Cut Wood Panel

Van Gogh Inspired (*39x35*) *The Dalmatian's substrate is a custom made birch wood panel cradled with 1x2-inch wood. The dog's head was cut from the substrate with a jigsaw. The format of these die-cut pieces is much like that of a top-out billboard–inspired by the graphic designer in me.*

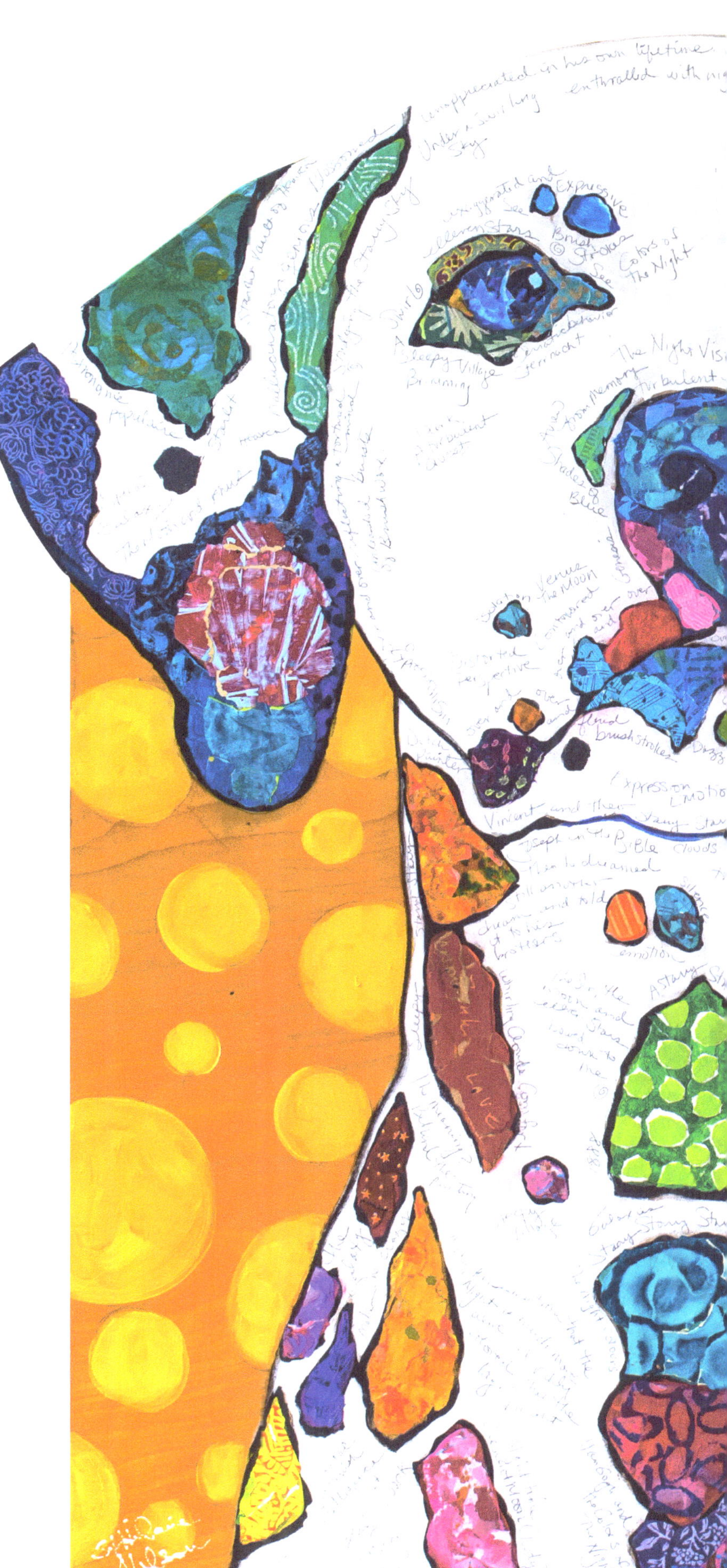

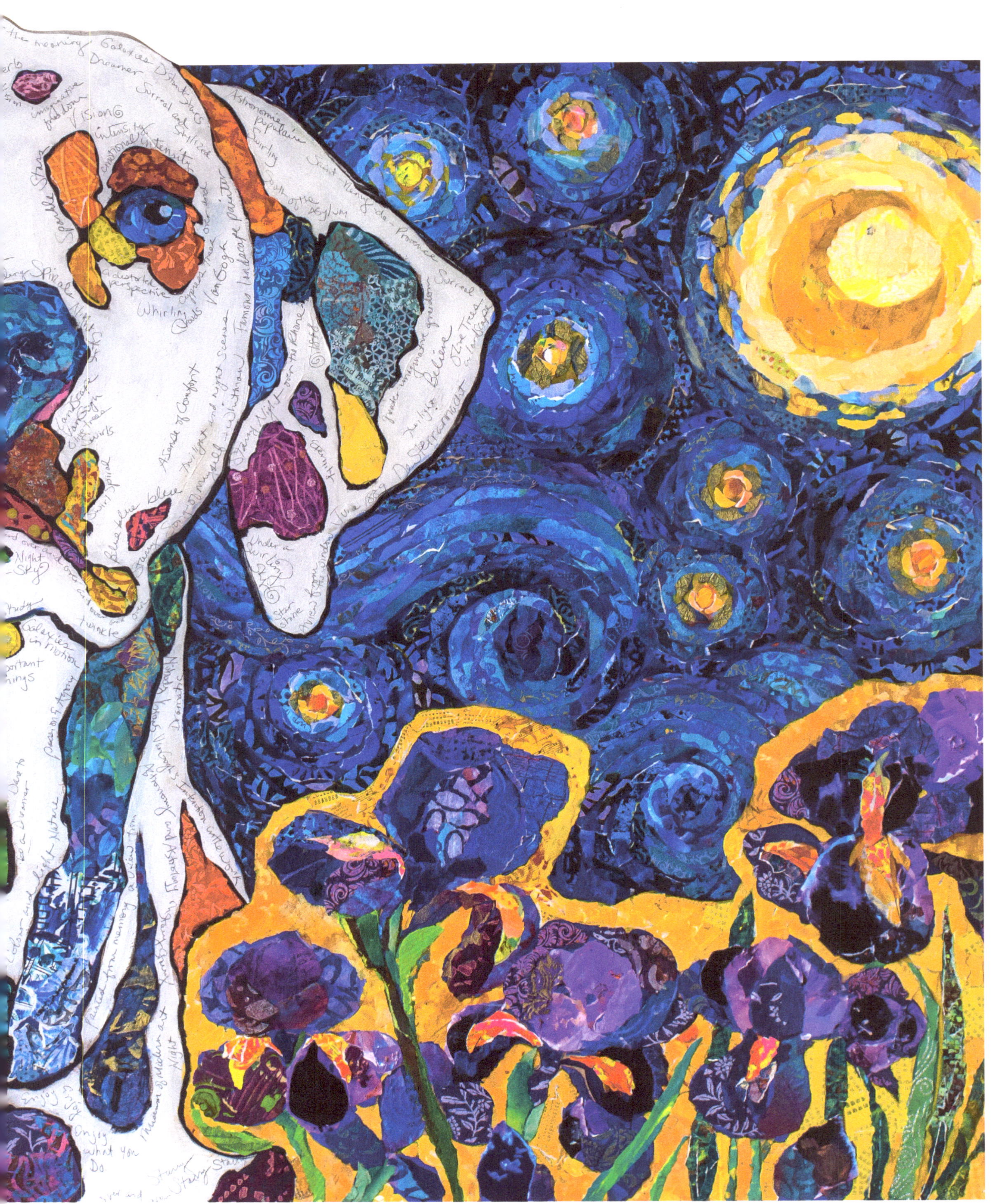

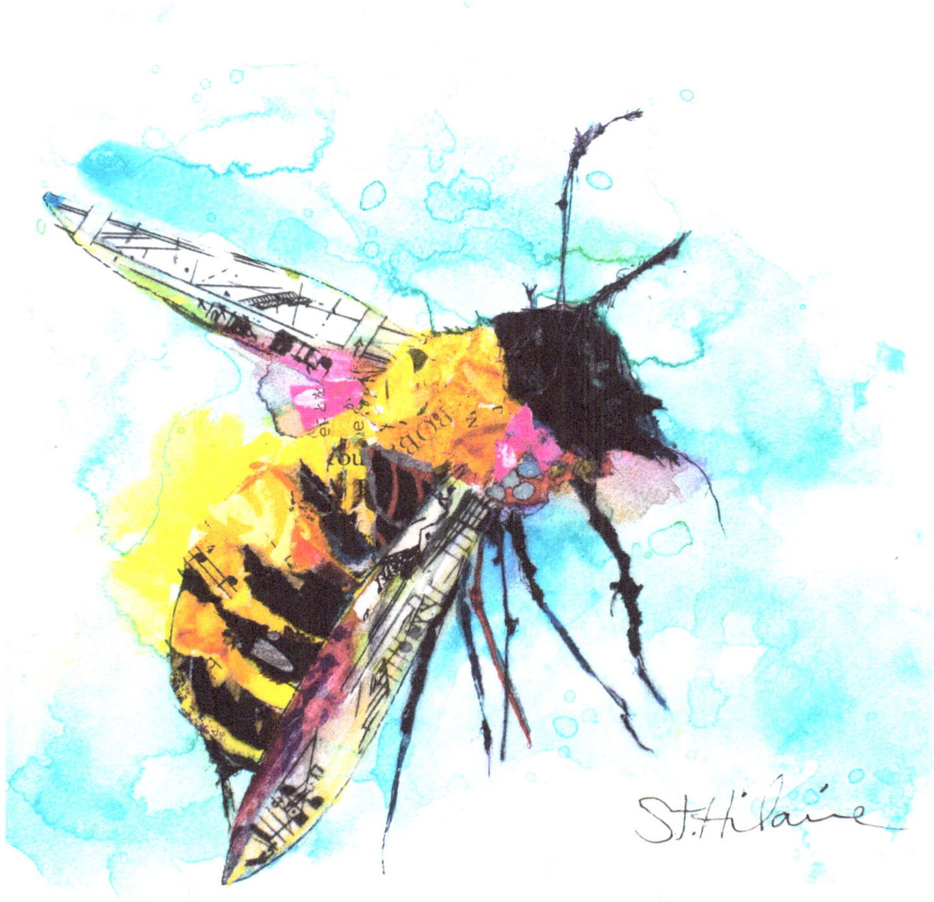

Ampersand's Aquabord

Above: **Bee Mindful** *(6x6) and Right:* **La Farfalla** *(8x8) The substrate for both of these pieces is Aquabord, a textured clay surface that absorbs water media like a fine paper. Aquabord allows colors to retain their purity and vibrancy. Aquabord comes in flat (1/8"), cradled (7/8"), and deep cradled (2") formats.*

For best results, it's a good idea to first "flush out" the surface of the panel with water using a large flat watercolor brush to release trapped air. Once the surface is slightly damp, it is ready to use. Follow directions on the product.

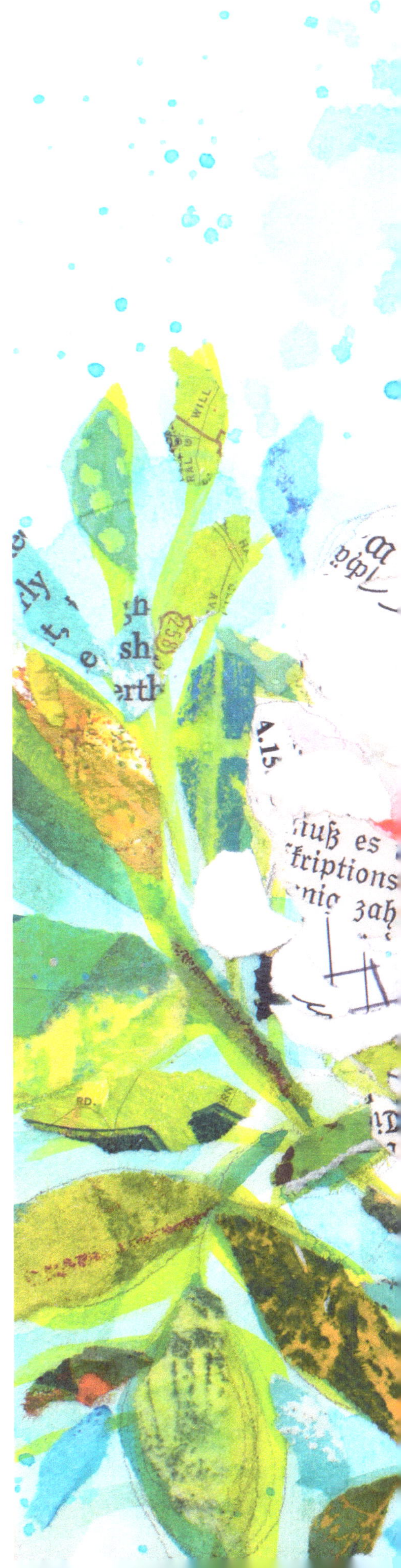

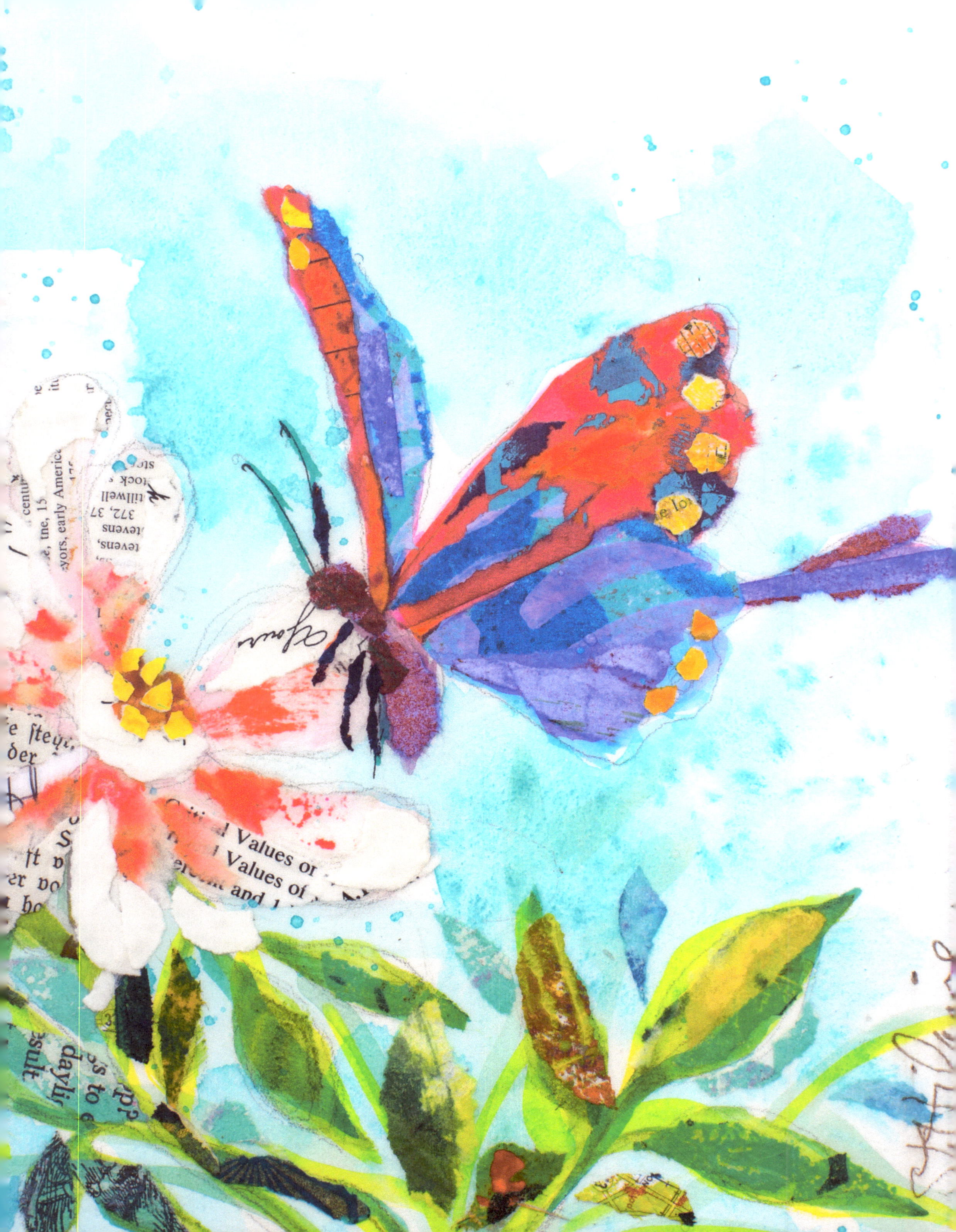

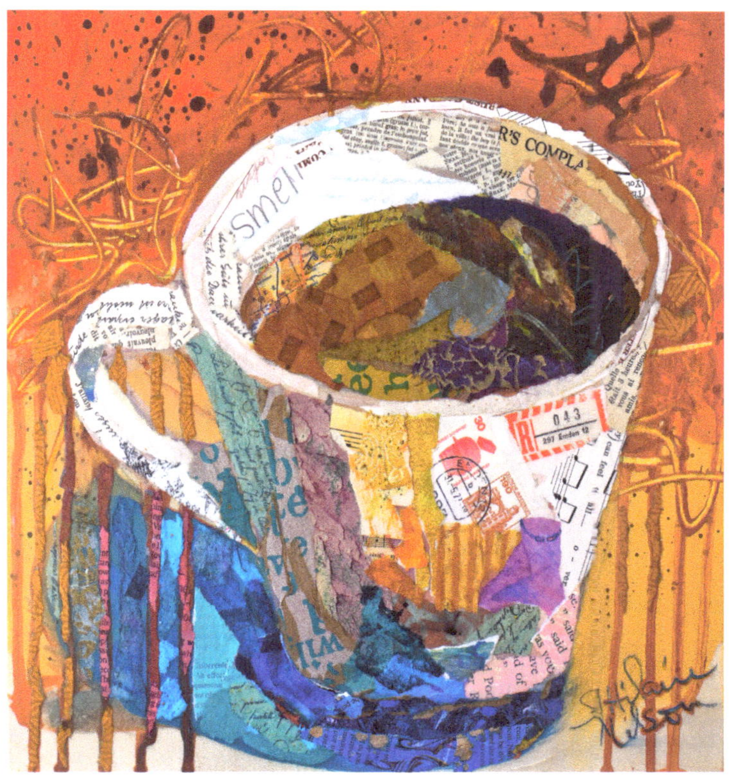

loosen up!

IT'S ALWAYS GOOD TO STEP BACK from what you are doing and consider how you can loosen up. Oftentimes we get too close, to caught up in our work, and don't take the time to loosen up. I have a few simple techniques I use to add spontaneity and a feeling of impressionism to my work.

Coffee Talk 1&2 (9x12, above and left) were exercises in working quickly and with limited materials. I set a timer for myself when creating the under-paintings on these pieces; limited time creates a sense of urgency, and eliminates the opportunity to get fussy with the details. I find that moving quickly inspires me to work in a looser style, and this is something I love to achieve in my work.

After the under-paintings were established, I limited my collage materials to a "scrap bag" of papers. Since I was only working with scraps, my full paper palette was not available–this inspired me to be more creative with color.

What can you do to loosen up? Be inspired by the process.

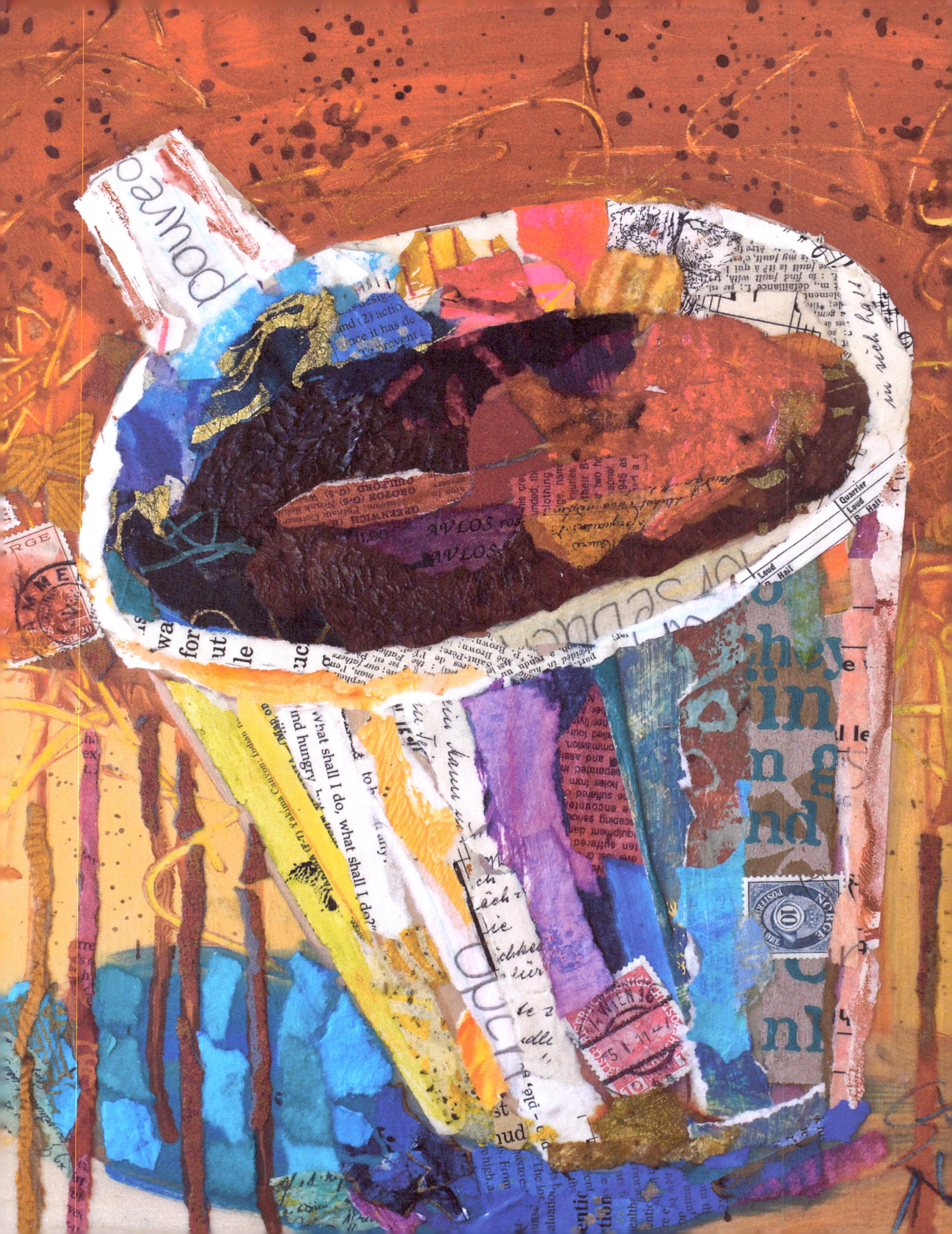

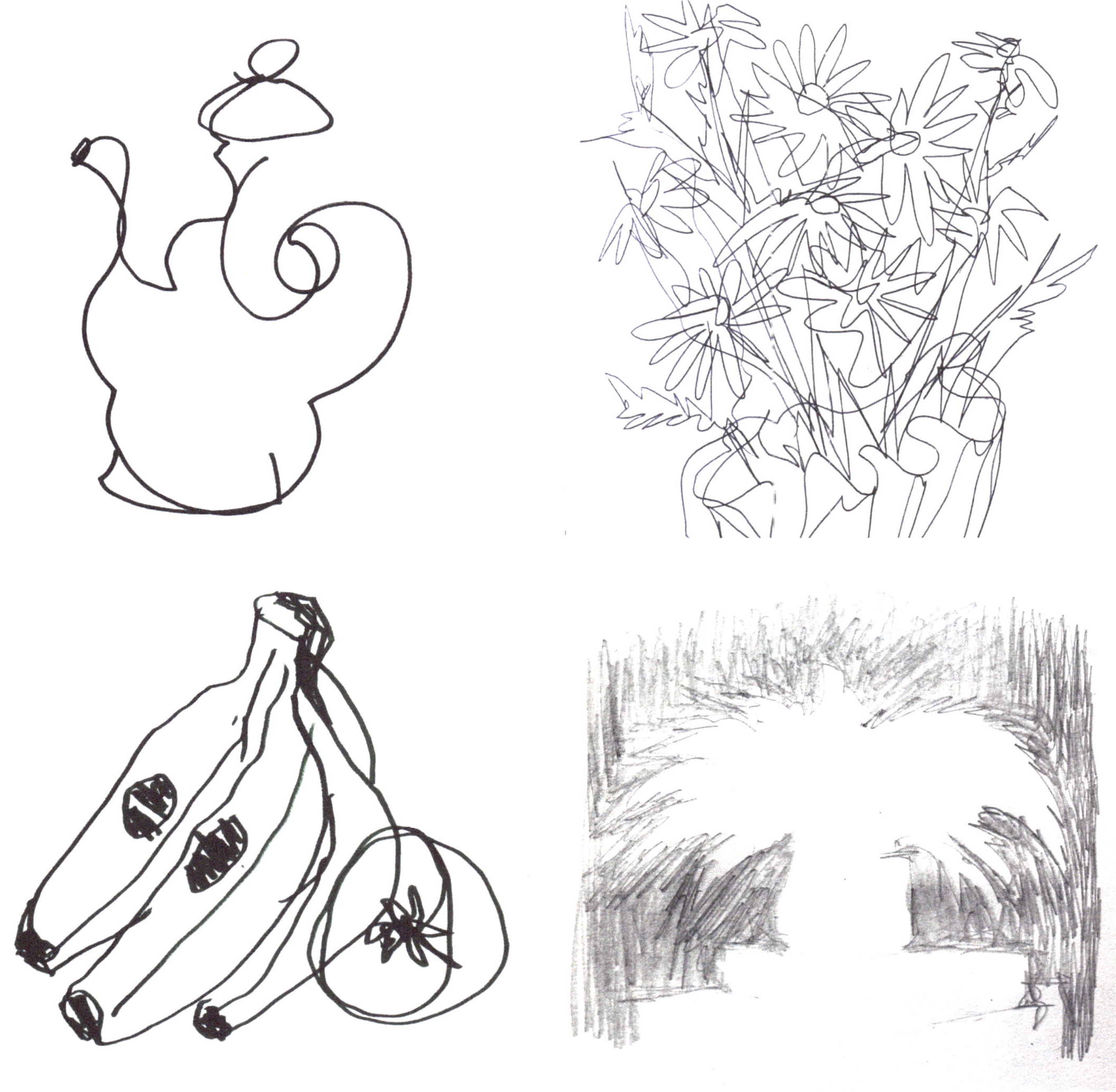

Exercises in drawing

FOR MORE PRACTICE and learning to loosen up, try these four basics lessons that every art student is familiar with and you should be too. **Top left:** blind contour drawing, this is a fun swirly teapot in my kitchen.

Top right: continuous contour drawing, these are some fresh daisies in a vase on my kitchen table.

Bottom left: non dominant hand drawing, I used my left hand to draw some items from the fruit bowl.

Bottom right: negative space drawing, focusing on only the area around this potted plant from my patio.

MIXED MEDIA COLLAGE INSPIRATION

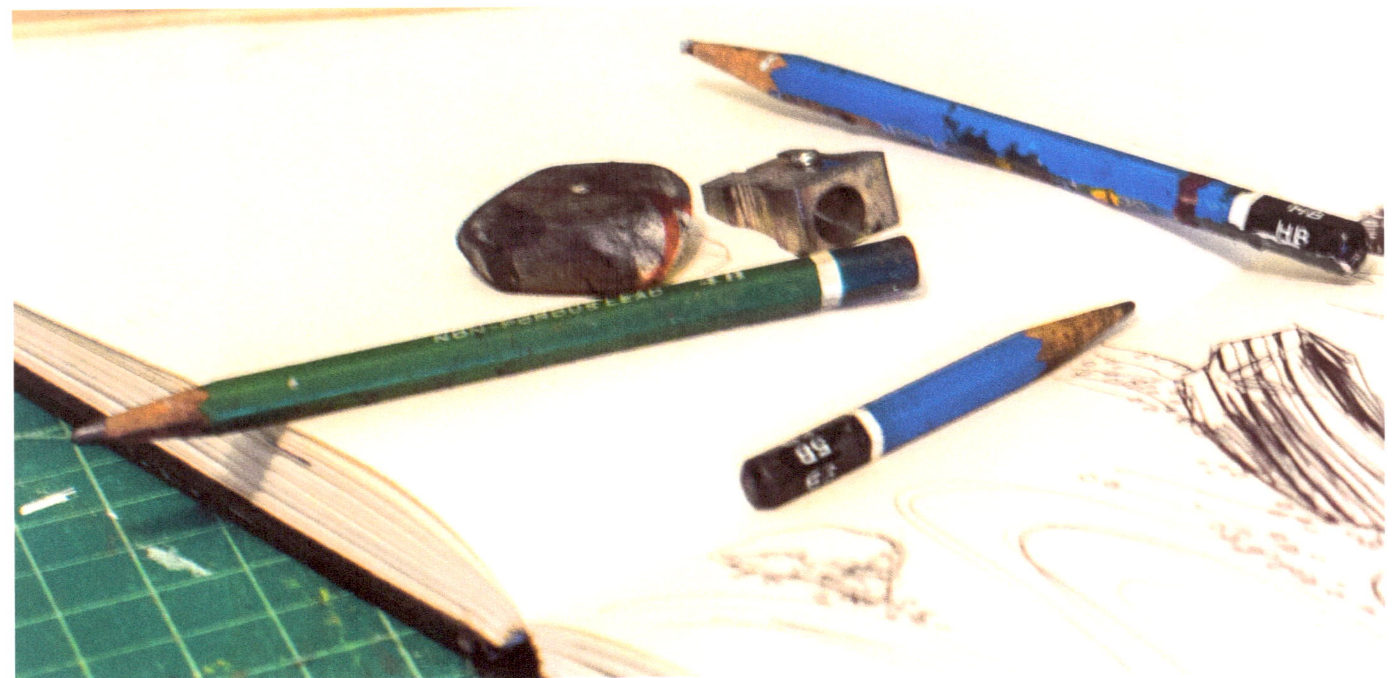

Blind Contour Drawing

This is an exercise in which the artist draws the contour of a subject without looking at the paper. It may seem crazy to suggest that you do not look at the drawing as you make it, but this is exactly how you achieve looseness. Fix your eyes on the outline of the object, and draw the contour very slowly, without looking at the paper. Oftentimes the results of this exercise can be inspiration for a finished piece of art. A few times through this exercise before you set out to actually sketch the subject of your painting, is a great way to warm up.

Continuous Contour Line Drawing

This is an exercise in which the artist focuses on line and shape. The goal is to create a drawing where you never lift your drawing tool from the paper. Focus on looking at what you are drawing (use a reference image or draw from life) as much as the drawing itself–do not stop moving your hand when you look up. Intersection of the flowing line creates some wonderful and unexpected shapes that may take on a more important role in the composition.

Non Dominant Hand Drawing

This exercise requires you to give up much of your learned control. By drawing with the non dominant hand, the artist gains an opportunity to be more free, since expectations of accuracy are lifted. During this exercise you should notice your line becoming more loose and fluid. Try making several drawings like this at the beginning of your studio time.

Negative Space Drawing

In this exercise the artist draws the shapes around the object rather than the object itself. Using good observation skills, and drawing nothing but the negative space, the positive form will be remarkably accurate. Your concentration should be on observing and drawing the space between objects.

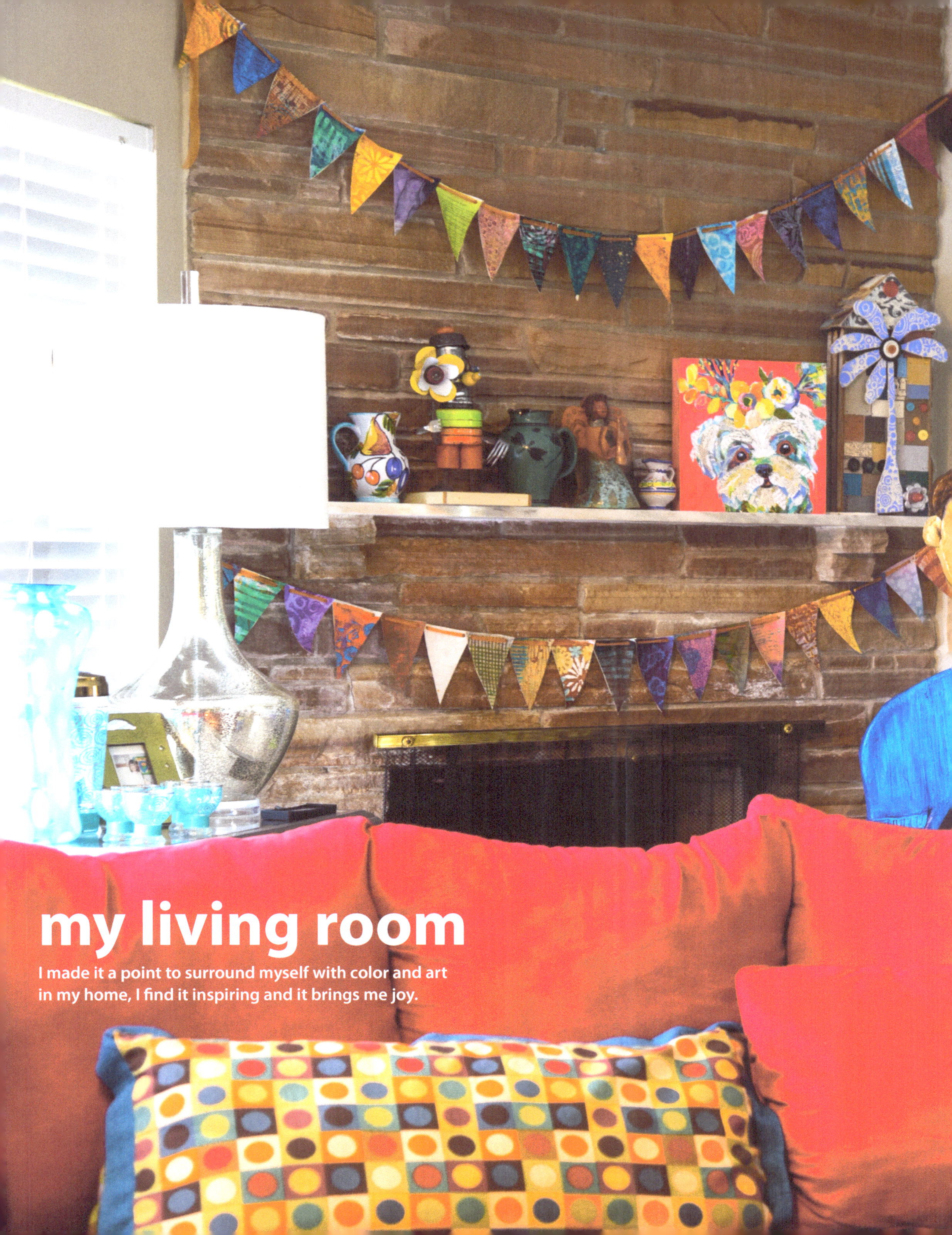

my living room
I made it a point to surround myself with color and art in my home, I find it inspiring and it brings me joy.

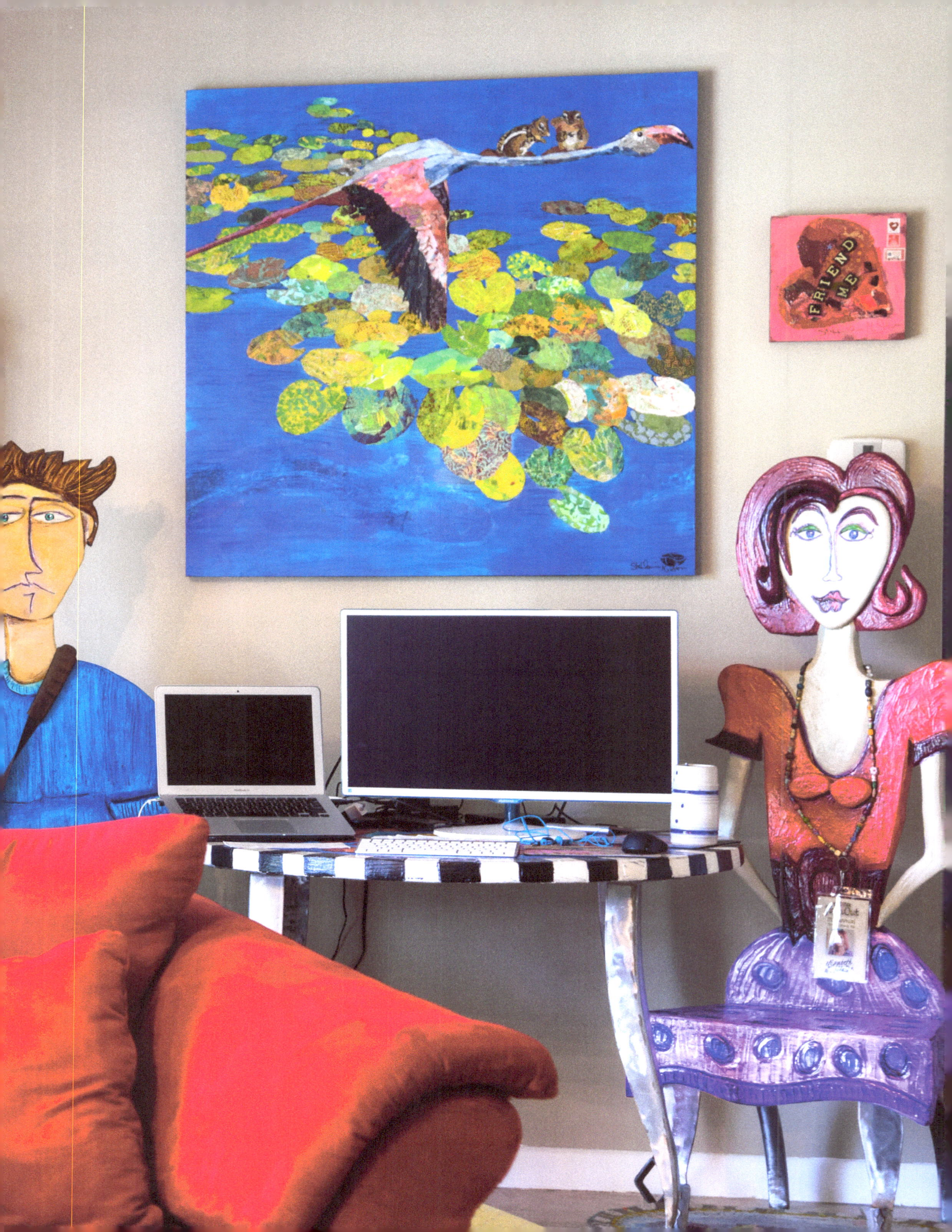

FRIEND
ME

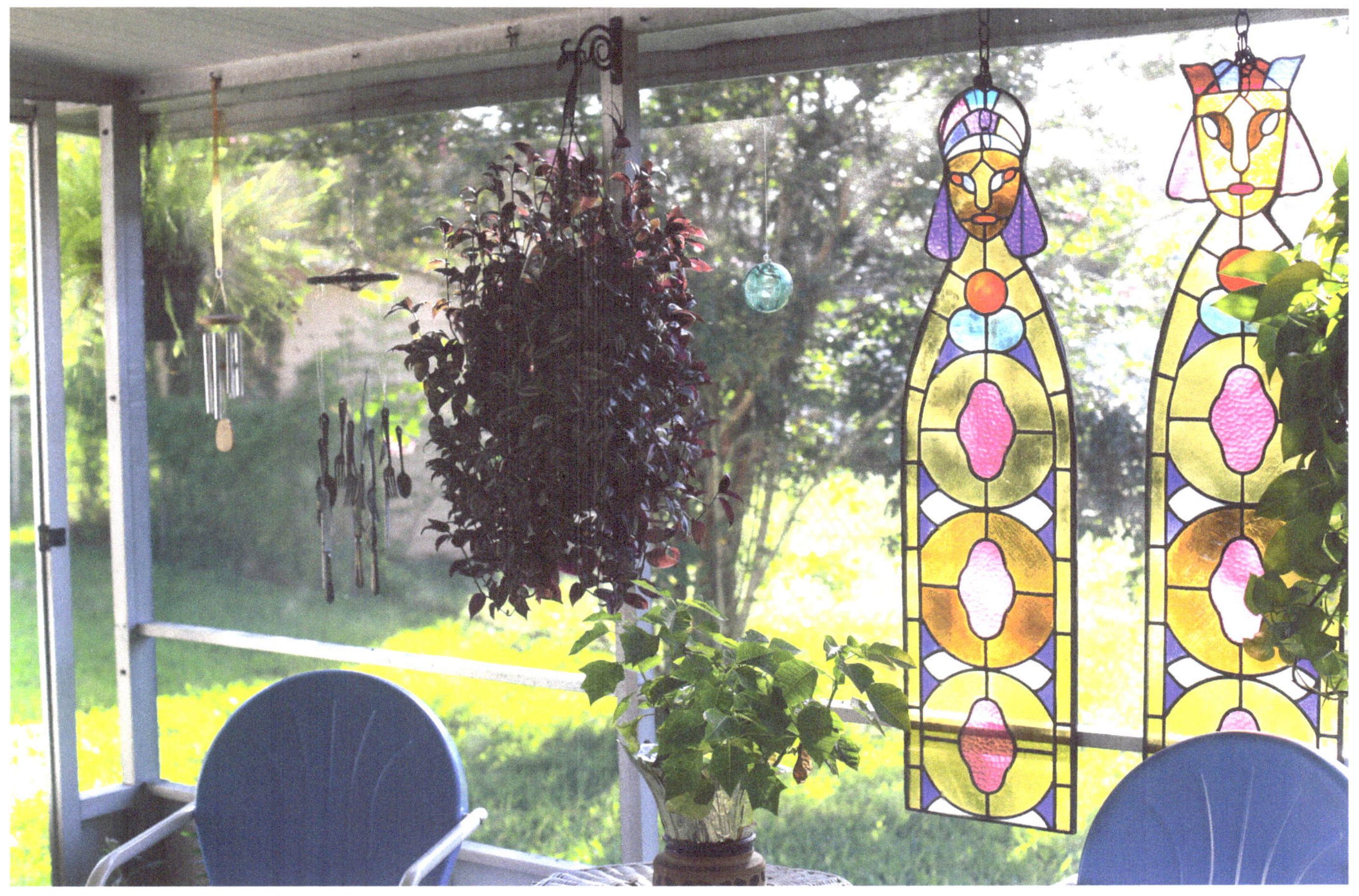

My coffee break spot, with hand-made wind chimes, blown glass, retro metal chairs, vintage stained glass windows and hanging plants.

An Artistic Space

SURROUND YOURSELF with things that stimulate your creativity and make you happy.
Whether it's your own work, art that you have collected, or an interior decor that features
your favorite colors—enveloping yourself in an artistic space helps to motivate creativity.
When the air conditioning technician came to my house for the first time, he looked at me
and said *"So colorful...quite the contrast from the previous tenants."* This made me smile,
and became a common theme with contractors who followed. I talked the property manager
into letting me paint bright colors over the freshly painted khaki kitchen and bathroom.
This seemed like uncharted water for him; I think he wondered what I had against beige.
Every morning when I come out into my living room with the red couch, two mannequins,
and pink metal mounted deer head donning an oversized pearl necklace, (just a few
highlights) I start the day with a smile and a sense of creative adventure.

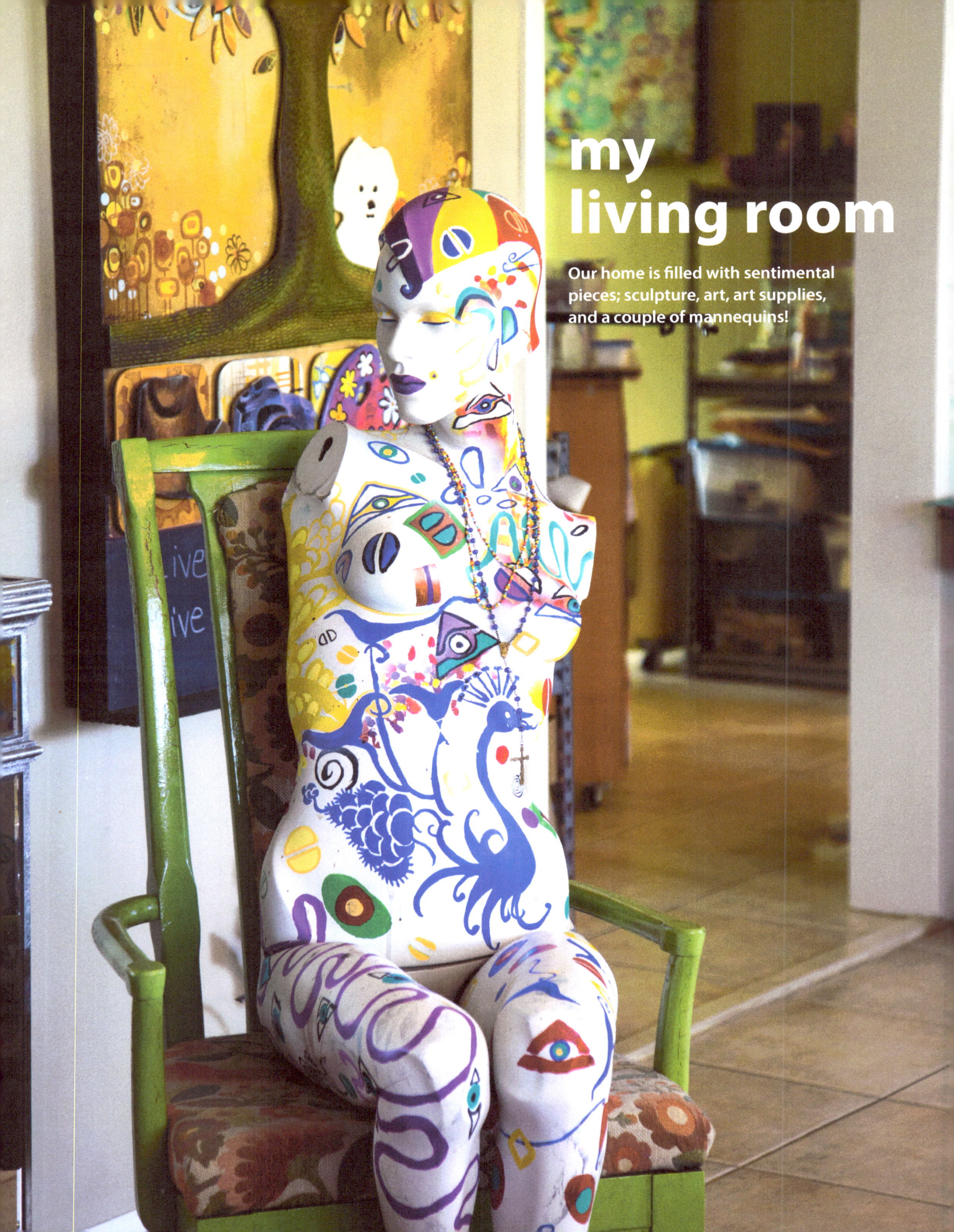
my
living room
Our home is filled with sentimental
pieces; sculpture, art, art supplies,
and a couple of mannequins!

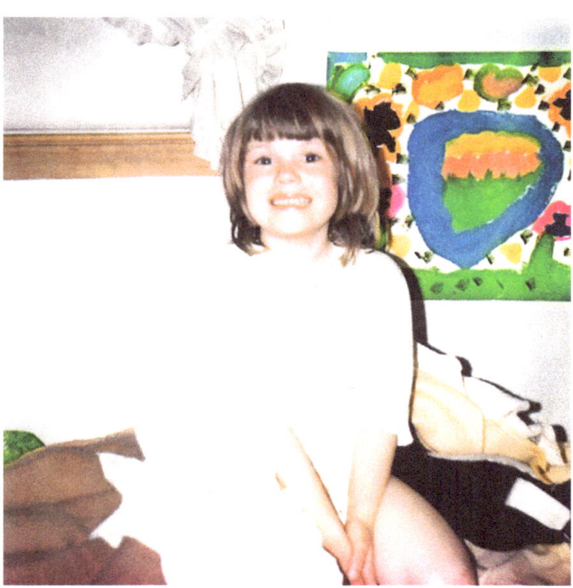

ABOUT THE AUTHOR

What sets the collage work of Elizabeth St. Hilaire apart is her use of unique, one-of-a-kind papers and imaginative imagery. Her signature collage style utilizes papers colored by hand, in every hue and texture needed for a complete paper palette.

St. Hilaire has self published several books on her collage process, available on her website:

Painterly Gelli Prints
Painting Paper

She is also published with North Light Books:
Painted Paper Art Workshop

Portfolio of work:
PaperPaintings.com

Email contact:
Elizabeth@PaperPaintings.com

Workshop information:
PaperPaintings.com

Work in progress:
FaceBook.com/PaperPaintingsCollageArtwork

Blog:
PaperPaintings.GrowingBolder.com

It is my sincere goal to inspire people, of all ages, to pursue their love of art. Whether it's a career choice, or for personal enrichment—go for it!

I also encourage you to find your style, your individuality, yourself. Color your hair green, wear mismatched clothing, dance to the beat of your own drum. "Life is not a dress rehearsal" as someone special once said to me. Do what makes you happy.

I am forever grateful to have been able to make something I loved into my living. But I couldn't do it without the support of people like you.

Thank You
For Being a Part of
My Art Journey,

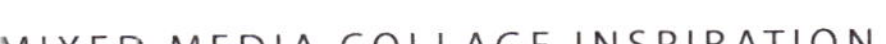

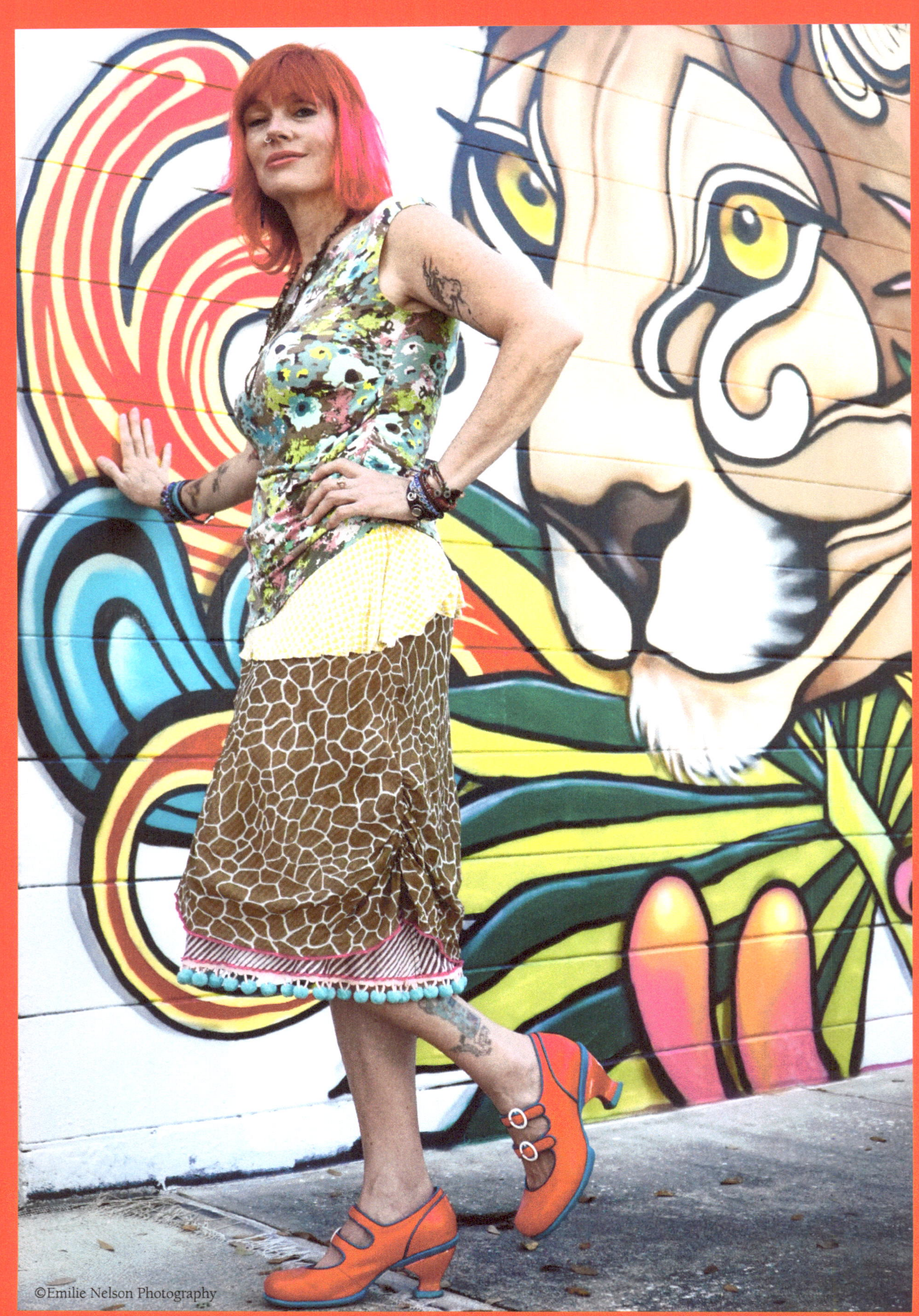
©Emilie Nelson Photography

www.ingramcontent.com/pod-product-compliance
Lightning Source LLC
Chambersburg PA
CBHW042149030726
47599CB00004B/667